1995–2010

TADAO ANDO

Francesco Dal Co

1995–2010

TADAO ANDO

PRESTEL Munich · Berlin · London · New York

Contents

Appendices

Echoes from another world

Francesco Dal Co

It has been sixteen years since Electa publishing first brought out a volume in which Ando's works from 1969*, either realised or planned, were set out in a systematic manner. Since then – that is, since 1994 – important developments have taken place in his work, with many more projects completed both in Japan and, increasingly, around the world. Sixteen years ago, FABRICA (Benetton Communication Research Centre) in Villorba (Treviso), was only in the planning stage and the only works that Ando had to his credit abroad were the Japan Pavilion for Expo '92 in Seville, the Gallery for Japanese Screens that he designed for the 1992 addition to the Art Institute of Chicago, and the Vitra Seminar House completed the year after in Weil am Rhein, Germany. Two years earlier he had entered – albeit without success – a competition for the Modern Art Museum and Architecture Museum, Stockholm.

However, from 1994 Tadao Ando's career took off and the period between 1994 and 2010 saw the completion of several projects around the world in addition to works in Japan. In the United States, he built two museums, the Pulitzer Foundation for the Arts in St. Louis and the Modern Art Museum of Fort Worth; in Chicago, he received a commission for a private residence. In Italy, there was the Armani/Teatro, a multi-use space in Milan, a villa in Treviso, the rebuilding of the Palazzo Grassi, and the restoration of the Punta della Dogana in Venice. The Langen Foundation in Neuss was built in Germany a small annexe referred to as a "meditation space" was created within the headquarters of UNESCO in Paris, France. Ando was also the master planner behind the new arts centre at the Château La Coste wine estate near Aix-en-Provence in 2010. In addition to the Pritzker Architecture Prize (1995) and the Premium Imperiale (1996), this professional success has earned him many other awards along with growing critical acclaim and media attention, testimony to which is a wealth of publications about him.

This summary would seem to confirm that there have been important changes in Ando's professional and private life, though it must be acknowledged that in his case the boundaries between the two arenas are not easy to establish. Given how marked these changes have been and considering the complexity of his works, it is perhaps surprising that they did not impact more on his architecture, in both theoretical and practical terms. Now that Ando is nearly seventy, it is worth exploring the nature of this coherence and his indifference to the circumstances in which his unique idiom manifests itself. To do this, the textual detail and critical analysis that accompanies each and every project and building in this volume is an attempt to set out the cultural bases as well as the models and traditions that provide a context in which to evaluate Ando's achievements throughout his career. Indeed, it is to his extraordinary contribution to architecture that this book is dedicated.

I

From the era in which Edward Morse published his pioneering yet still very relevant book *Japanese Homes and Their Surroundings* (1885), many like him have been struck by the general monotony of most Japanese cities: a bird's eye view takes in a seemingly endless panorama of roofs without chimneys spreading out like a densely woven carpet. This homogeneous impenetrability has been commented on by Goffredo Parise, amongst others, who noted that, "in Japan, cities are measured by the decimetre".

In reality, the decimetre as a unit of linear measurement is not the most appropriate means of calculating the dimensions of the residential fabric of Japanese

*Dealt with in the book *Tadao Ando* by F. Dal Co. Currently out of print, it can be regarded as a companion or first volume to the present one. It would be advisable to read the following pages taking into account the essay *The Architecture of Betrayal* by the same F. Dal Co, published in the 1994 edition.

Fabrica, Benetton Communication Research Centre, Treviso, Italy, 1992–2000.

Pulitzer Foundation for the Arts, St. Louis, United States, 1991–2001.

Modern Art Museum of Fort Worth, United States, 1997–2002.

Art Centre Château La Coste, Aix-en-Provence, France, 2006–2010.

cities, even if the words of Parise do express a reality. Whether seen from above or from the maze of streets that criss-cross it, there is of course another dimension to a Japanese residential quarter. Instead of a linear form of measurement, we substitute another means of calculating the surface area: in Japan the proportions of the *tatami* are taken as a reference. In houses, *tatami* are arranged on the floor in such a way that the corners of two of the mats are always in contact with the side of a third. They use the more common sizes of *Kyō-ma* and *Edo-ma*, comparable to the *ken* unit of measurement (circa 180 cms), and determine the room and floor dimensions according to a scale derived from the proportions of the human body. In fact, as Bruno Taut explained in *Houses and People of Japan* (1938) "the measurements of the body are of maximum importance. Every detail in the Japanese house is in perfect harmony with the measurements of the human body and this is the key to the aesthetic effect that it produces."

These and other observations that are inevitably inspired by traditional Japanese achitecture also define its character and can be summed up by simplicity, a word that the literature returns to again and again, as does Morse. Forty years or so after the publication of Morse's book, the idea was then enriched by Taut when he superimposed the concept of *Einfachheit* with its overtones of "smoothness", "unpretensiousness" and "discipline" to describe an architecture that was modest and at ease with itself but at the same time bound by rules. In these terms, it has been rendered synonymous with artistic perfection that according to Taut reaches its apotheosis in the Imperial Villa of Katsura. This perfect manifestation was proof indeed that "Kunst ist Sinn – in der grössten Einfachheit liegt die grösste Kunst" or, "art is sensation – in its greatest simplicity lies its greatest artistry".

Occupying areas measured by the decimetre and thanks to the disciplined simplicity of an order imposed not just by the *tatami* but other factors, Japanese homes are repetitive references to the "fullness of the empty". As Karl Löwith writes, if the void carries in the house the echo "of the metaphysical background that resonates everywhere in Japan", then the rooms that make it up are more or less faint reflections of the place appointed as the celebration of the void, the *sukiya*. Kakuzo Okakura has familiarised us with the characteristics of the teahouse and has explained how the *sukiya* is a place that belongs to the cult of simplicity offering "a display as extraordinary as it is lacking in show", to quote Giangiorgio Pasqualotto in words similar to those of Taut.

In various works of Ando, it is possible to observe *mises en scene* that allude to these kinds of displays. Fidelity to the genre represents a code and illustrates its specificity. For the most eloquent proof, we need only look to the Azuma House and the building constructed in the park in Utsuboin, Osaka as well as the Gallery Noda in Kobe. The first was completed in 1976, the second in 1993, and the third in 2010. Each one occupies a different type of plot but all have common characteristics. Despite having been built well over a decade apart from each other, the three houses are closely related: all are presented as closed volumes annotated only by a two-fold punctuation, in one case represented by apertures cut geometrically that scan and provide scale to the outer walls, and in the other formed by a series of cylindrical holes produced by puncturing the braces that anchor the formwork for casting the concrete. The planimetric variations generate internal spaces that are linked like the rhythms of the heart, systolically and diastolically – an alternation similar to that of the dynamic interplay between emptiness (exhaling) and fullness (inhaling) that tests itself in a series of meditation and breathing exercises. The plans and the sections coldly register the change of circumstances that have to be interpreted, the implications of

Hasso-seki teahouse of the tea master Kobori Enshu in the Temple of Konchi-in, part of the temple complex of Nanzen-ji, Sakyo-ku, Kyoto-shi, 17th century.

Dojinsai teahouse of the tea master Ashikaga Yoshimasa in the Togudo Pavilion, Temple of Jisho-ji also known as Ginkaku-ji, Sakyo-ku, Kyoto-shi, 1486.

Opposite page: Rokko Housing I, Kobe, Hyogo, 1978–1983.

4 x 4 House, Kobe, Hyogo, 2001–2003.

Chichu Art Museum, Naoshima, Kagawa, 2000–2004.

Right: 21_21 Design Sight, Minato, Tokyo, 2004–2007.

Kanden-an teahouse of the tea master Matsudaira Fumai that belonged to the Arisawa family, Matsue-shi, Shimane-ken, 1792.

However, it is not enough to understand the ultimate value of his *œuvre* and the reasons for its success in Japan and on the international stage. It is necessary to turn now to what have been described as "circumstances", and to *metis*, the "flair" one needs to possess in order to liberate oneself from it, as Jean-Pierre Vernant explained.

III

Circumstances then. "Circumstances, *circum-stare*, and if I look to European semantics (*peri-stasis* in Greek, *Umstand* in German)," writes Jullien in *Pensare l'efficacia*, "it is so that each time it signals, 'that which is around'. But what is 'around'? Around the projected subject which demands that I am the subject of an enterprise and portray myself as an island battered by waves from all sides: there is the sea with its waves in constant motion, threatening".

How does one respond to the friction of circumstances? Are there analogies between the ways in which Japanese and Western architecture have contrasted this friction? We have made references to work that should not leave doubts in this regard. The friction of circumstances shapes the practice of architecture in the West; it does not have the same effectiveness in traditional Japanese architecture where continuity prevails instead. Isn't the *sukiya* actually a demonstration of this, an "island" where void and fantasy dwell, countering "the threats of the surrounding sea" with sublime indifference?

Its size also protects the *sukiya* from the waves that surround it. Its dimensions correspond to five *tatami* as a *sūtra* of Vikramaditya prescribes. The *sūtra* relates how, in the smallest of rooms, the said Vikramāditya is able to welcome Saint Manju and eighty-four thousand disciples – an allegory, explains Okakura "of the non-existence of space for the truly enlightened". In order to reach such a place, it is necessary to complete various "paths to self-illumination". The first is fulfilled via the *roji*, the stone path that leads "randomly" to the teahouse and "has the function of breaking the links with the outside world". This is the world that architects also share with those whose lives pass by at the mercy of circumstances. In order to overcome the friction, it is said you need "flair", a quality that Ando certainly possesses and which has allowed him to obtain the success his career afforded him. However, his success doesn't come from his ability to adapt, as seen specifically in his widely recognised work outside Japan, but rather from his indifference to changing circumstances.

The theme of a *continuum* re-emerges once again. Ignoring it makes it easy to fall into banality when speaking of "flair" and not understanding how the *metis* of which Ando has offered much evidence coincides with the indifference that he reserves for circumstances in his work. Eliminating the fear of repetition is the key to this indifference. In Ando's case, repetition doesn't have anything to do with the concepts of "reproduction" and "reproducibility", which are at the root of a misunderstanding that it is easy to fall into. This is when the formal characteristics and the construction options observed in his works are considered expressions of style – a mistake that Ando, for understandable professional reasons, is not worried about correcting. Style is a form of adaptation to circumstances, to the inconstancy of taste, to changes in expectations, to material conditions, to constraints, to commitments, to mentalities, to surroundings, to culture; style reproduces and is reproduced, but it does not itself repeat.

It is this repetition that characterises the buildings of Ando instead. From the very first ones we have mentioned it has been a building choice, for example the removal of the structural – covering dichotomy – achieved thanks to the use of volumes obtained from floors in cast concrete that have the potential to always be the same. The formal implication of this syncretism is

Post supports, Tokyo.

Lindera fencing (1919) near the inner gate of the Imperial Villa of Katsura, Kyoto, 17th century.

the absence of originality, the high point of style. The style is drawn out, as are his buildings when the volumes that compose them are put together in an exceedingly satisfying manner. Yet the prolixity is also always mitigated by the repetitive use of materials and by the techniques of construction and of restraint in the treatment of details in these cases. The indifference to originality and the cult of repetition has evidently many points of contact and Japanese architecture offers a clear demonstration of this. In traditional architecture, the disposition of space tends to follow the indications of a complex wind rose; design conceptions and building solutions remain unaltered over time; the ways wood is selected and cut, joints shaped, and components tied together all presuppose the use of tools that have not needed to evolve. It is the intervention of consciousness and expertise, the end of which is self-conservation. The tools do not announce the advent of the machine and the artisan is not the forerunner of the workman. Everything about a carefully crafted Japanese house has examples as convincing as the one we are able to observe ourselves in the ties, which fasten the vertical branches of lindera to the more robust horizontal bamboo in the fencing of Katsura Villa with perfection and grace.

It is worth recalling a more prosaic detail suggested by Parise in his book on Japan, *L'eleganza è frigida*. In one of its most beautiful passages he observes the millimetric precision with which four posts were tied together to form a cage around a tree that had just been planted in a street in Tokyo. This was in 1981 and Parise noted, "it was a work that was always done by hand, that tradition demanded to be done by hand. But why? The only answer that Cartesio was able to suggest to Marco (the alter ego of the author in the story) was for aesthetic reasons, for reasons that had to be respected: tradition, the organic form of the tree, the harmony between the materials (the tree and the string) and man's contribution. All in all, it was about the level of awareness needed to turn this work of fencing in a tree into a work of art." For aesthetic reasons, writes Parise, who goes on to explain that "aesthetics" here have nothing at all to do with "originality", a pale modern reflection of the deocentric idea of art. The separation between "aesthetics" and "originality" then describes the limits occupied by the terrain of "making". In Japan, the final goal in making consists in its repeating itself, indifferent to the passage of time, fulfilling itself – according to Löwith, "when it becomes the perfect vision of the truth of things and the 'nothing-other-than' of the appearance is transformed into the precious simplicity of the 'being-so-and-nothing-else'."

"It is this way and no other" would possibly describe the walls in cement for which Ando is known. Asserting their form, they intervene as a barrier between the spaces that they define and the world "on the outside" that admires them though does not know how to interrogate their aloofness, their inscrutability, their apparent coolness. If the formwork utilised to make them describes sequences on similar surfaces that recall those separating *tatami* (even to a naïve observer), then the technique has come close to the elimination of the insignificant. For this reason, in the constructions that come closest to the attainment of this result, the concrete surfaces assume a sheen similar to those that silk fabrics possess and a consistency similar to that of *shigarami-gami*, the paper that in Japan is mixed in snow and worked only by hand. For the very same reason, those themes that suggest to clients outside of Japan the indifference that Ando reserves for "his circumstances", allow us to measure the distance that separate them and us from that which they evoke.

Church of the Light, Sunday School, Ibaraki, Osaka, 1997–1999.

Post supports, Tokyo.

Punta della Dogana Contempory Art Centre, Venice, Italy, 2006–2009.

Right: Punta della Dogana, Venice, Italy, 2006–2009.

Looking back on 40 years of architecture

Tadao Ando

The 1970s – the differences between architects of the same generation and our separate points of departure

In 1978, an exhibition was organised that was to tour ten cities in the United States. It was titled "The Japanese New Wave" and it brought to an international audience the work of seven young architects who were at the onset of their careers. I was one of those architects.

Much of the work exhibited had been produced within an urban context. In Japan, that amounted in most people's eyes to a poor architectural environment, one lacking in style where buildings reflected the personal taste of their occupants. The solutions we presented were at once quite radical and completely different from those of our contemporaries, and they gained worldwide attention for us.

During the 1960s, a time of posturing and polarisation in the art world, the critics of Modernism were gaining ground and momentum. Mainstream architecture had seen the great masters replaced by a new breed of artists like Louis Kahn, who gave a Modernist twist to Classical formalism, the New York Five, who showed off their "deconstructionism", and Aldo Rossi, whose highly original work with monuments sought to help the city remember its past.

It was within this avant-garde context that the work of the young generation of Japanese architects was welcomed. But the trajectory in Japan was different from that of our "Western" counterparts. Unlike the latter, whose rejection of the Modern Movement came from exploring it to its absolute limits, reaching an exhaustion point if you will, we had never "understood" Modernism in this way. Its failure as a universal language meant that it never established itself as a deeply rooted principle in our country; it hadn't really become something to rebel against. Instead, we developed a set of critiques based on historical imperatives, deconstructionism, ecological theories, self-building, etc.

Each of these lines of enquiry had already been tried and tested from the 1960s onwards, but the work of the New Wave carried a special charge. It played with the old boundaries and was ready for new departures. I was a radical along with many of the other architects of my generation, but I kept a distance from the Postmodernism that had become so fashionable in Japan, and from those critics who "opposed a social system based on the Modernist doctrine". While my contemporaries were making clear their distaste for Modernism – often in a showy, attention-hungry way – I was seeking to develop my architecture around its very origins.

I think it is quite likely that the path I followed was a result of being self-taught and from having received no formal academic training as such. It was during my formative years, outside the institutional channels, that I became focused on "direct vision" as the essential element for a work of architecture, rather than entrusting myself to abstract notions of a technical or theoretical nature – for me it was about the concrete. I thought it was important to visit the buildings and the cities in person, and in this way I would gradually discover their real essence. That would be my starting point. Then, during my late twenties, I took off on a long trip to Europe and the United States to see for myself firsthand how architecture had developed in the Western world, from classical times up to the present. I confess that I did not have much of a foundation to build on, and I wanted to familiarise myself with the most famous monuments from each historical period. I believe it was this type of approach, characterised by simplicity and a sense of urgency, that proved positive and allowed me an encounter with the works that was free of prejudice.

It was during this period of reconnaissance that I was struck by a strong "will to construct", expressed both within the buildings and in the cities I explored. It was a quality that was quite absent in the Japanese consciousness. Moreover, in engaging with the works that form the corpus of Modernism this way, I was able to appreciate just how heterogeneous they were. Even if they both belong together as the founders of the Modern Movement, the architectural works of Alvar Aalto from Finland and Le Corbusier of Switzerland show marked differences in relation to the spatial characteristics that their structures embody. And, in the works of Le Corbusier, space is manipulated quite differently, for example in the buildings from the "White Period" or the Ronchamp Chapel.

What, then, is Modernism? Can one claim that its ideals have been fully achieved and that, for this reason, as a movement it has nowhere further to go? Sensitive to the dreams of early Modernism, I recognised its infinite potential rather than its limits. I saw a role for Modernism's formal principles and their practical application in an architecture of the future. I was against the way in which Modernism had been exploited for the financial ends that have become so dominant they exclude all others, and where profit and utility take precedence over style and quality. It was in recognising its diversity, its inherent contradictions, and the disparate approaches to Modernism that made my work quite distinct.

A spatial prototype halfway between the abstract and the concrete

One of the principal Postmodernist themes throughout the 1960s and 1970s was the denial of any connection with Modernism. In particular, certain American architects such as Robert Venturi, who had published a book entitled *Complexity and Contradiction in Architecture*, and Charles Moore, a supporter of the grassroots architecture movement, who had elaborated on a theory and a style of relativism in modern architecture. Under the direct influence of this movement, it was becoming the norm among the younger generation to give expression to theories of populism and decorativism through an architectural kitsch.

Faced with the frustrating prospect of having to design office blocks that only took into account the functional aspect of the building, or poor-quality suburban developments that looked the same everywhere, even I could sympathise with Venturi's pronouncement that "Less is bore", an ironic play on the more celebrated motto of Mies van der Rohe "Less is more". However, I had never let myself be seduced by the trend of cladding buildings in the Pop style, or be swayed by historical precedent or by the appeal of the play of forms to express "multiplicity".

One of my motives was to find a likeness to the situation I was living at the time. I was a novice architect and, what's more, I studied independently. Most of my commissioned work was for low-cost single-occupancy dwellings on tiny plots in densely populated urban centres. The debate surrounding this was carried out in the language of high art, which for me was too abstract and divorced from reality. Another reason, and a more personal one, was that I preferred metaphor to simile. For example, in the dispute between the "vernacular" and the "featureless", planners that turned to Postmodern theories thought traditional village architecture was strictly bound by its local setting. They would apply a stock formula based on the specific context. I would instead hold that the essence of the problem lay in preserving the spirit concealed behind the form handed down, instead of applying a simplistic genealogical formula. The "spirit of the village" expressed itself in a wish to return to the most commonly used materials and construction methods that produced houses which were well adapted to the local climate – in a way, which met the needs of their occupants. In wanting to conceive of a vernacular style for a contemporary city, I was now called upon to consider and make sense of how space can be used to welcome the existence of people rather than resort to the superficial symbolism, construction methods and materials that are in such wide use today.

So I began to construct urban dwellings in the form of simple units that were compared to hollow pipes. They were formed in reinforced concrete on both the inside and the outside. I imagined a simple, strong aesthetic in balance with the environment, where light and space were articulated into a narrative in the interior. It was an attempt to rehabilitate the minimalist aesthetic of "Less is more", in the sense that I sought to eliminate all the superficial elements and to simplify expression. Modernism dealt with the language problem from a purely aesthetic point of view, separating it from real life. In my work, I was taking a risk on being able to harmonise a real and concrete part of life with its abstract representation.

The Row House in Sumiyoshi

Completed in 1976, the Row House in Sumiyoshi, also known as Azuma House, is the work that provided the model for the Courthouse. Closed to the city on each side, and with a microcosmic interior arranged around a courtyard, this was to become a characteristic form of my architecture. In one respect, the house possesses qualities quite different from those of the functional rationalism that was influential in residential building styles of that period. Located on a "narrow slot site", the blank walls appear to be uncompromisingly closed off to the outside world. An internal courtyard takes

Row House in Sumiyoshi (Azuma House), Osaka, 1975–1976.

up one-third of an already tiny plot and interrupts the usual circulation of the interior. Given that it was such a small-scale project, it was quite surprising that it generated so much controversy. "This house is an act of violence perpetrated by an architect who has sacrificed the lives of its occupants and ignored every link between the building and its surrounding environment," typified the tone of the critics who, from my point of view, failed to understand what I was doing. Yes, I had made radical decisions, but far from ignoring the needs of daily life, I had carefully reflected on every aspect related to being human, the relationship between architecture and the city and how they all impacted on each other. I had contemplated deeply what was necessary for life in that locality and what gave it meaning. I eventually arrived at the conclusion that despite being in the centre of the city, to co-exist successfully with nature was an essential part of our existence. Paradoxically, it was because of this that the house was closed off to the outside. An empty internal space was circumscribed, making it possible to experience the changing seasons, as harsh or pleasant as they may be, by giving the elements priority over and above more conventional comforts.

The use of comparatively few materials – in particular reinforced concrete for both the outside and the interior – mixed with a search for geometrical abstraction that was carried through to the most minute details, was developed from the idea of "subtraction", taken in this case to its logical conclusion. Severe restraints imposed by the site and the available budget were also factors. For this reason, with regard to the materials, particular attention was paid to tactile qualities. I wanted to bring out their delicacy rather than their brute strength, their smoothness rather than roughness; to render them soft to the touch in ways familiar to the sensibility of the Japanese, accustomed as they are to houses made of wood and paper. I was persuaded of the need to exhibit all of the qualities linked to the actual material as the house had been deprived of all the inessential elements and reduced to an ensemble of bare forms.

In this way I tried with these purified units of reinforced concrete to create a prototype that offered infinite options for manipulation which, on the one hand, would dramatise the harshness that comprises the life of man, bound inextricably

Rokko Housing I, Kobe, Hyogo, 1978–1983.

as it is with nature and, on the other hand, to reach a totally simplified abstract representation.

It was fortunate that I had the chance to inscribe this house there, anomalous as it was, in the otherwise uninterrupted sequence of the row. It was my own audacity, which you could put down to my age at the time, the courage of my clients, and the construction company that then made it possible to see this difficult project through to completion.

It was thanks to the Row House project, with its continuous demands for solving complex problems – reconciling the tenets of Modernism and the vernacular with the needs of the clients and the day-to-day management of formal and practical questions – that I was able to find myself as an architect in an otherwise anonymous quarter of Osaka.

The development of the "closed unit"

After completing the Row House in Sumiyoshi, I started on other small-scale urban residences that allowed me to further explore the expressive potential of the "closed unit". During the same period I had begun designing modest commercial buildings using the same scheme of composition in which I would include open spaces in the form of dramatic voids for use as public areas. In order to achieve a completely confined space, in which to create an abstract microcosm of nature that allowed an encounter with the elements, I had developed the idea of a universal architecture that infused itself into the city by manifesting a closed, introverted character. It has come to be known as "guerilla style".

After about ten years in the profession, however, I began getting chances to work in different contexts from the ones I was used to. At that point I no longer felt a need to build walls along the edge of the plots or to cut myself the necessary space into the urban fabric of the city. Now able to work more freely in areas immersed in nature, I began to search for a new vocabulary to supercede that of the "closed unit". During this period of great change for me, between the end of the 1970s and the first half of the following decade, I worked on such projects as Rokko Housing, which was a housing complex, the Koshino House and the Time's Building.

With the Rokko Housing, it was the first time that I confronted the theme of public housing and, in this case, it was

Koshino House and addition, Ashiya, Hyogo, 1979–1984.

Time's I, II, Kyoto, 1983–1984.

quite a sizable project. It was also the first time that I had worked on a collective residential project. Two fundamental themes emerged here: a design that gave integrity to the whole but at the same time individualised a solution that met the challenge of building on a south-facing, 60-degree grade.

To this end, I adapted a geometric grid to the configuration of the terrain and took advantage of the irregularities in the landscape to integrate contrast within the whole. This allowed marginal areas to be utilised as public spaces – transitional neutral zones between nature and the built-up areas.

The solutions ultimately adopted were a clear consequence of the difficulties imposed by the site and were for this reason applicable only to that specific case. However, the personal experience I gained in the process of a project based on such a "dialogue with nature" became a precious point of reference at a time when I was beginning to work on much larger architectural visions. I followed up this experiment at Rokko in phase II, III, and IV.

With the Koshino House project, I had the advantage, to begin with, of what was for me a superb setting: a village location on a densely wooded hillside. Further, I had been given free rein with regard to the programme and its eventual size. Finally, I had the possibility not only to approach for the first time the relationship between a building and open spaces, but also to consider a different set of challenges from the one posed when building small residential units in central urban locations. Great possibilities existed here in bringing in line elements of the composition with the individulisation of a type of domestic space more at home with natural surroundings. I looked for ways to work with the topography of the place, as if the house was governed by an autonomous geometric order. Inside, the spaces had an affinity to those of the Row House, made up of aestheticised "boxes", but the play of light and the views introduced by openings cut into the walls conferred on the space a singular character. In this way, it was a design originally conceived as a study in light. This discovery, made whilst working on Koshino House, signalled the start of a new phase of development for me in my work and the beginning of the end of the "closed box".

Commercial buildings are seen as having little cultural value and are often ignored. The Time's, a project planned for

Church on the Water, Shimukappu, Hokkaido, 1985–1988.

Church of the Light, Ibaraki, Osaka, 1987–1989.

a riverside complex located by the Takase River in Kyoto, gave me the opportunity of raising the profile of such developments and give them a role in providing more accessible space within a city.

With this theme, I wanted to achieve a pleasing public space that made a positive contribution to an urban environment while also making the case for buildings with a river frontage that had been overlooked in previous urban regeneration programmes. I put forward the suggestion of a building organised around a public space that was open on one side to the river and worked as a sort of garden promenade. In Time's I approached the question of a building's relationship with nature in a quite different way than in the past. Instead of creating in the interior a microcosm assembled around a closed courtyard, where human contact with the elements is made, I sought to open up the building and integrate the architecture with the exterior surroundings. The construction of a context that allowed the incorporation of nature into the building has now become a recurring theme in my work.

The Rokko Housing, the Koshino House and the Time's building – each one of these projects represented a different attempt to destroy the "box" and to set up a dialogue between the building and its surroundings.

The theme of place

In my career I have been given the opportunity to design two churches, both around the same time, towards the end of the 1980s. The first of the two projects was the Church on the Water, a chapel set amidst an extraordinary landscape on the banks of an artificial lake on the island of Hokkaido. In the second, known as the Church of the Light, I was hoping to create a symbolic space using the vocabulary of minimalism manifest in the elements of reinforced concrete and light – a design objective that had to be achieved within severe budget constraints.

I believe the direction that my work took during this period, and the achievement of a "oneness" between the buildings and nature, was clearly manifested above all due to the spiritual component that lay behind the completion of these religious works. Once these projects had been finished, however, at the end of the 1980s, I decided to stop working

Children's Museum,
Himeji, Hyogo, 1987–1989.

on residential and commercial edifices and instead concentrate exclusively on public buildings, in particular museum complexes. By increasing both the scale and complexity of the projects, I was able to single out a unique theme of research – the paring down of superficial elements – and this was to become the objective of my work.

This theme was about "the creation of a context within architecture that was done in such a way as to express the character of the place in which it dwelt". It was a theme that I had explored up until the 1980s by elaborating on various architectural prototypes, the first one of which was the Row House in Sumiyoshi. The character of a place – that is, the complex quality that it possessed – included things such as its natural characteristics, conservation issues involving the presence of existing buildings, and old traditions that had endured there.

In working within surroundings where the landscape had special seductive qualities (marked by a certain beauty in the type of land or by more intangible qualities like its state of wildness), I was looking to capture the spirit of the place by incorporating abstract references to the topography of the site and harmonising the marginal spaces into a pattern, all as part of the overall project. From the outside this appeared to consist in staging a battle between man and nature. From the inside, however, it was a matter of using the actual architectural language to create a mechanism that allowed human beings to interact with the natural world around them.

The Children's Museum and the Museum of Literature in Himeji were the first of these structures that I designed; they were also the first works in which I explored these themes in any depth. Such methods of architectural planning, narrowly bound to the site, came to define a form of design known as "site-craft". At the same time it was an attempt to respond to a type of architectural planning that was beginning to attract the attention of public authorities and which required areas that allowed for the interaction of interior and exterior spaces.

The programme concerning the Chikatsu-Asuka Historical Museum near Osaka once again called for a building that was radical when seen in the historical context of the location. I proposed a structure that wasn't trapped in the

Museum of Literature,
Himeji, Hyogo, 1988–1991.

Chikatsu-Asuka Historical Museum, Minamikawachi, Osaka, 1990–1994.

Sayamaike History Museum, Osakasayama, Osaka, 1994–2001.

Suntory Museum, Osaka, 1989–1994.

Hyogo Prefectural Museum of Art and Kobe Waterfront Plaza, Kobe, Hyogo, 1997–2001.

Oyamazaki Villa Museum, Otokuni, Kyoto, 1991–1995.

International Library of Children's Literature, Taito, Tokyo, 1996–2002.

conventional canons of museum design. The stepped roof of the museum allowed for a panoramic view of the tombs and graves scattered throughout the grounds, and the museum site was traversed with pathways allowing visitors to interact peacefully with the artefacts. I used this idea again in a modified version in the History Museum in Sayamaike, also just outside Osaka. The attempt to integrate the building with its surroundings, however, required me to go further in order to transcend the limitations that I was up against.

The Suntory Museum and the Hyogo Prefectural Museum of Art were both cases in which I sought to realise an ideal relationship between architecture and location. With two spots facing the water, I erected new public buildings along the seafront, creating a strong link between the site and the sea. In order to do so I had broken down a number of barriers, not only in the physical sense of spacial limits but also from the point of view of jurisdiction, by intervening in the areas governed by the state, the prefecture, the city and the private sector. These were works on a much larger scale than the experiments of the past such as the Time's building.

The Oyamazaki Villa Museum and the International Library of Children's Literature were planned such that the dialogue with the site took into account the connection with the existing buildings. In interventions like these, in which the themes required the conservation and "recycling" of that which was already there, I made a pledge with myself to do something more than just introduce new architectural elements as if they were an appendage grafted onto the inside of an existing shell. My aim was to establish an interplay between the old and the new. By means of the energy released from this ideal collision, it was possible to create a connection between memory and the future.

Omotesando Hills, a luxury complex that juxtaposes commercial spaces and residences in one of Tokyo's most exclusive avenues, was an intervention of new buildings. Here, the theme was complicated by the fact that I wanted to maintain a conception of place that would be familiar to what existed there. Japan had always adopted a political short-sightedness as far as urban development was concerned, giving priority to the economic aspect of interventions. As a consequence, we devalued the importance of community and

Omotesando Hills, residential and commercial complex, Shibuya, Tokyo, 1996–2006.

Left: Awaji-Yumebutai, Awaji, Hyogo, 1993–1999.

Right: Vitra Seminar House, Weil am Rhein, Germany, 1987–1993.

FABRICA (Benetton Communication Research Centre), Treviso, Italy, 1992–2000.

Armani / Teatro, Milan, Italy, 2000–2001.

Palazzo Grassi Renovation, Venice, Italy, 2005–2006.

Punta della Dogana, Venice, Italy, 2006–2009.

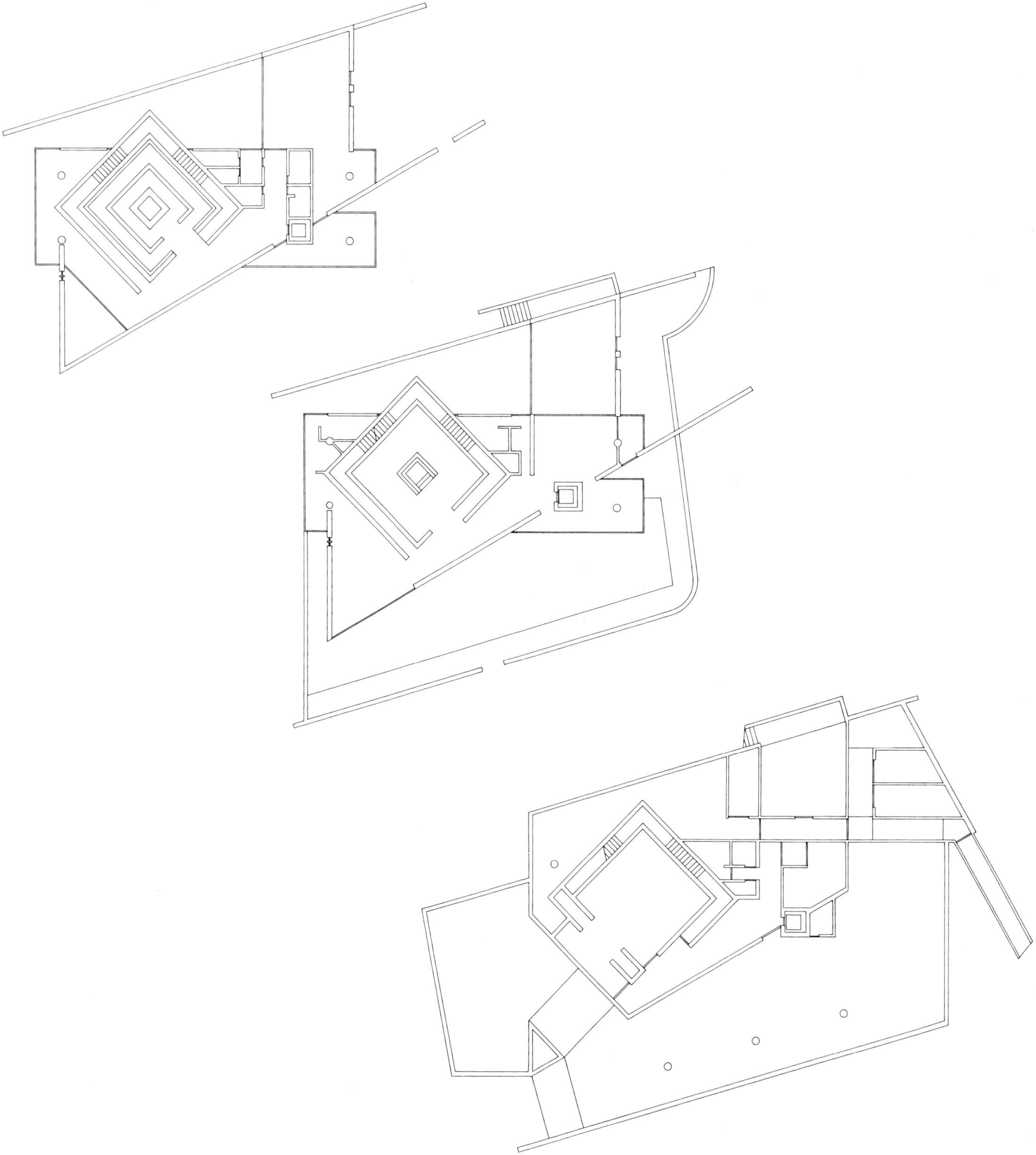

Left: Plans of the first floor, ground floor and basement of the library.

Right: A view of the east façade and the view south-east of the archive library.

External and internal views of the lounge space in the cylinder head north-east of the library.

Opposite page: Elevations and sections of the library.

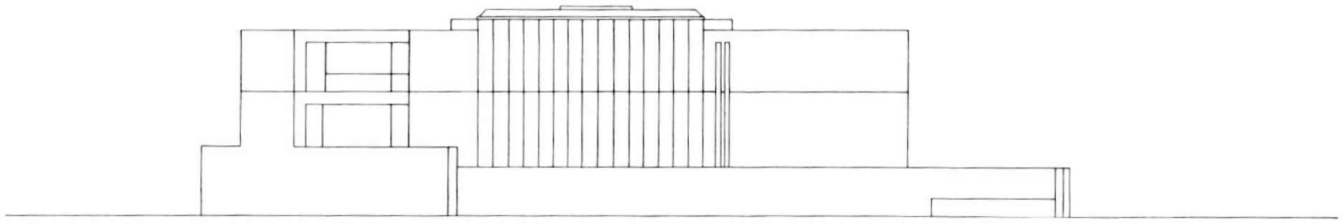

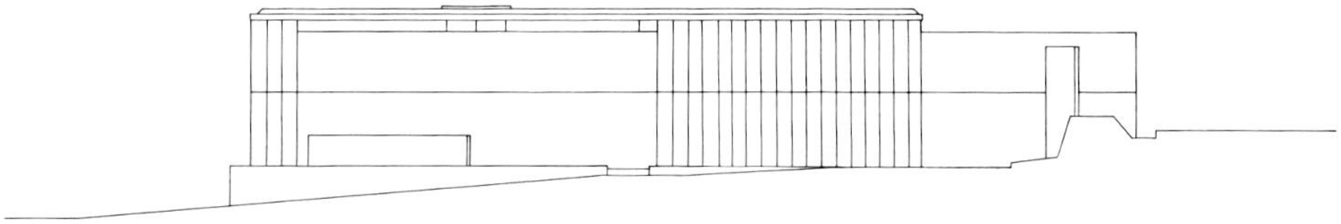

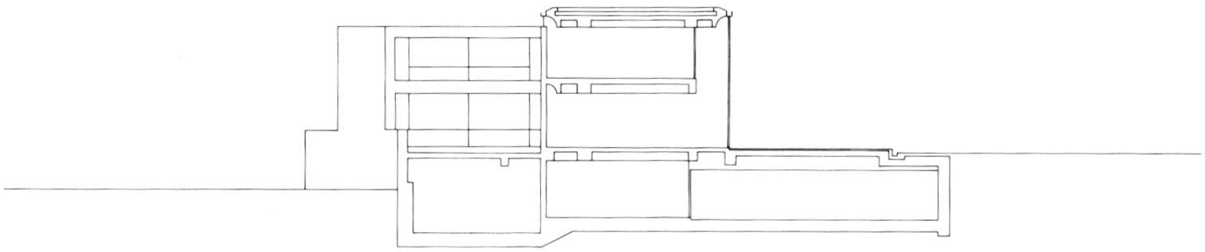

Benesse House Museum

Location Naoshima, Kagawa, Japan
Design 1988–1990
Construction 1990–1992
Site area 44,700 sq m
Building area 1,775 sq m
Total area 3,643 sq m

Naoshima is a smallish island in the Inland Sea of Japan. The site is perched atop a narrow promontory on the southern tip of the island and overlooks the gently lapping waves below.

The museum is oriented and designed so that visitors can reach it directly from the ferry landing. After crossing a wharf, guests arrive at a terraced square that is the entrance to the complex itself. The terrace doubles as a stage for outdoor events and houses the entrance to an underground annexe of the building. Only once you have ascended the stairway with stone walls does the main nucleus of the museum become visible.

Because the complex is situated in a spectacular national park, more than half of the building's footprint is under-

Sketch of the project highlighting the entrance.

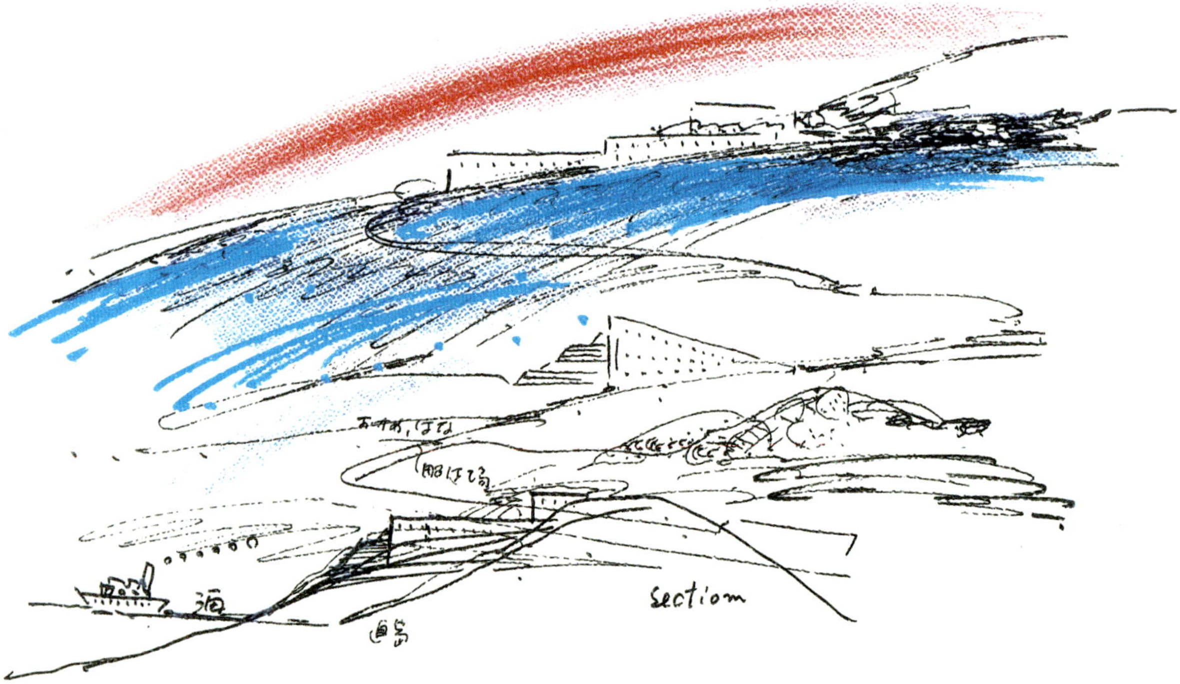

Study sketches.

Right: Views of the rotunda from the south-west and the graded stairs.

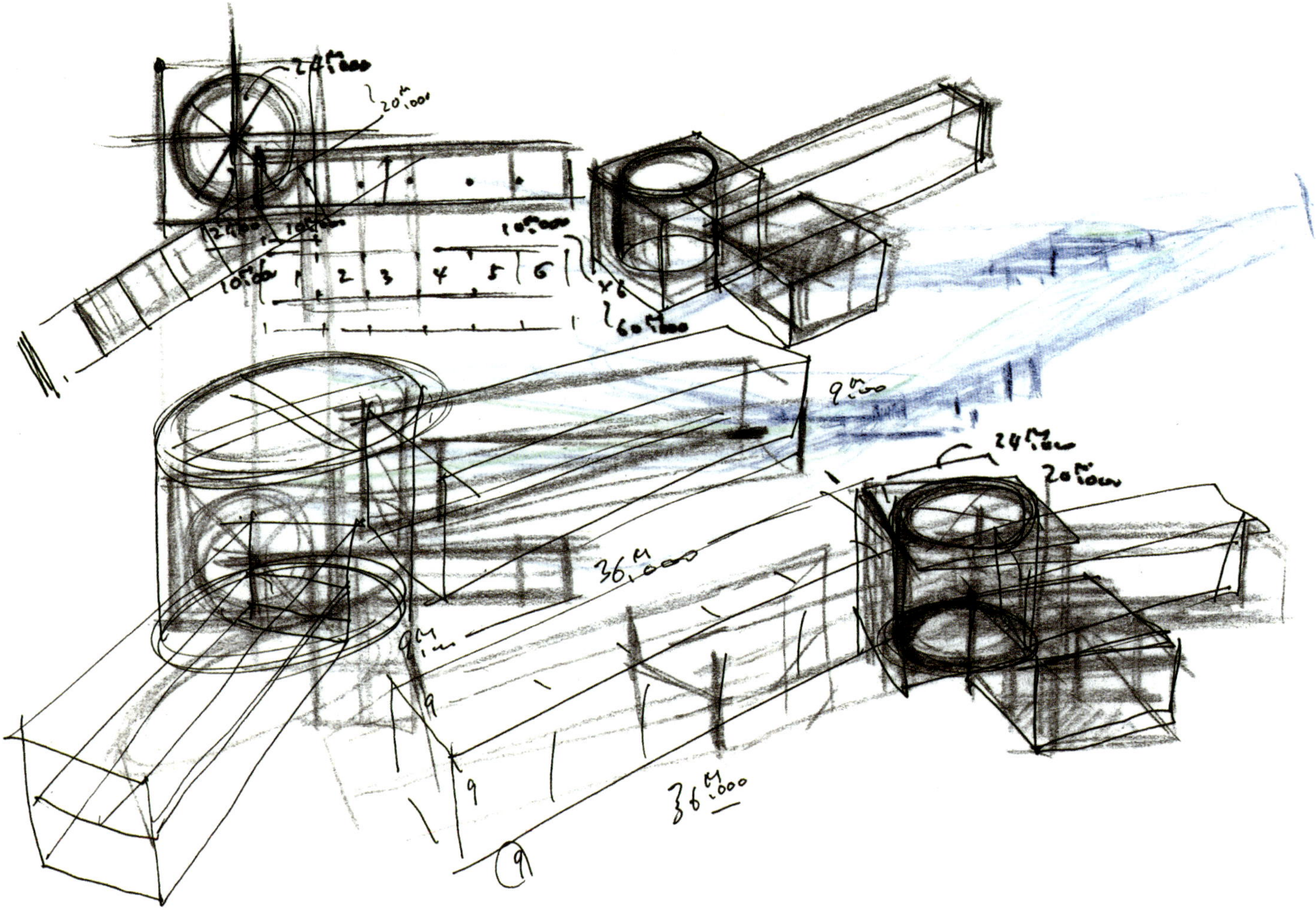

Left: Views of the covers towards the Inland Sea of Japan and view from the steps of the wharf with the gallery exhibition forum for open-air events.

Right: Elevations and sections.

ground, a concept that does well to minimise the visual impact upon the surrounding terrain.

Upon ascending or descending the ramp, visitors pass through the main entrance of the building and access a large, two-storey subterranean gallery that is about 50 metres long and eight metres wide. The wing containing the hotel, the gallery and graded terrace all face the coast, allowing the serene seascape with boats and dazzling sunsets to sweep into the interior of the building. Around the complex are pathways periodically punctuated with vista points from which to relax and absorb the ocean views.

Much like the sculptures outside in the museum courtyard, this building was placed amidst an expansive natural landscape, dug into the earth in order to generate a new landscape.

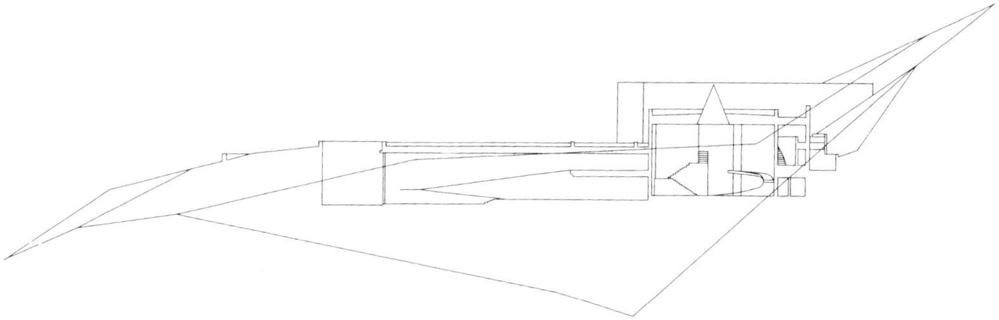

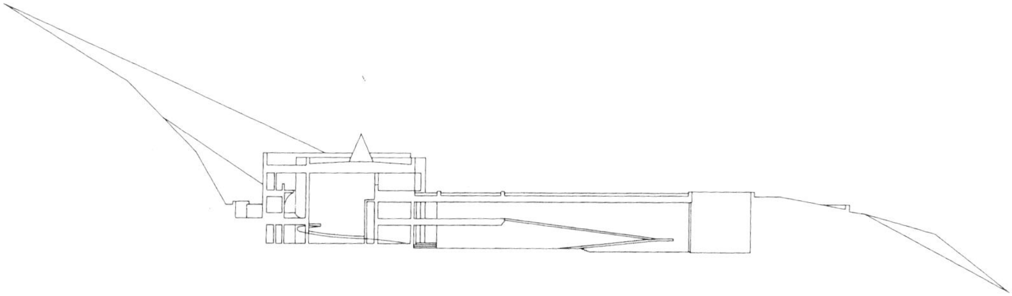

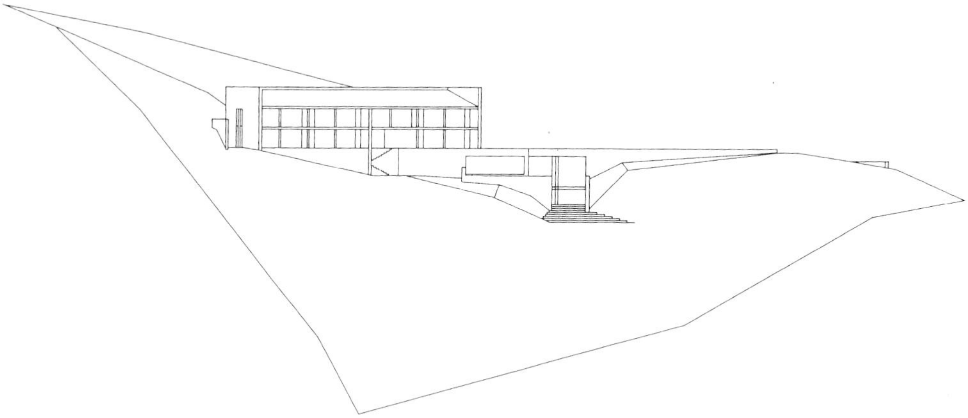

Plans of the second floor, first floor and basement.

Opposite page: Perspective from the access ramp and a beautiful graded terrace overlooking the coast.

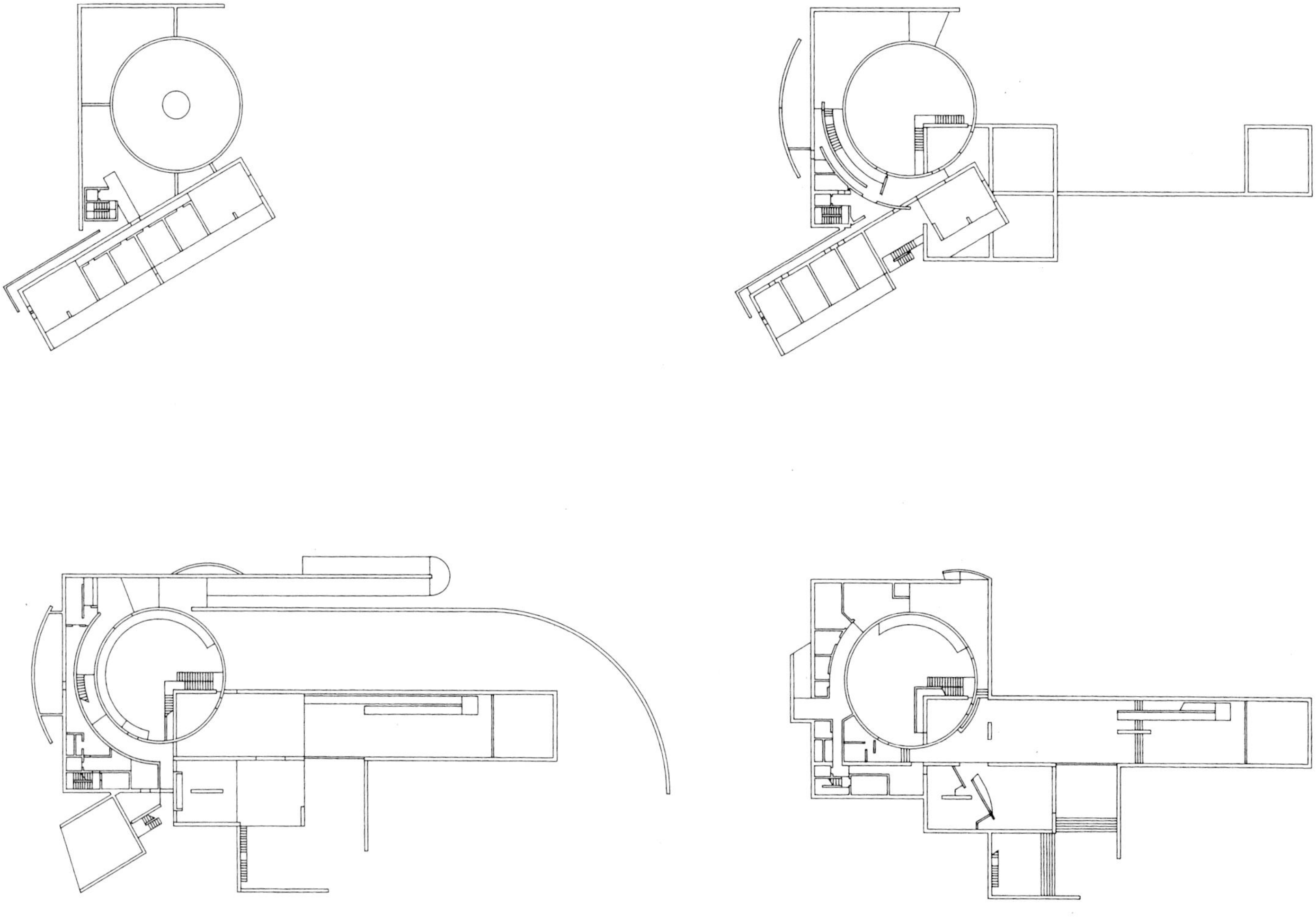

LIVE AND DIE
PISS AND DIE
SPEAK AND DIE
FEEL AND DIE
SHIT AND LIVE
HEAR AND LIVE
YOUNG AND DIE
RUN AND DIE
STAND AND DIE
STAND AND LIVE

Interior views of the exhibition gallery.

Study sketches.

Right: View from the sea.

Location Osaka, Japan
Design 1989–1992
Construction 1992–1994
Site area 13,429 sq m (museum and plaza)
Building area 3,984 sq m
Total area 13,804 sq m (museum); 2,697 sq m (plaza)

This project explores water and its importance in contemporary society, more specifically its role in everyday life and experience. The project transformed part of the seaboard in front of the museum into a plaza 100 metres long and 40 metres wide that slopes down toward the water through a sweeping system of ramps and stairs.

The philosophy behind the project was to turn a museum into a theatre. It also shows the common link between Ando's projects and water. Much like a theatre is a connection between the audience and the show, this project is a connection between the audience and the art. The museum is a link to the ocean, a place to enjoy the breeze and the sound of waves breaking on the shore, and it is a venue where the sun sets on both the water and on the crowd around you.

The steps are a grandstand for spectators, who can watch several stages at once. To accent continuity between the plaza and the sea, five pillars at the water's edge are replicated over the breakwater 70 metres from shore. The building consists of a huge volume drum, or inverted cone, that has a diameter of 40 metres at the top and is intersected by two rectangular prisms. The drum contains a sphere 32 metres in diameter that houses an IMAX theatre.

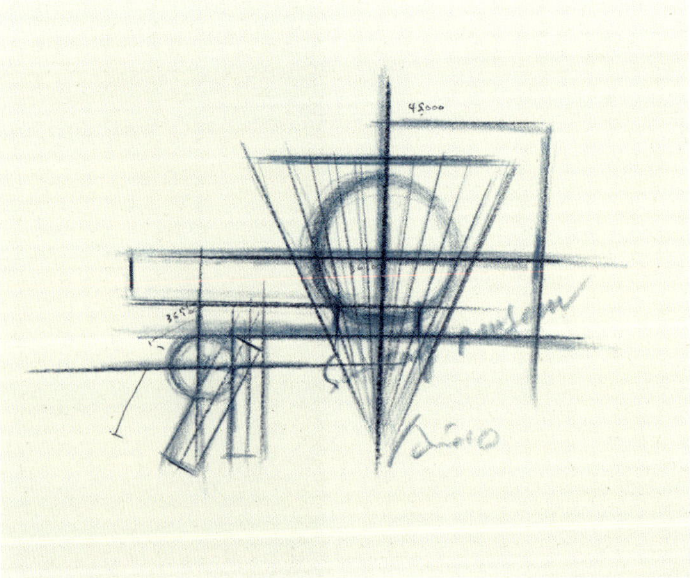

J.C.T.C.

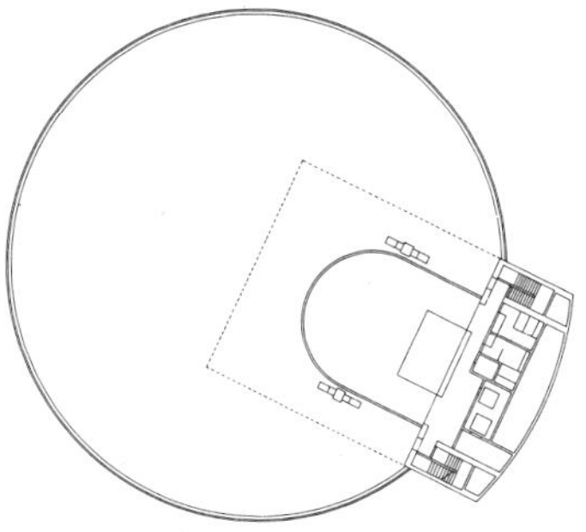

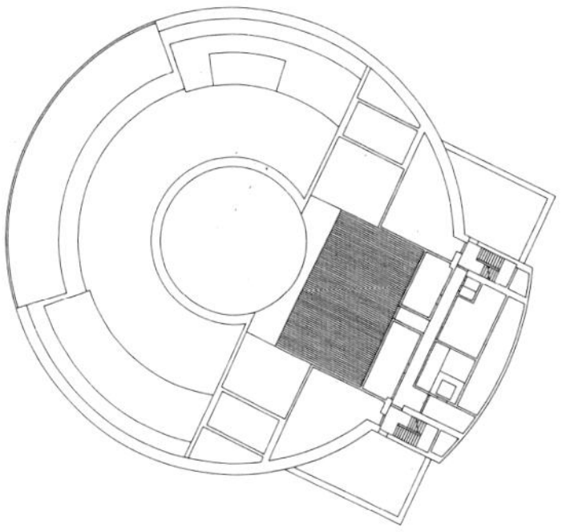

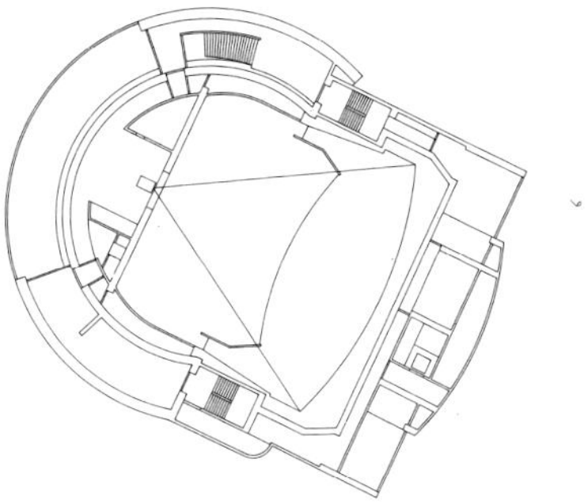

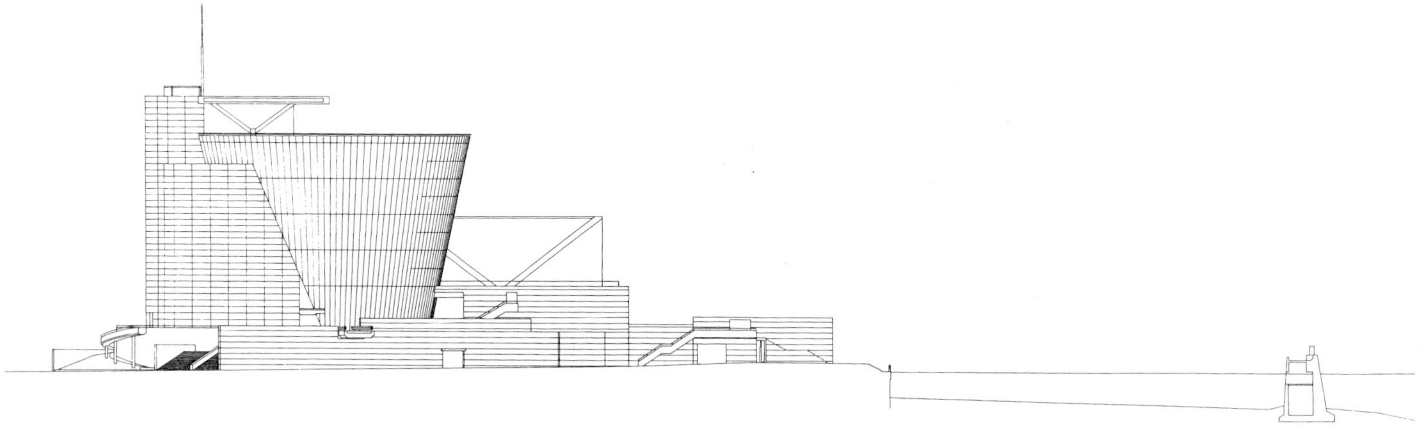

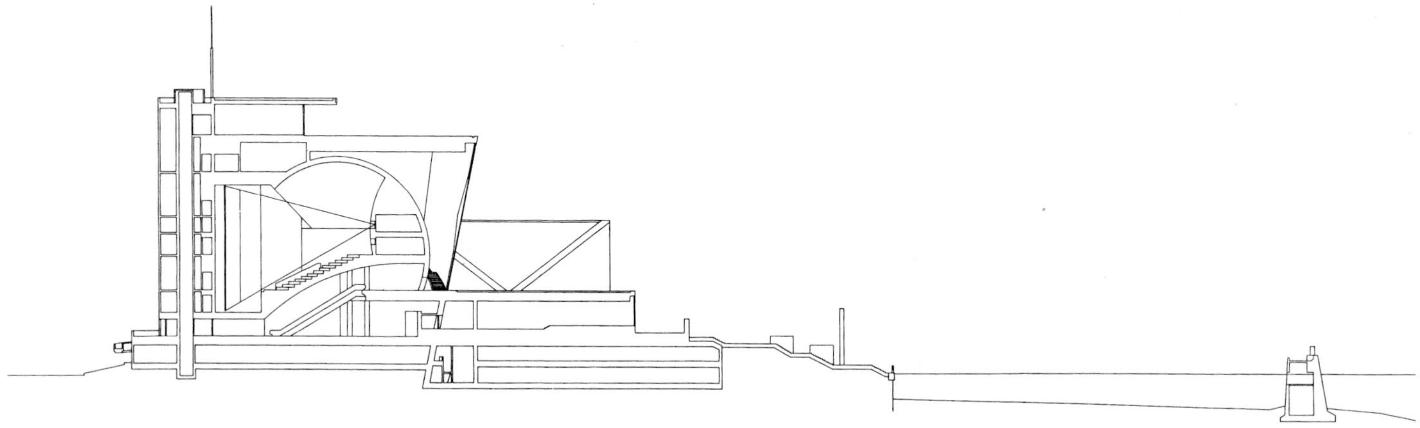

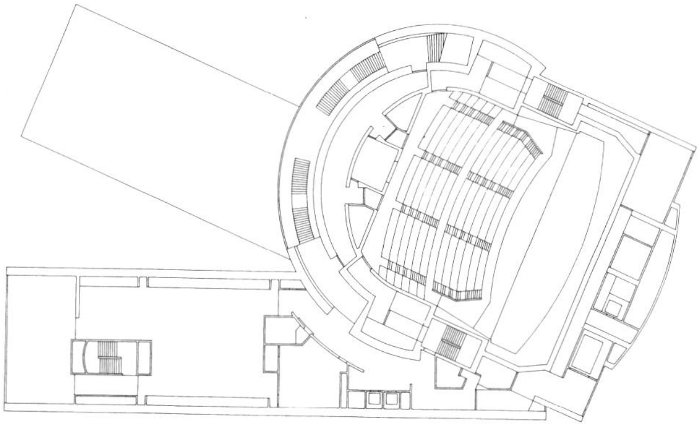

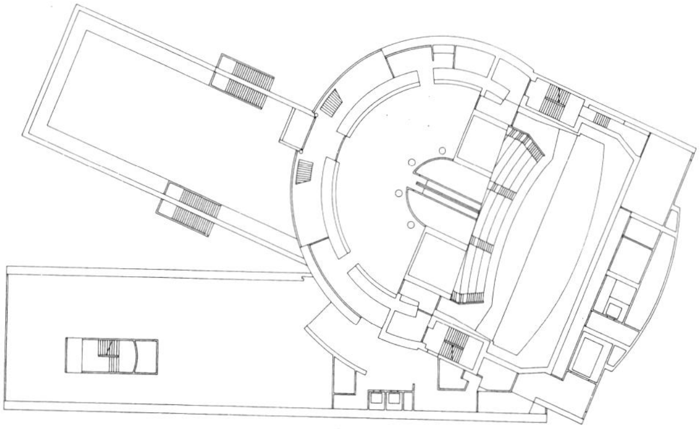

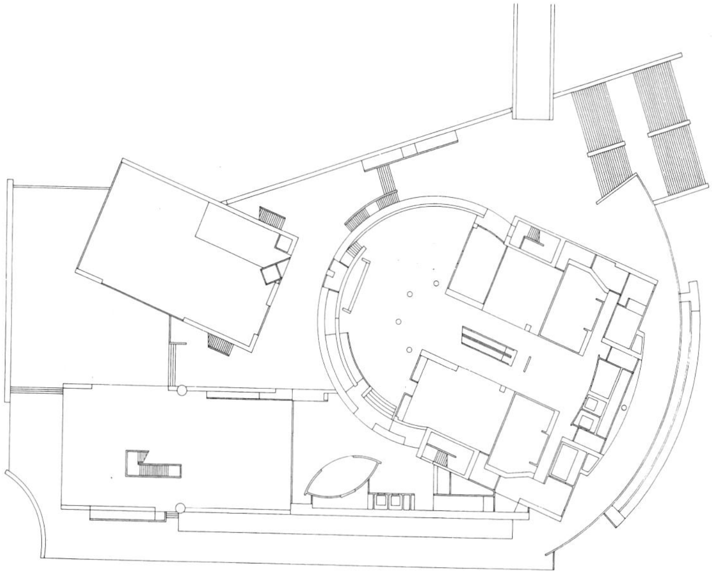

Opposite page: Plans for the eighth, seventh and fifth floors, sections and northern elevations.

Plans for the first, third and fourth floors.

Interior view of the entrance and the IMAX Theatre.

Right: View of the stepped plaza on the western side.

29

Inamori Auditorium

Location Kagoshima, Japan
Design 1991–1993
Construction 1993–1994
Site area 1,846 sq m
Building area 810 sq m
Total area 1,613 sq m

This auditorium was commissioned by the founder of Kyocera, Kazuo Inamori, for his alma mater, the University of Kagoshima. The idea for the oval space was taken from a previous design created in 1989 for the restoration of the Nakanoshima City Hall, where it was proposed that an egg-shaped room be placed inside the existing structure to establish a harmonious contrast between old and new. At Inamori's request, this solution, which had been passed over in Nakanoshima, was recovered the following year for the university's auditorium. Inamori's concept was that the modern design would act as a catalyst and inspiration to the students at the university, who themselves are charged with shaping the future.

Unlike the town hall in Nakanoshima, however, the egg-shaped hall here emerges from the interior through to the exterior. Strictly speaking, this volume is an ellipsoid whose oval projection is evident in plan, elevation and section. Unlike the churches of Borromini in Rome, which are characterised by repeated and combined use of oval shapes, the all-round visibility of this volume can simultaneously convey unity and continuity of form.

As the structure of an egg comes from the rotation of an ellipse, it therefore has two foci that create a trajectory and a dynamism that is lacking in a sphere. What makes this structure of interest is that it has the potential to offer the very definition of an awe-filled space. A form with two centres can symbolise the coexistence of old and new, local and global, individual and collective, and so on. The main aspiration of this project was therefore to establish a fruitful dialogue between these opposite behaviours in order to promote dynamic and creative behaviour.

In the history of architecture there are countless examples of oval forms being used – take Michelangelo's Campidoglio, for example – but none have three-dimensional ovals. This is one of the things that inspired the experimentation with this figure. The second was the techni-

View of the oval room through the exterior window.

Elevation and views of the front entrance.

Following pages:
Plans of the second floor, first floor and basement.

Front and reverse shot of the access ramp to the room and an inside view of the auditorium lit through optical fibres.

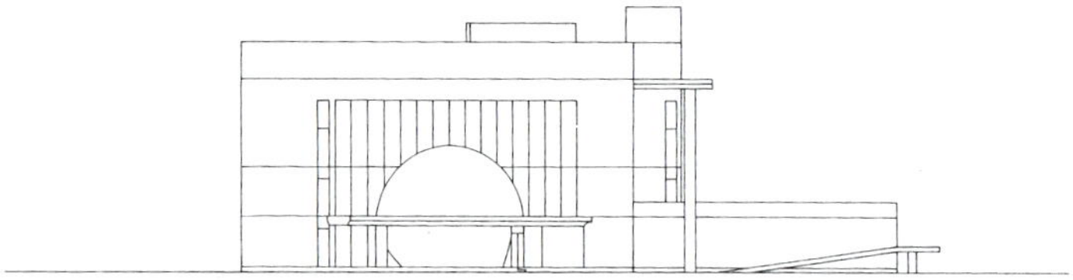

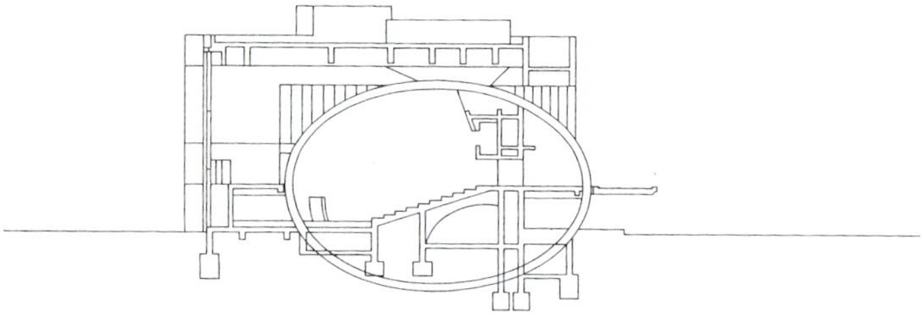

cal challenge represented by the difficulty of implementing such a structure in exposed concrete.

The design for the construction of the oval shell casing was done with the aid of a computer, but the concavity and convexity were the result of craftsmanship by local carpenters. Putting up the concrete formwork for this project was also very different and far more complicated than erecting a standard vertical wall. A further obstacle revolved around the problem of giving equal curvature at every recess and termination of the oval.

The outer wall that surrounds the egg accents the external quarter-ellipse whose curvilinear segment is emboldened by a glazed colonnade that creates a visual continuity with the surrounding vegetation. A spiral ramp emphasises access to the room, approaching and then moving away from the line of demarcation between the exterior and the interior. The auditorium lighting is created using a system of fibre optics together with a natural light source that provides a starry sky effect.

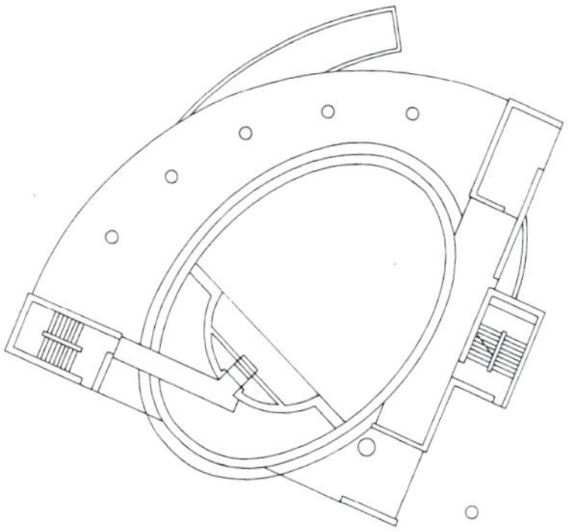

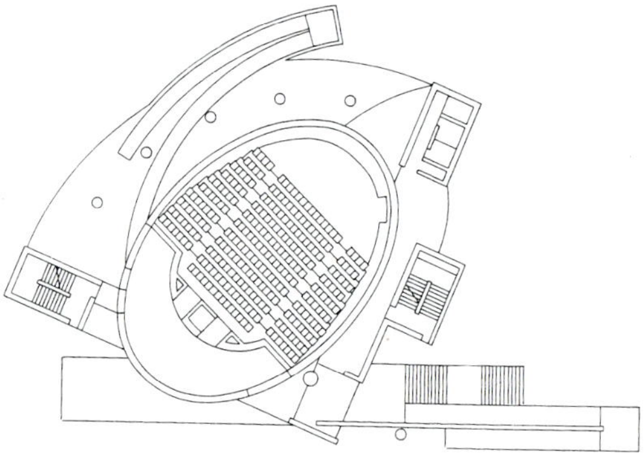

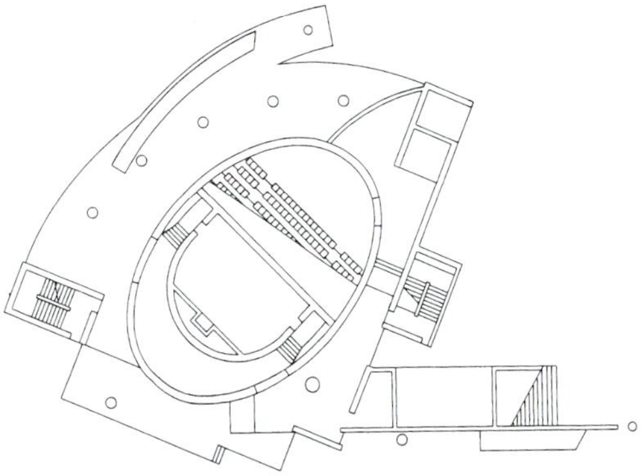

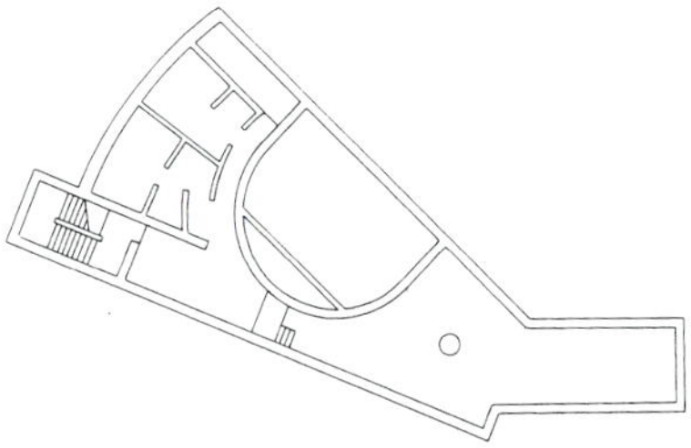

Nariwa Museum

Location Nariwa, Okayama, Japan
Design 1991–1993
Construction 1993–1994
Site area 7,608 sq m
Building area 1,490 sq m
Total area 2,691 sq m

Nariwa is a provincial town in Okayama Prefecture located north of Kurashiki. For many years it has had a flourishing economy thanks to the copper deposits in the area. Nariwa-cho is famous for its rural houses called Fukiya, with their distinctive red ochre colour.

The museum here is located between an old villa surrounded by a stone wall and a steep slope facing south. It consists of a concrete cube fenced in by its own perimeter.

Arriving at the museum, visitors are first greeted by the old stone wall, which shows the patina of time. Then they climb a long staircase built around the L-shaped concrete block and are presented with a panoramic vista of the cultivated slopes to the west and the large body of water interposed between them and the museum. The main objective of the project was to transform this building into a meeting place between nature, culture and history.

Sketched study and view of the pool on the south side.

The entrance through the stone wall to the east and a terrace at the south wing.

Opposite page: The entrance foyer.

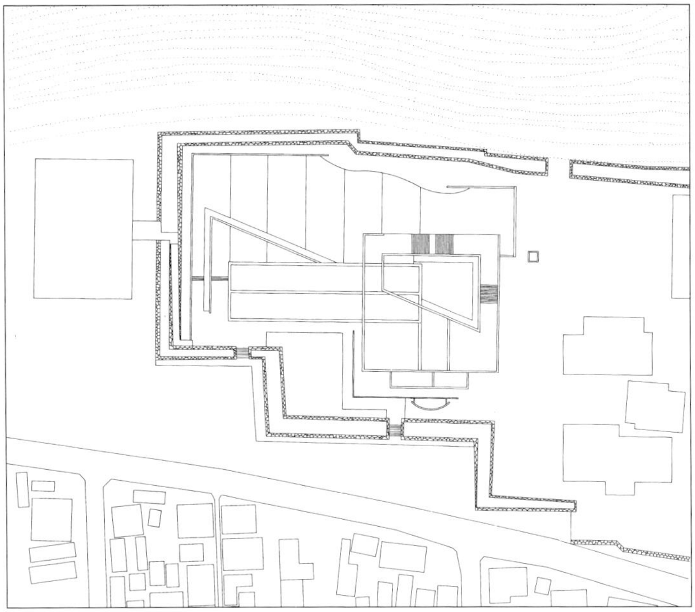

Site plan and axonometric draft.

Right: Plans of the first and ground floors.

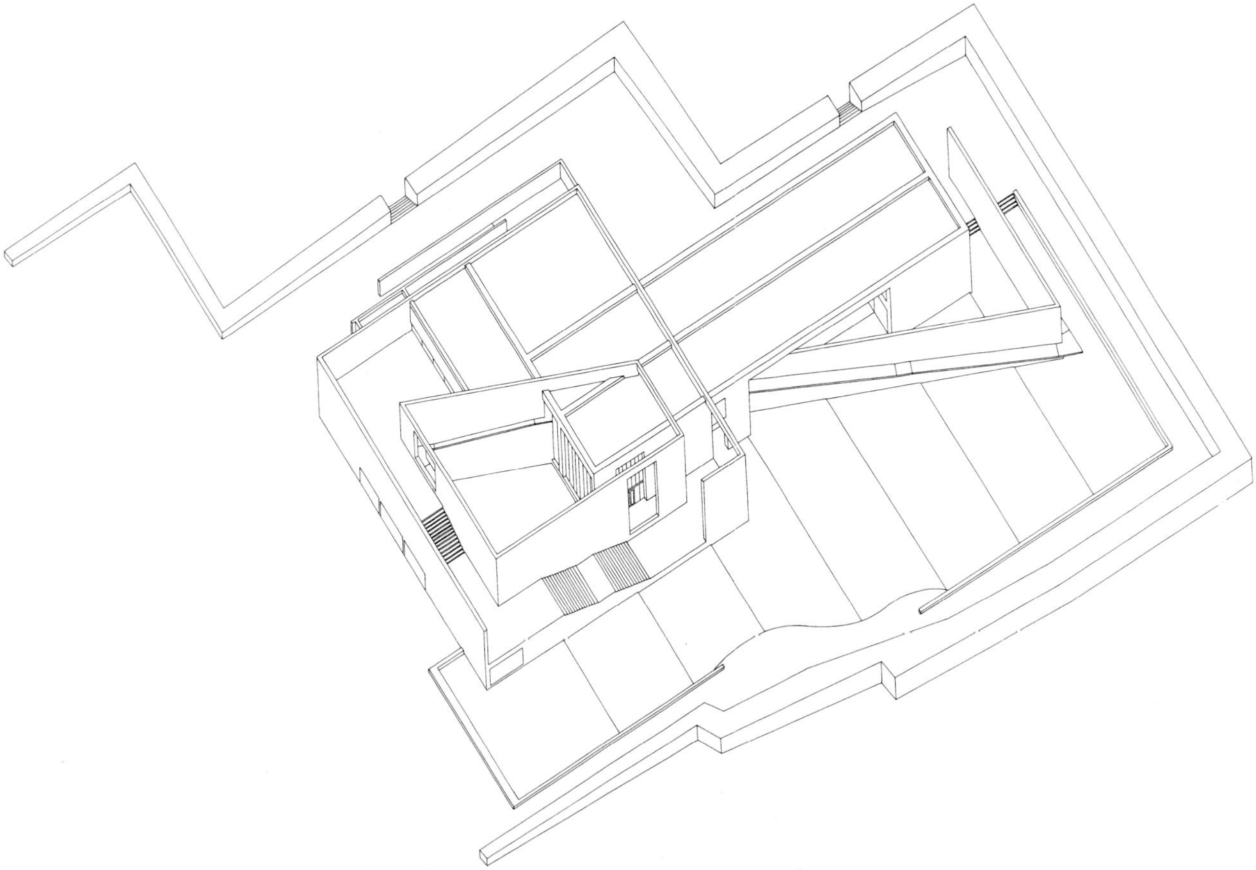

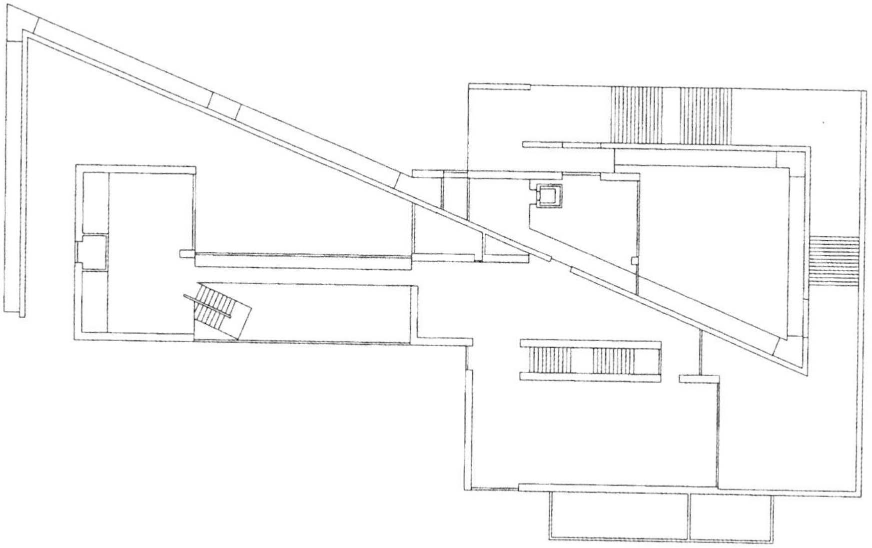

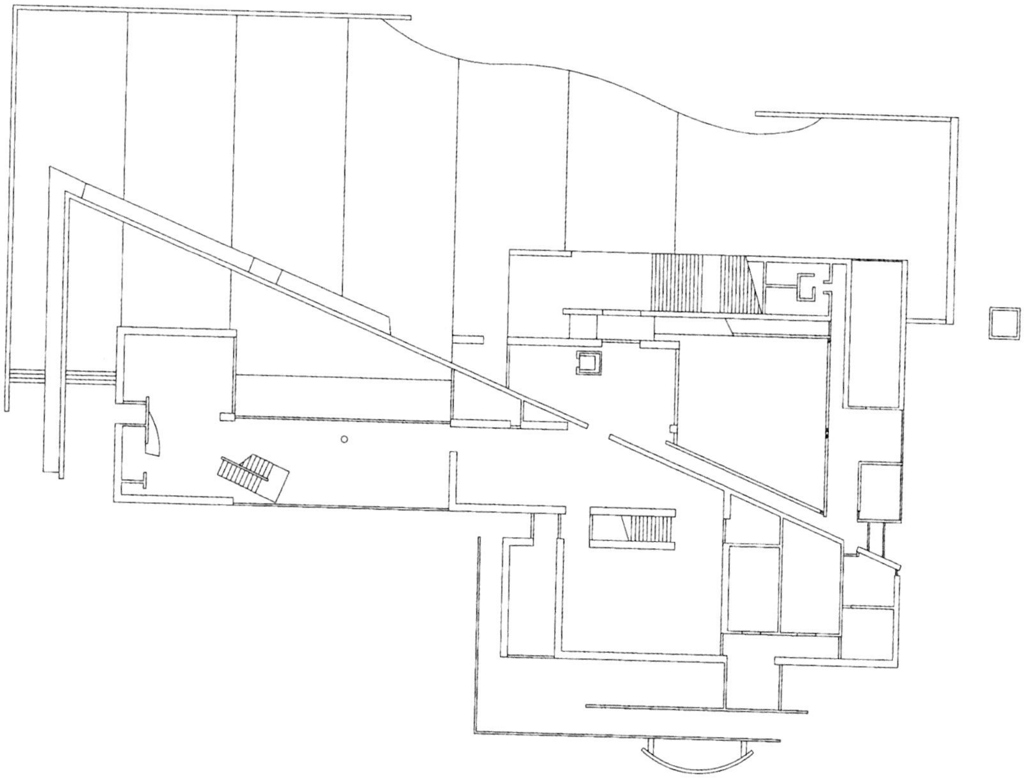

Southern elevation and cross-section.

Right: Internal view of a room and hall access.

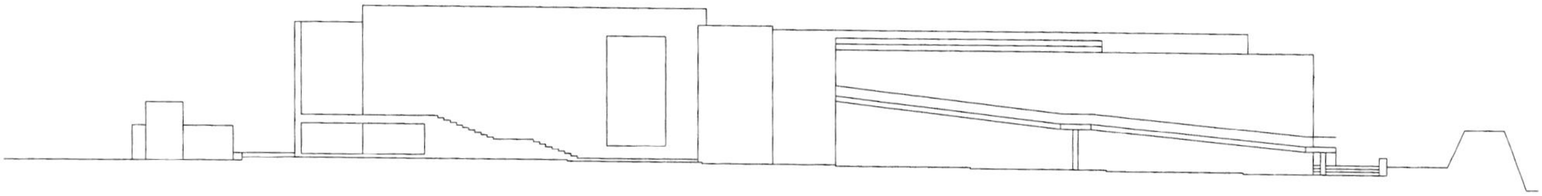

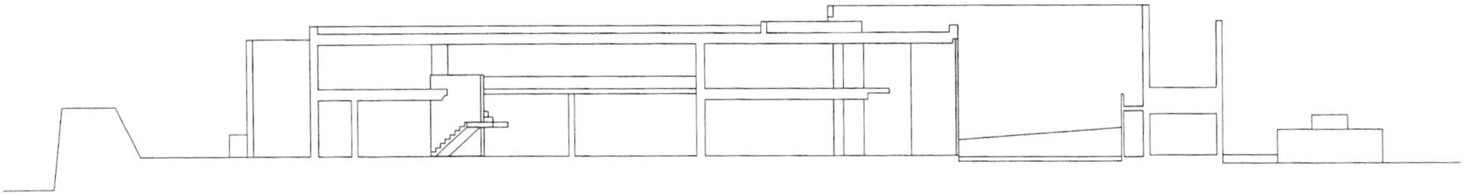

Location Osaka, Japan
Design 1991–1993
Construction 1993–1994
Site area 346 sq m
Building area 204 sq m
Total area 973 sq m

This project concerns the headquarters of commercial lighting supply company Maxray. The design called for offices as well as a showroom, but the framework of the project presented some difficulties because the lot – owned by the firm since its founding – is located in the middle of a crowded area of shops and artisans (Shitamachi) and was characterised by an irregular L-shape.

After some initial uncertainty, mostly caused by the differences between the industrial activities planned and the surrounding environment, Tadao decided to take the job due to both the low expectations and passionate resistance to the project on the part of the client's (an old friend of Tadao's) objectors. It was also an opportunity to graft something new into the vibrant and popular atmosphere in Shitamachi. The idea of an introverted and withdrawn settlement was present from the first site inspection and, as Tadao had already experienced in the past with the model of the Row House in Sumiyoshi, placing a core at the centre of the building would help to transcend its conventional intended use. In fact, it would create an extraordinary microcosm, even in a simple box for offices.

The result is a full-scale atrium reaching up six storeys and surrounded on three sides by the company's offices. Not only that, the showroom as well as all of the other rooms can be used as exhibition space for Maxray's lighting products.

The atrium is the vital core of the building. It receives light and air from above and distributes them to all the other floors. It is also a versatile and flexible space that can accommodate different types of events, from conferences and lectures to exhibitions. Its scale may appear disproportionate in relation to the other spaces, but Tadao felt the reduced dimensions of the building required an element of delineation and a particularly ample and internal volume that was rife with potential.

Street views and images of the covered atrium.

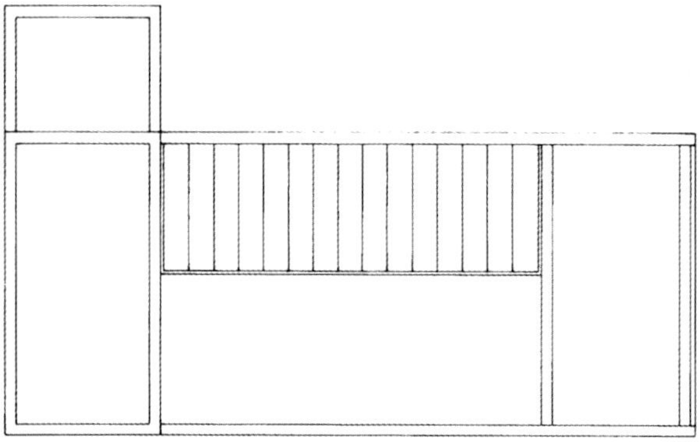
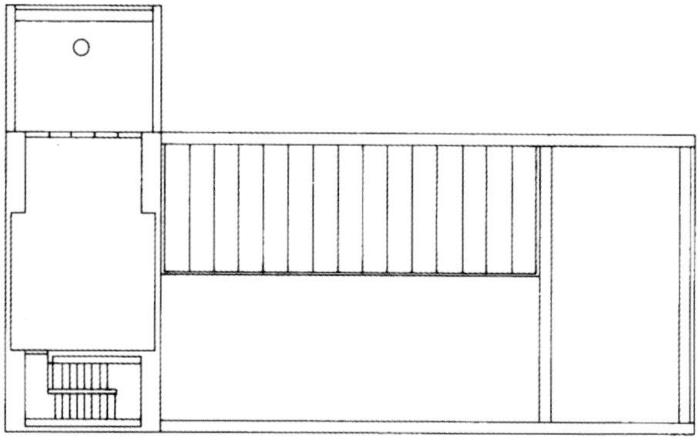
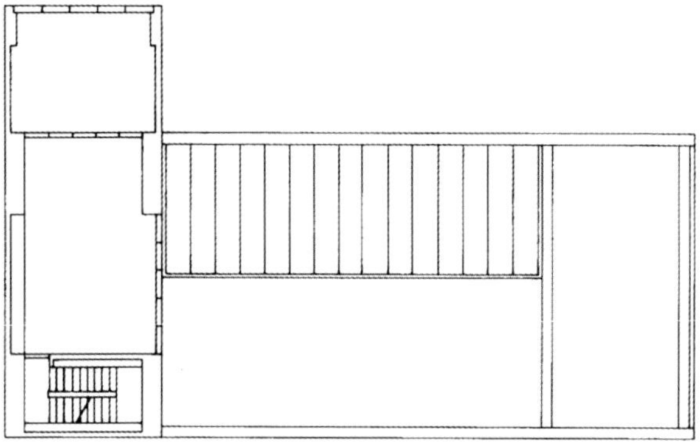
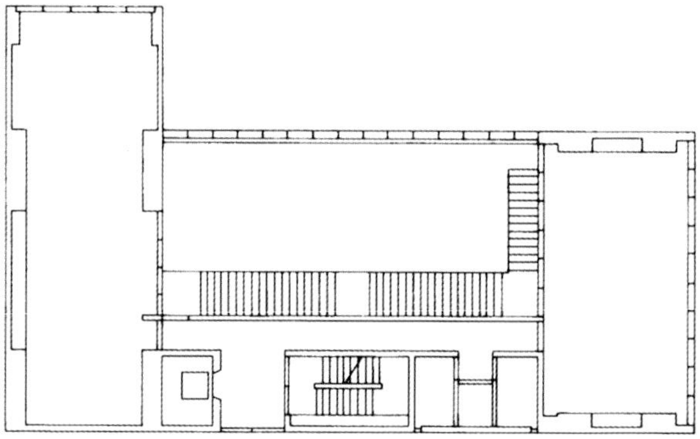
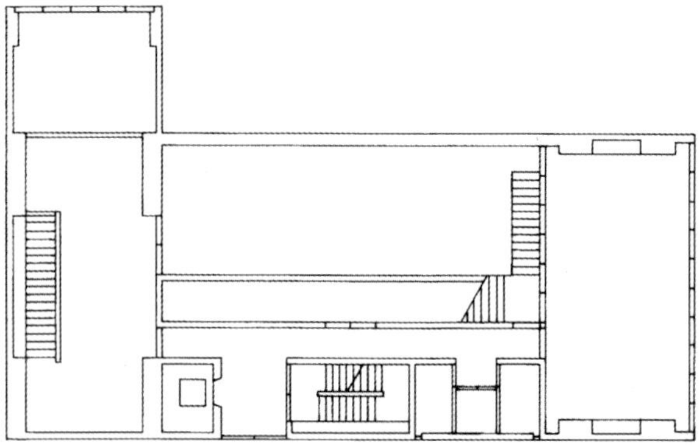
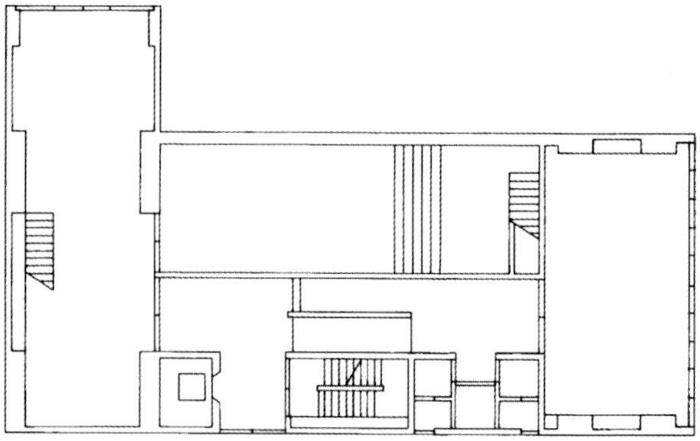

Left: Plans of the covered floors – sixth, fifth, third, first and ground.

Right: Sectional and axonometric draft.

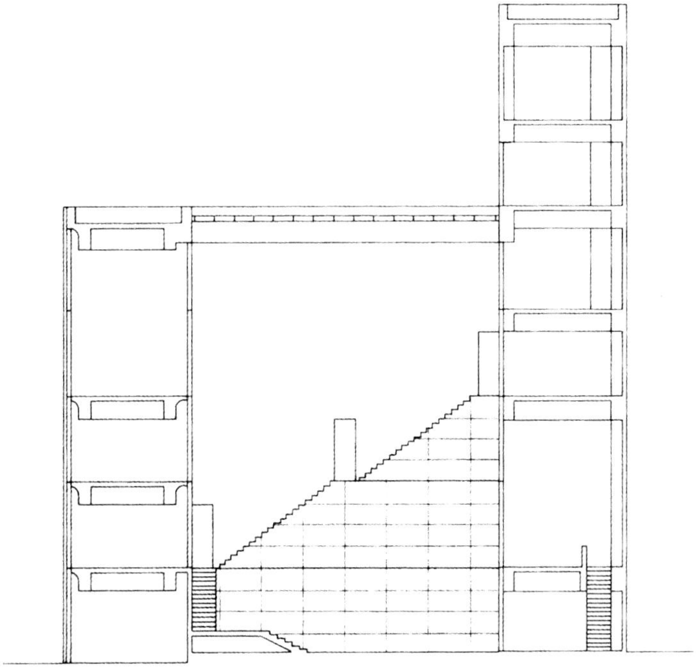

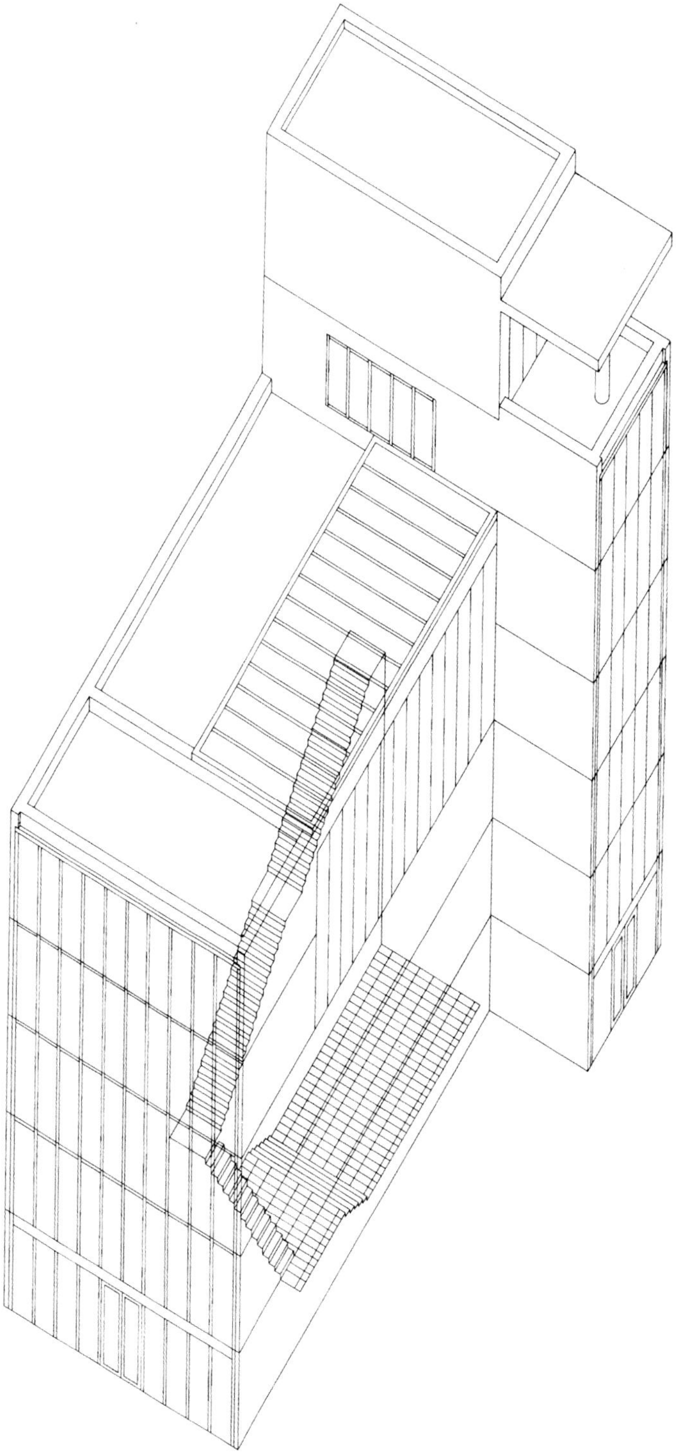

Location Otokuni, Kyoto, Japan
Design 1991–1994
Construction 1994–1995
Site area 5,482 mq
Building area 439 sq m (restored); 262 sq m (new)
Total area 731 sq m (restored); 72 sq m (new)

This project aimed to convert an old villa built in the 1920s on the outskirts of Kyoto into an art museum. The mansion was built in an era when Western architecture had not yet established itself in Japan. The original owner had taken inspiration from Tudor architecture, which he became familiar with and learned to appreciate while studying in England. The stylistic imprint is evident in every detail of the construction.

The project was born out of a strong interest in triggering an interaction between this eclectic architecture, with its expressive elements, and the open space of a modern new building. The existing building has now been juxtaposed with a cylindrical underground gallery that is just over six metres in diameter, covered and surrounded by greenery to achieve continuity with the grounds.

A straight staircase set at the entrance to the villa connects with a tunnel that links the gallery to the existing structure, forcing visitors to cross the old building to reach the new. The latter is placed underground to respect the historic villa and leave the memories of the past intact.

The villa itself now houses a collection of ceramics while the new gallery exhibits contemporary Impressionists, including Monet's *Water Lilies*. The two environments, while differing greatly, still communicate with each other and offer guests wildly contrasting spatial experiences.

Surrounded by nature, art enthusiasts can view the works on display in a place where past and present coexist in harmony. A pond of lotus flowers in the garden creates a connection between the interior and exterior, between the real world and the creative attempts of humans to transfer that world onto canvas.

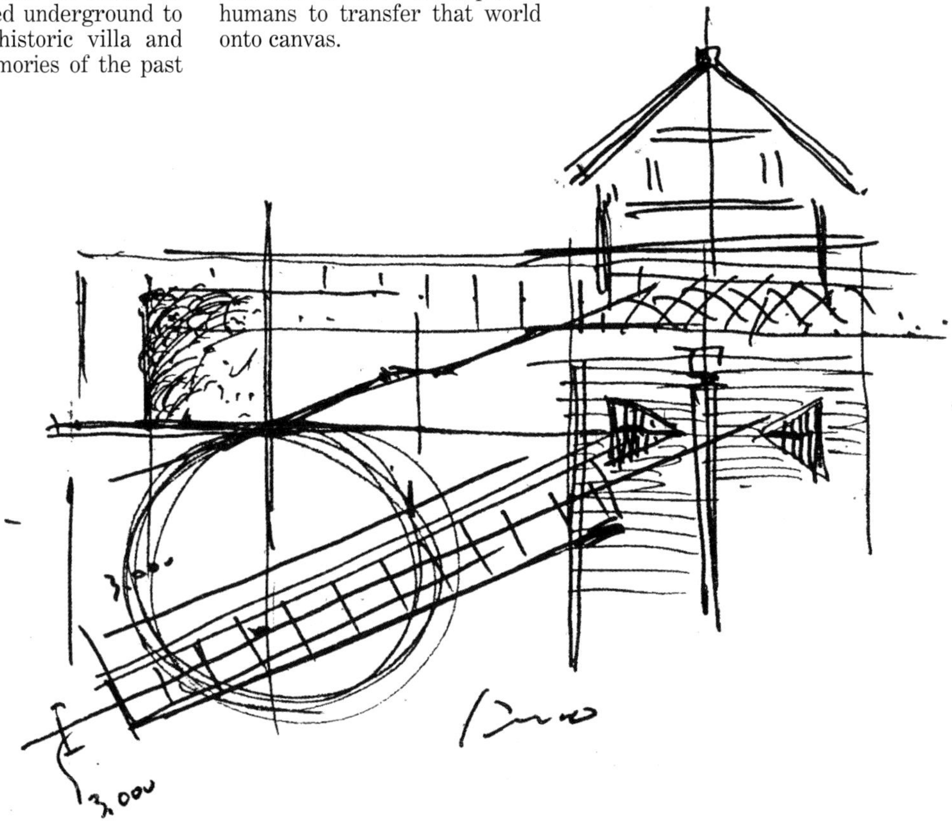

Studio sketch.

Right: View from above.

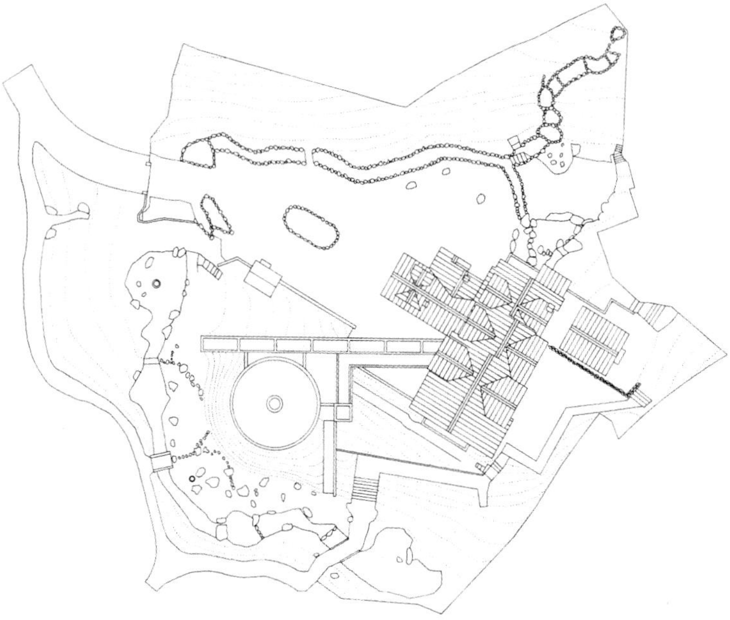

Planimetric diagram and plan.

Right: View of the new wing of the villa and the southwest perspective.

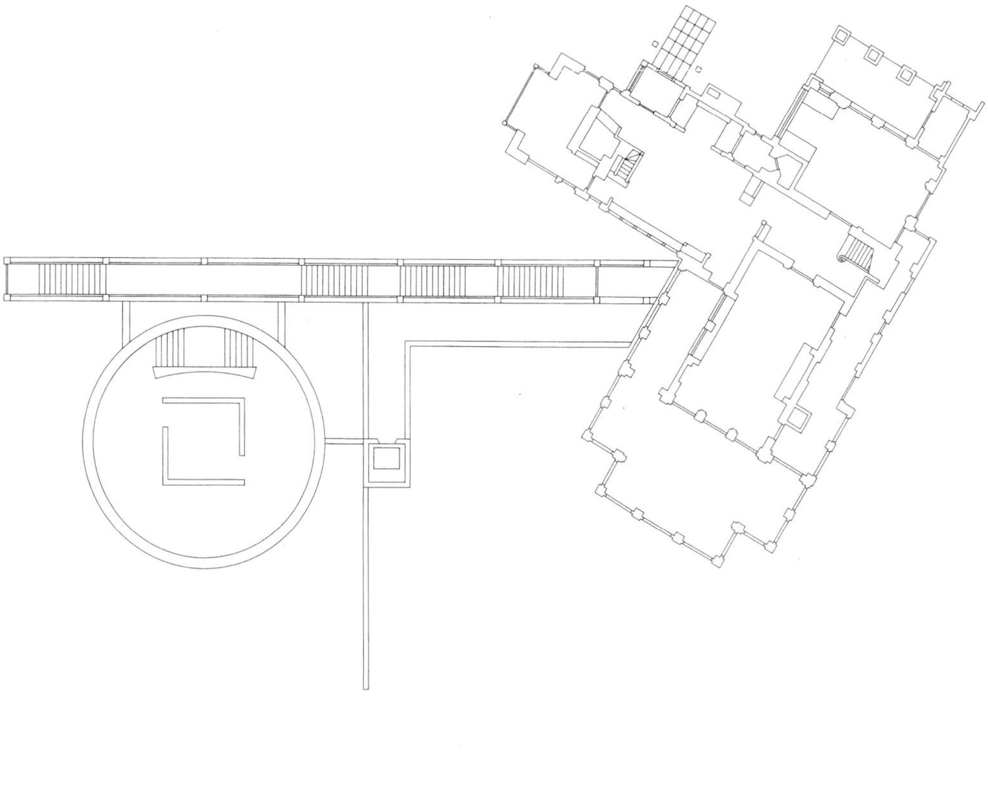

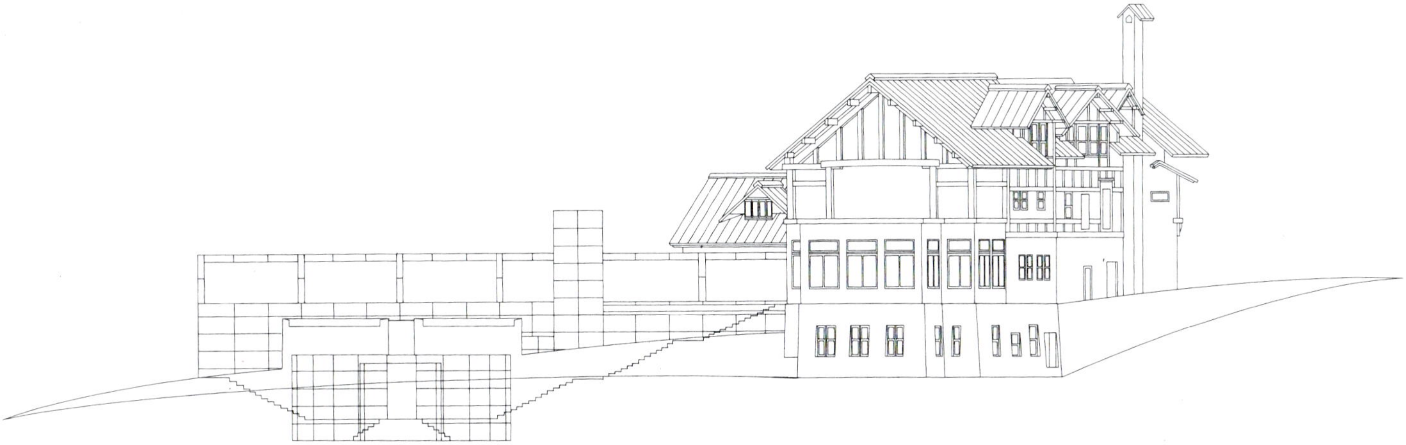

Left: Views of the stairway access to the underground room.

Cross-sections and elevations of the northwest and southeast.

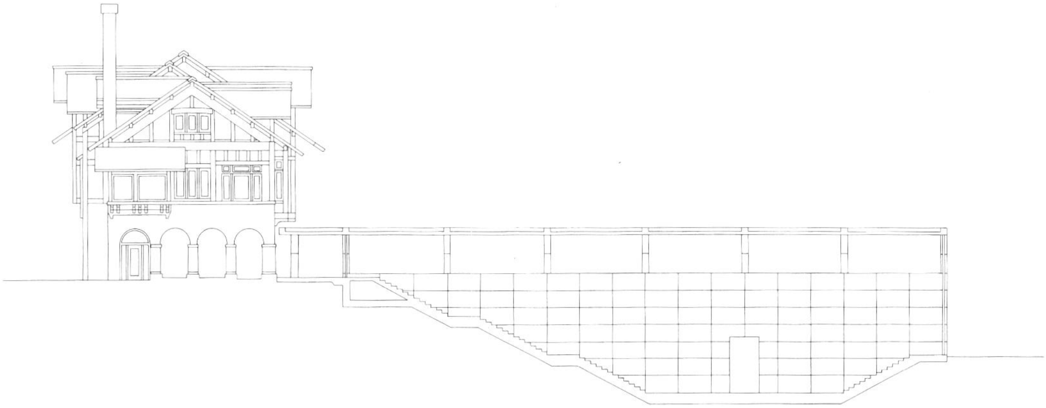

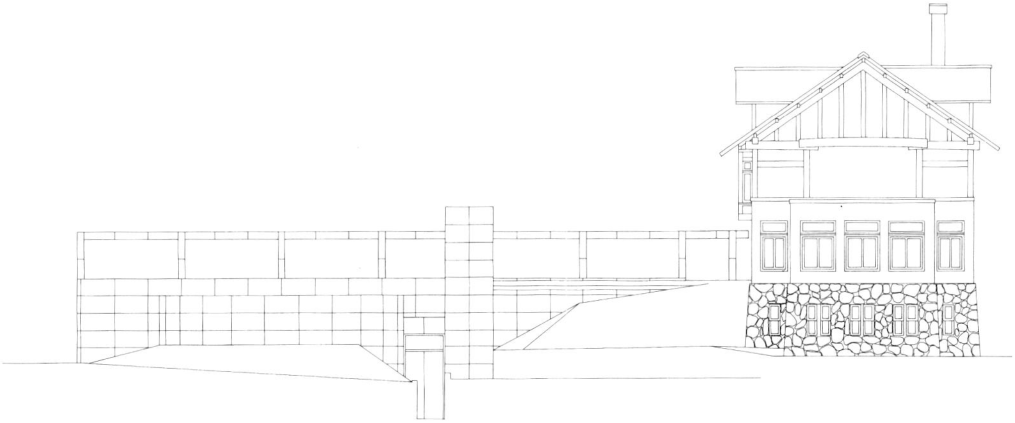

Aerial view of site and axonometric plan.

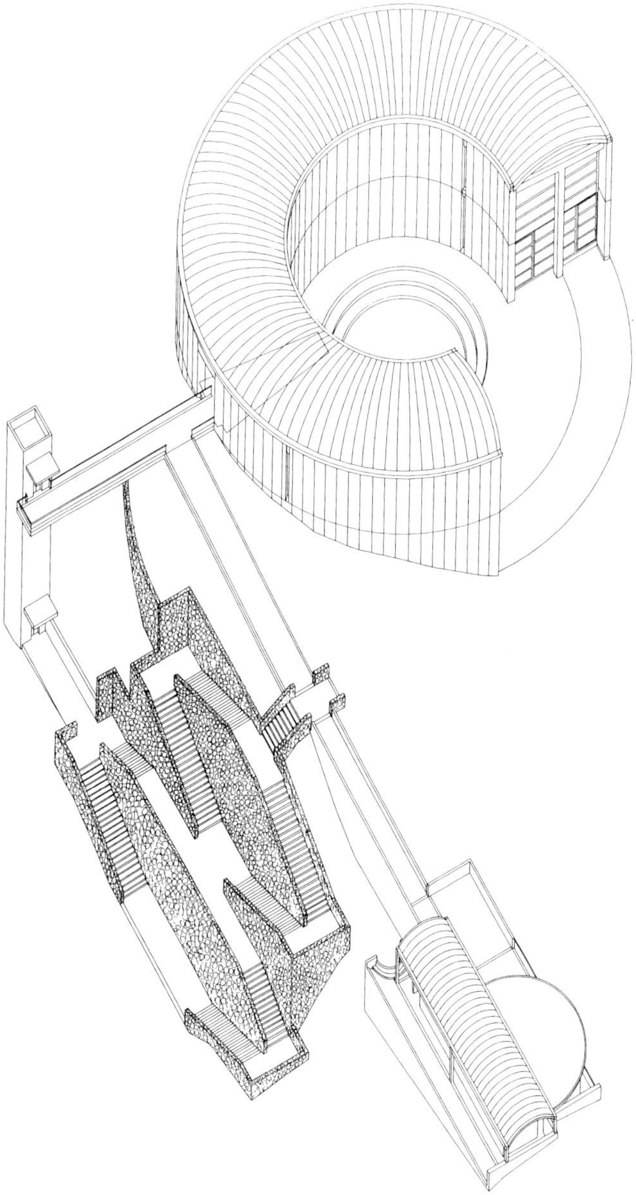

Location Gojo, Nara, Japan
Design 1991–1993; 1996 (annexe)
Construction 1993–1995; 1996–1997 (annexe)
Site area 10,450 sq m
Building area 801 sq m
Total area 2,235 sq m

The city of Gojo in Nara Prefecture began its development about 200 years ago during the Edo Period. Located at the intersection of important communication routes, it is still famous for its traditional houses and cultural attractions.

When I was first approached regarding this project, the location of the museum had not yet been chosen. The final decision to build on the site that it now occupies was taken on the basis of my proposal to locate the building on top of a hill overlooking the city. This resulted in some difficulties for the contractors, but the opportunity for the inhabitants of the city to benefit from a work of architecture in a site with obvious symbolic value was very attractive indeed.

I wanted to reforest the hilltop totally so that the museum could be constructed in a sheltered corner of the new woodland. The circular gallery at the centre of the building offers the opportunity to enjoy a view of the city below. Most importantly, to make the most of this design, two new elements were incorporated within the building: a room for tea ceremonies and a meeting space. When it was completed, my hope was that the entire building at the top of the hill would come to be used as a social centre and meeting place for the entire local community.

Inside the building the walls are of exposed concrete while outside the same concrete structures are covered with panels of galvanized steel, a material with its own unique characteristics. In particular, it seems able to absorb elements, such as wind or light.

Indeed, the architectural expression of the complex cannot be separated from its shape and the materials used. Each material possesses qualities that I have used in order to inspire emotive communication with people who actively enjoy architecture. The galvanized steel provides more strength than concrete surfaces, and fluoropolymer treatments on it may increase resistance to wear and tear. From the perspective of the materials used, this project was experimental in nature for me. I am attracted by materials that, like all living creatures, age and decay with time.

Historically speaking, the best projects have this quality, and from this point of view the way the exposed concrete deteriorates is in and of itself stimulating. I of course hope that the people for whom I have so far designed private homes share this line of thinking. With public buildings intended for large numbers of people, however, we must pay close attention to the problems of attrition and maintenance, and for this reason I must continue experimenting with new materials.

Tadao Ando

Plan of the entry level and basement.

Right: Prospect and view of the front.

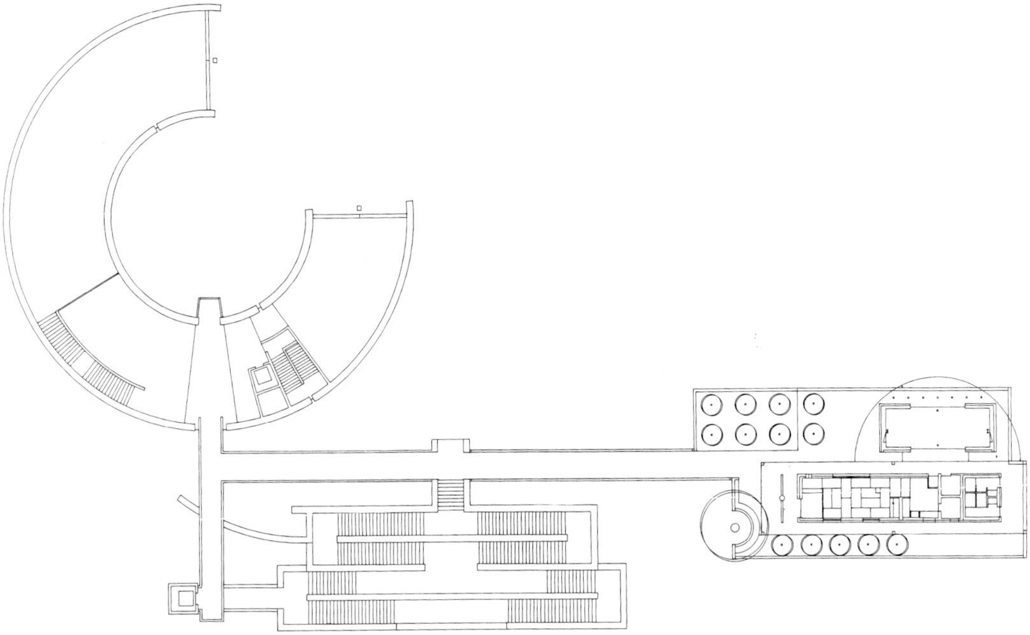

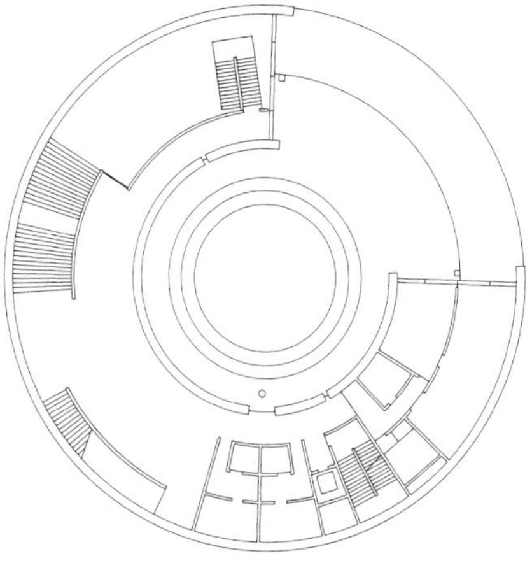

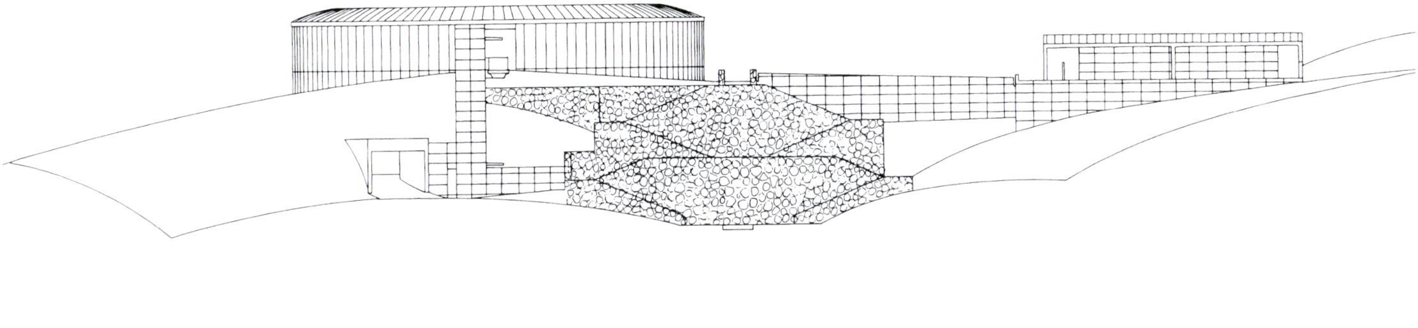

View of the entrance to the museum.

Right: Cross-section from the entrance and view of the courtyard.

The courtyard and the exhibition space.

Site plan and aerial view of the primary school.

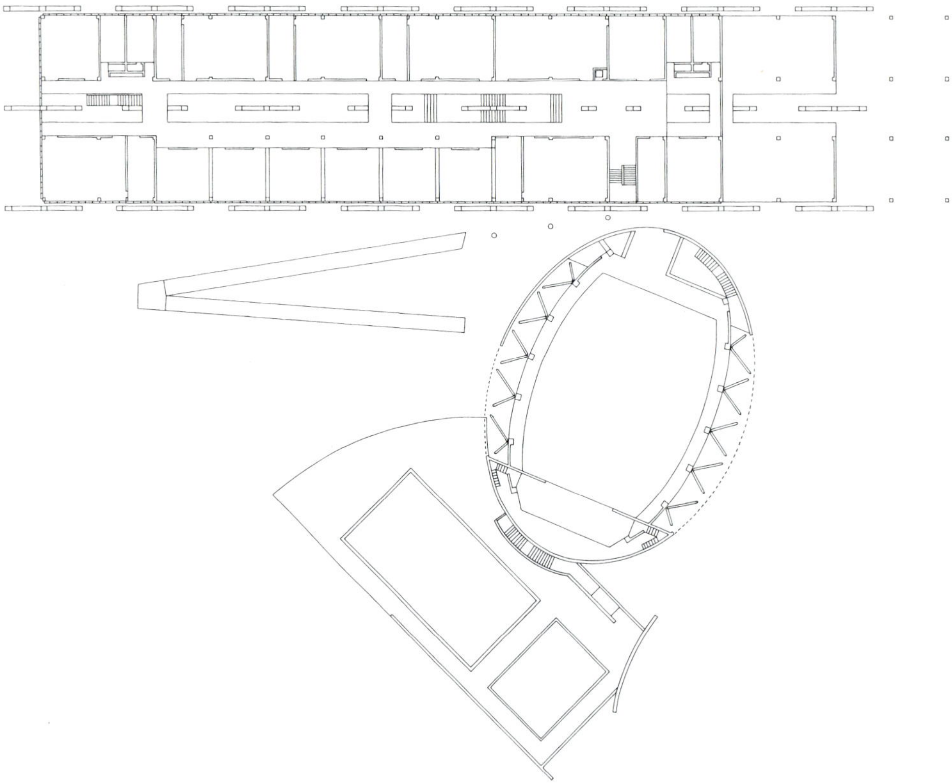

Every detail of the project, from designing the overall concept down to the expressive details of the individual buildings, are intended to establish a distinct contrast with nature in order to emphasise the beauty of the natural surroundings here. Given the grandeur of those surroundings, the buildings were indeed challenged to compete.

The scholastic buildings are aligned along an east-west access and erected on a simple structure of inclined concrete pillars interspersed with open spaces. The ancillary services, gym and swimming pool, formed as elliptical volumes, are configured along an axis that creates an angle of 22.5 degrees with the east-west axis.

The various interior spaces are arranged in a linear fashion. A long gallery lit by skylights runs along the east-west axis and acts as a sort of spine from which the classrooms are laid out on either side. The main outdoor area and the continuum of open space along it is intended for the pupils, but can also be used for community events and activities.

The very minimalist structure here has helped to create a series of environments that are free of predetermined functions, which provides an ideal platform to unleash the unlimited potential of children.

Tadao Ando

Left: Plan and perspective view of the primary school.

Views of the school.

Detail of the inclined pillars in front of the school and a view of the access to the first floor of the gym.

Opposite page: Perspective view of the primary school and views of the central gallery inside the two buildings.

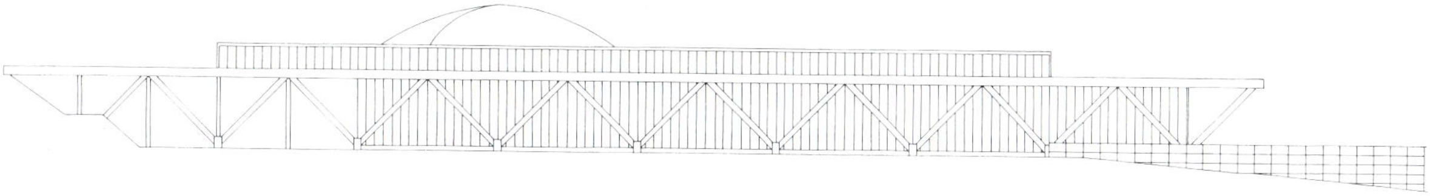

Location Chicago, Illinois, USA
Design 1992–1994
Construction 1993–1997
Site area 1,935 sq m
Building area 403 sq m
Total area 835 sq m

This site is in a quiet residential neighbourhood near downtown Chicago, and though the north-south lot is long and narrow, the goal was to create a comfortable living space while developing a relationship with the surrounding environment.

The building has two wings on a north-south axis connected by a terrace, a living space and a ramp. Private spaces for the client's family cover three floors in the south wing (12 square metres per floor), while the public spaces like the entrance and guest rooms are in the two-storey building (12 by 6 metres per floor) to the north.

Between these two wings, extending from north to south, are the six-metre-wide roof terrace and a living space delimited by a stone wall that borders the courtyard. The six square metres to the west of the terrace are now a pond while the space below the roof terrace overlooking the garden is the central hub of the residence: the living room.

The pond and courtyard connect to the house with an elegant ramp that filters movement outside. The two residential blocks are closed to the outside, but they are open towards the courtyard.

Despite the rigorous geometric composition, a semicircular wall under the northern wing was introduced to preserve an existing poplar tree. It was the first major building by Ando's studio in the United States.

Detail of the water garden on the western front (left) and a studio sketch.

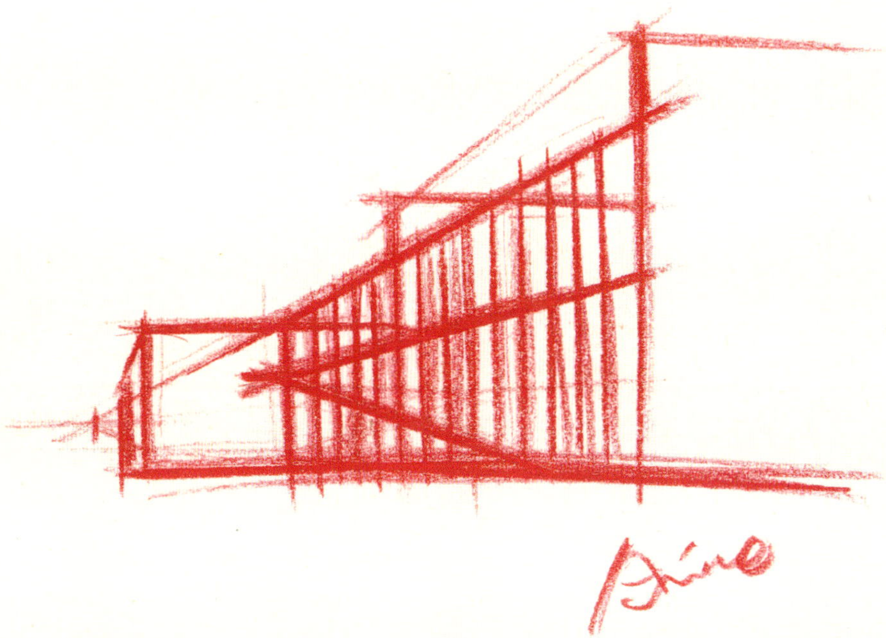

View from the northwest and a studio sketch (right).

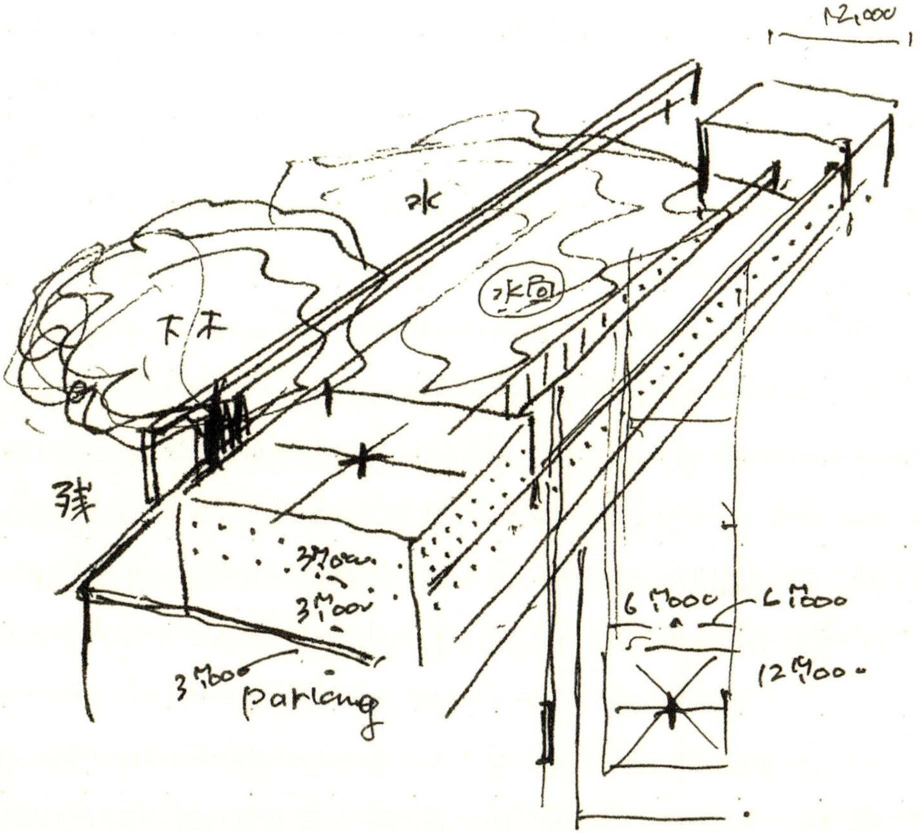
水
parking

A view from the water pond of the entry building and north wing leading to the lounge and roof terrace.

Right: Studies of the living room and view of the terrace from the front of the north wing.

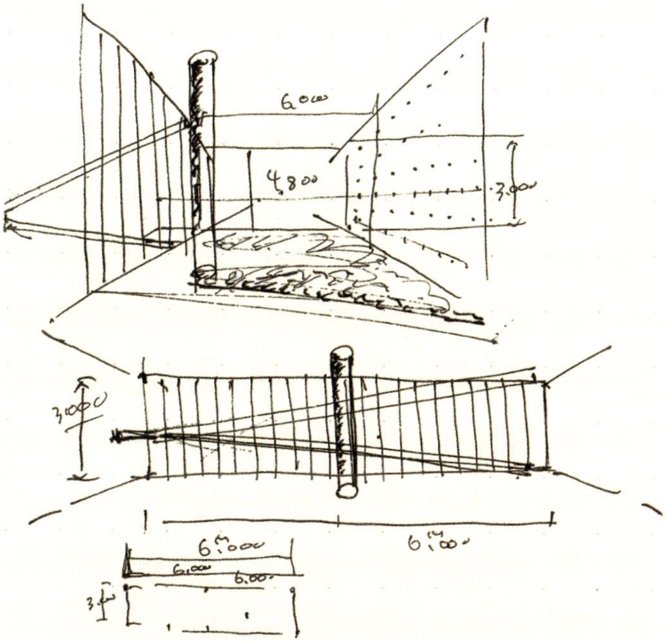

Longitudinal cross-section of the buildings and external view of the ramp in front of the living room.

Right: Plans of the basement, first and second floors.

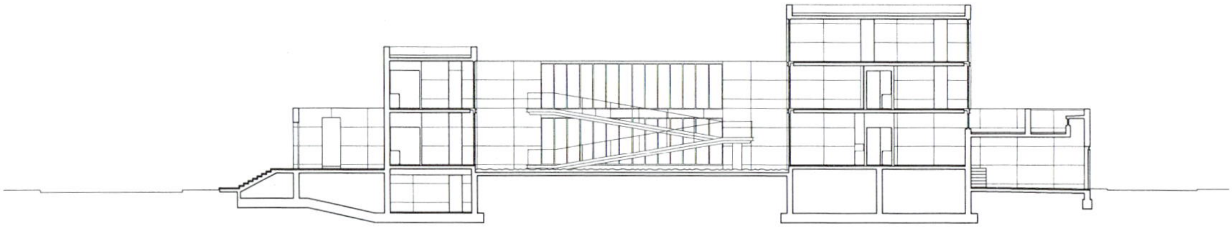

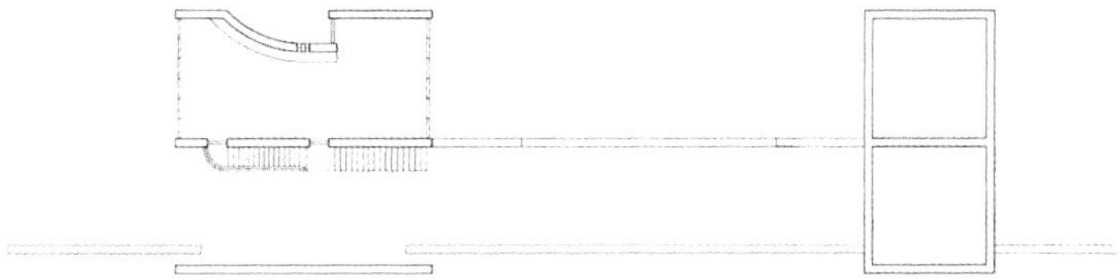

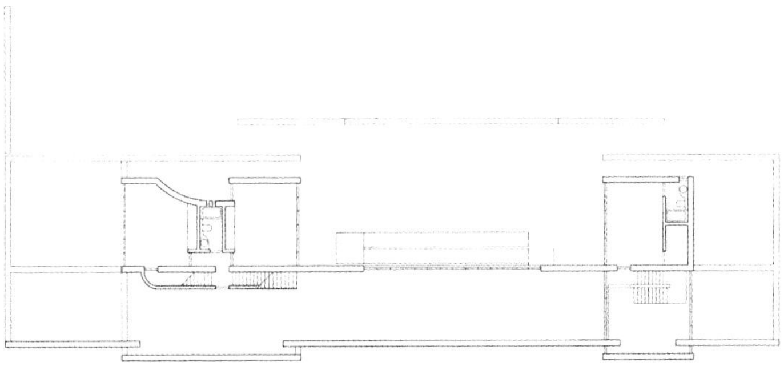

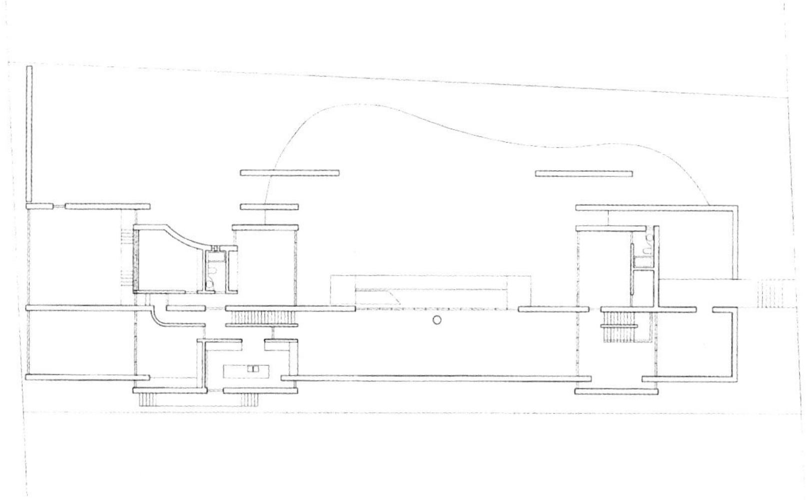

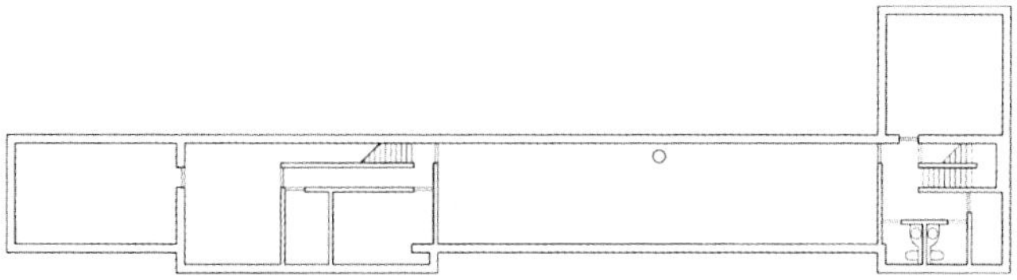

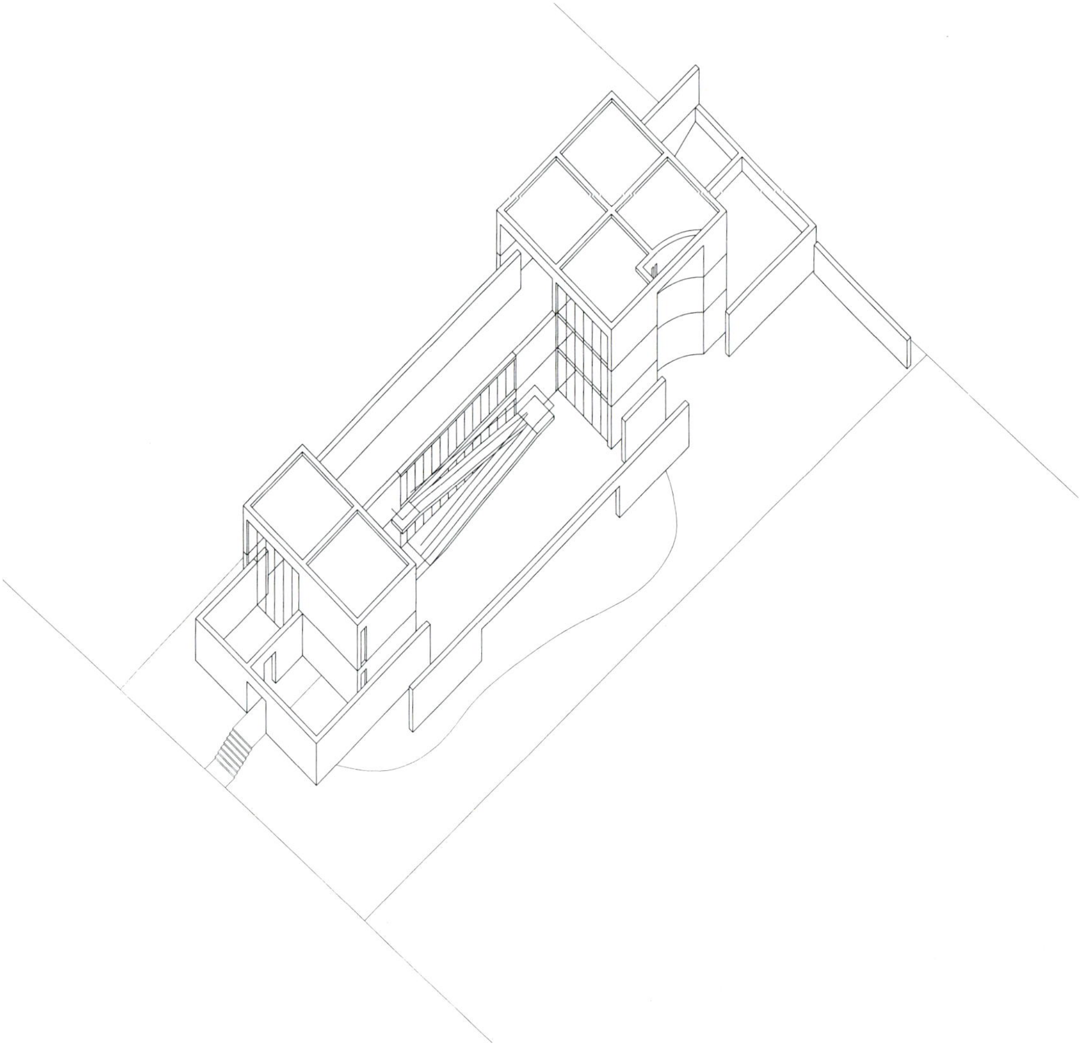

Left: An axonometric sketch and views of the courtyard from the various levels of the main residential block.

View of the living room from the hall entrance.

Rokko Housing III

Location Kobe, Hyogo, Japan
Design 1992–1997
Construction 1997–1999
Site area 11,717 sq m
Building area 6,545 sq m
Total area 22,221 sq m

Developed as an independent proposal around the time that Rokko Housing II was being constructed, Rokko III is a modular housing project that became an integral part of the urban regeneration and reconstruction plan for Kobe after the Great Hanshin Awaji earthquake of 1995.

With the third phase, the development was divided into three levels: the lower (Rokko I), the middle (Rokko II) and the top (Rokko III). As in phases I and II, the basic idea, and a provision of the plans for the housing units, is that the units follow the unevenness of the landscape and ensure that all residents enjoy individuality in each of their abodes.

In phase III, however, the ground conditions were more diverse, and it was impossible to differentiate individual units due to construction costs and commercial expectations. With this in mind, attention was subsequently focused on enriching the public spaces that separate the residential units. A stairway extends the axis of the second phase from north to south, which is intersected by areas of greenery stretching from east to west.

Public and secluded plazas form points of intersection, which in turn create public connections. A fourth project in the complex is currently being built on a neighbouring slope of Mount Rokko.

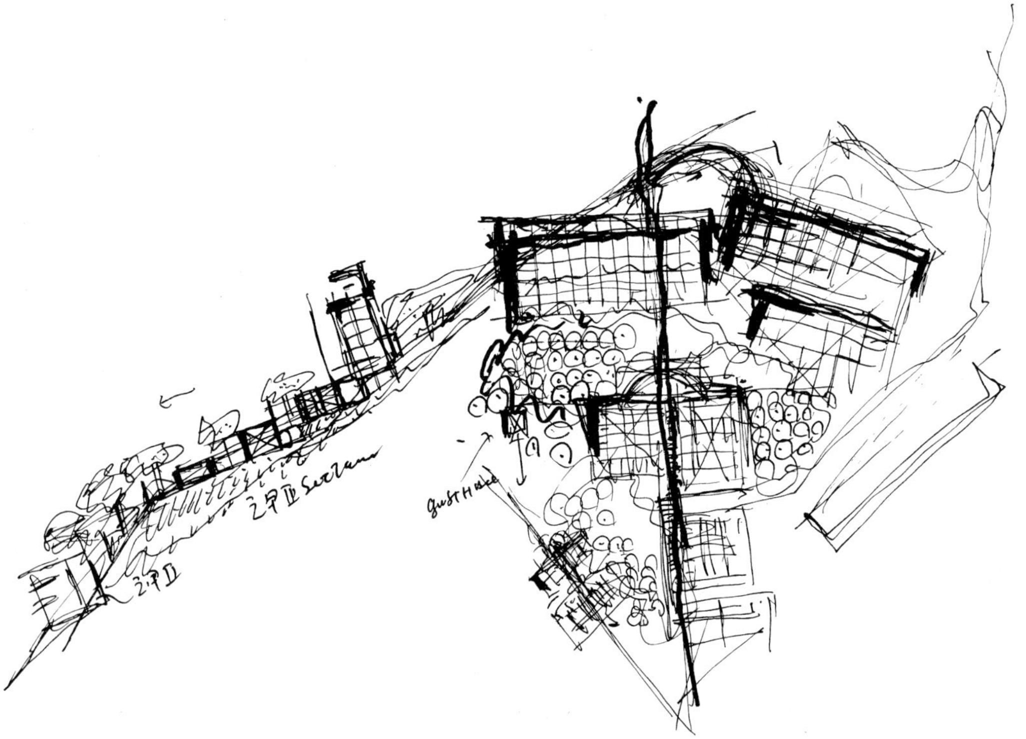

Preliminary planimetric sketch.

Right: Overhead view from the southwest of the three housing estates built from the early 1980s through 1999.

research centre. The lot on which the villa stands, being bordered by a railway line, inspired Ando to create wherever possible a protective barrier for the body of the building against this less than desirable presence. For this reason, the building, which faces the railway line, is now flanked by a series of concrete columns that continues along the border of the site while the old villa is reflected in a pool of shallow water. The long section that houses the new additions (laboratories, classrooms, gallery, cinema, etc.) is rather more open, with a schematically configured oval rotunda and a varied system of steps and stairways all facing the countryside to the rear towards the vast manufacturing complex built for Benetton by the Scarpas.

The old villa was gutted and now houses a small auditorium and offices. Grafted onto it is a long, multi-level corridor, generating variously illuminated spaces that expand and contract in height and length and which can be exploited for various uses. Since much of the volume, defined by the rotunda, is actually underground, the building presents itself through a series of trilithic floors and areas produced by the typical concrete construction often associated with Ando. This is a nod to Europe's architectural legacy that also allows the new spaces to exhibit their own character.

Fabrica is now a sort of small, bustling city. Possessing monumental vistas and discrete corners, it is enlivened by contrasts of the immaculately maintained

Views of the underground rotunda.

old walls, which are trapped or leaning against new concrete surfaces that have become a hallmark of Ando's architecture. The complexity of the areas and various levels that cross the building's axis can really only be appreciated once one has had the opportunity to observe the linearity of the concise volumes emerging from the ground. It is an amazing ensemble. The simplicity of the casings and the structures that rise from the earth masks the articulation of the interiors. Take, for example, the smug virtuosity apparent in the configuration of the exhibition gallery, which penetrates the ground in a spiral form.

The old villa is the head from which the spiral departs. A long, largely camouflaged, straight spine (from which free volumes are detached) help to define a diverse space and are a clear expression of the conclusions made in recent years from Ando's experimentation.

Those who visit the building will appreciate the uncompro-

Benesse House Oval

Location Naoshima, Kagawa, Japan
Design 1993–1994
Construction 1994–1995
Site area 53,369 sq m (incl. museum)
Building area 693 sq m
Total area 598 sq m

This project was for an annexe to the Benesse House hotel that was originally built in 1992. Located on the side of a hill, it was part of a complex of buildings that brought museums, galleries, conference facilities, a hotel and a restaurant all onto one site. The extension, which was 40 metres higher up at the top of the hill, is linked to the existing core of the unique Benesse complex by numerous walkways as well as a funicular monorail.

With an oval plan and only one level, the building is set in the heart of a forested area that boasts a lovely variety of plant and tree life. The annexe also offers vista points from which to appreciate the lush vegetation and spectacular views of the Seto Inland Sea.

In order to protect the environment, part of the new structure and its garden was set underground, as in the exisiting one. The oval itself measures 40 metres on its long axis and 20 on the shorter one. Luxury accommodation here includes four double guest rooms, two suites and an in-house café. The central courtyard also has a large pool with an oval shape measuring 20 by 10 metres on its long and short axes, respectively. It forms a sort of liquid sculpture and is enclosed by a portico that could be used as an outside gallery.

Inside the Oval, an L-shaped wall was constructed with the same type of stone used for the access to the main building. Water features were then made an integral part of the entrance design and used to link areas around the structure. At the edge of the complex, water flowed directly into the sea and and the verdant hanging garden appeared to be an extension of the surrounding vegetation. Fusing with the landscape and the sea, the Oval and its wonderful garden offer a completely different nature experience.

Left: View from above looking towards the Seto Sea.

Sketch for planimetric drawing.

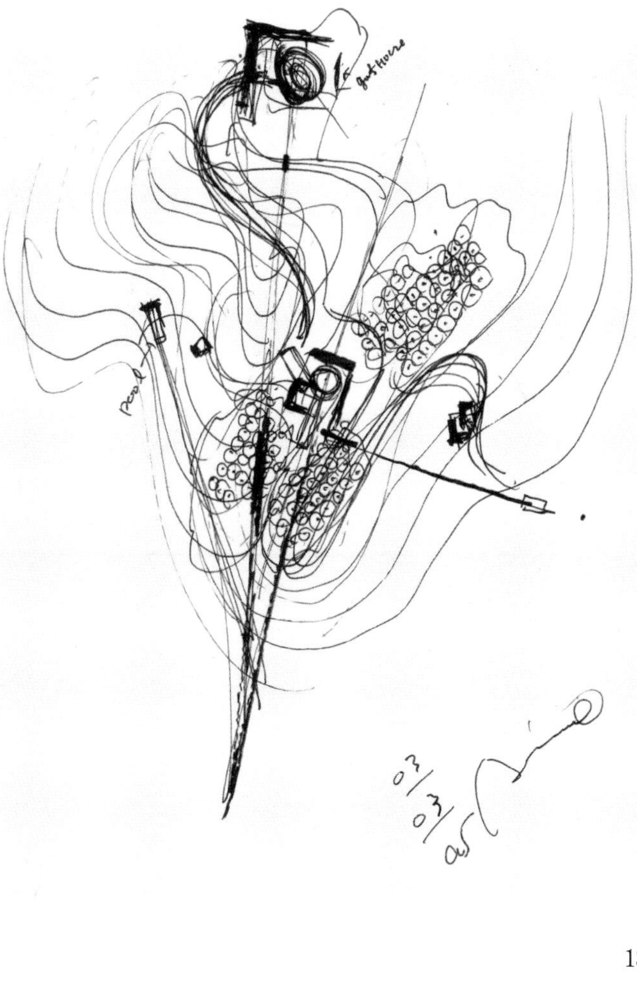

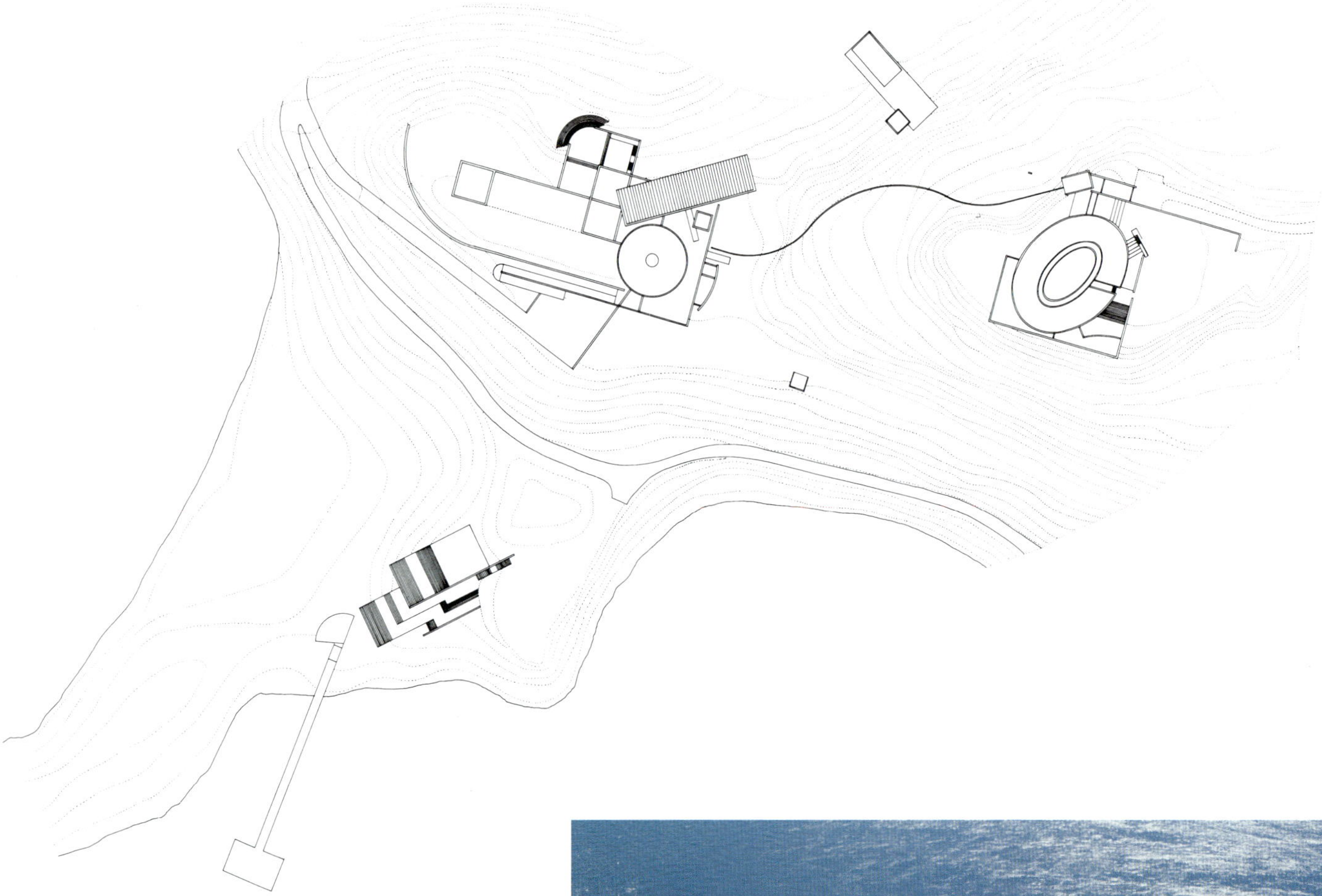

Left: Planimetric study and aerial view of the architectural complex in the landscape.

Right: Projected altimetric design and view of the terrace.

Following pages: The water court.

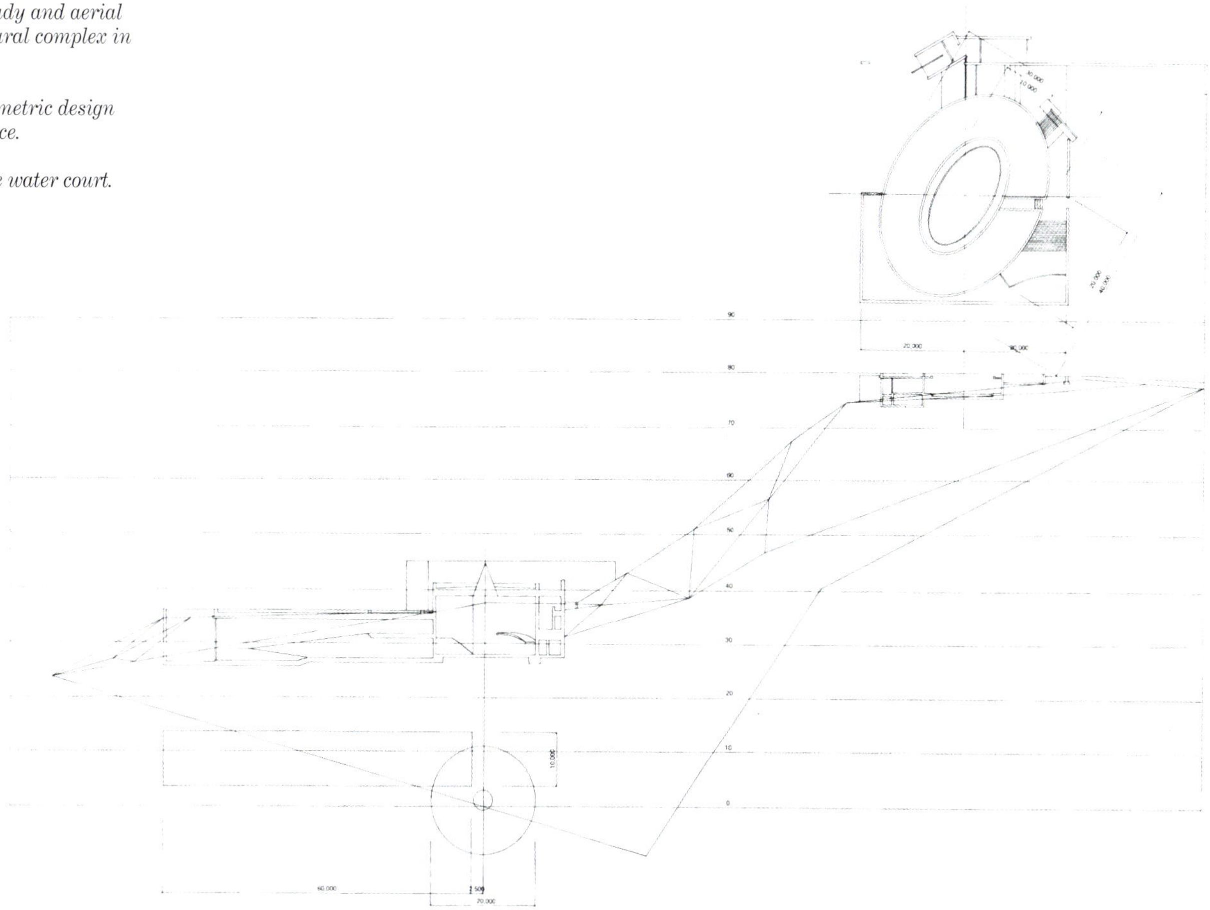

ACS Cardholder Copy
EXCLUSIF.
94

Ayabe Community Centre

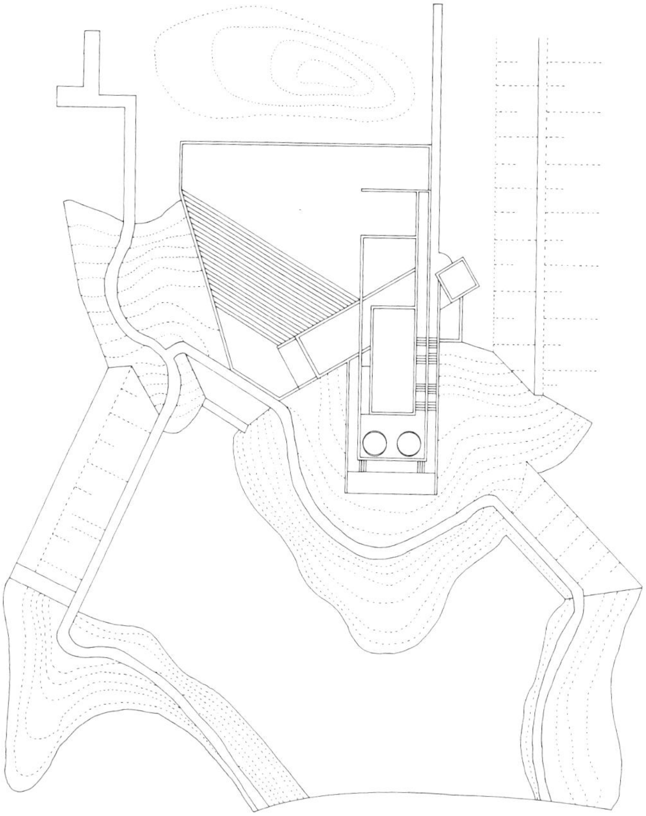

Location Ayabe, Kyoto, Japan
Design 1993–1994
Construction 1994–1995
Site area 19,775 sq m
Building area 526 sq m
Total area 596 sq m

The Ayabe Community Centre is located within an industrial park set inside a densely wooded and mountainous area about an hour's drive from Kyoto. The aim of the project was to build a place that could serve both the business community and provide a resource for local residents. The spaces inside include an atrium, a multi-purpose area and conference rooms.

The complex was meant to be at the centre of the park and was conceived to harmonise with the surrounding landscape. Following a steep, tree-lined path that winds its way through the park, you reach a long concrete wall and a tranquil expanse of water. Walking alongside the wall you come to the naturally lit atrium with huge glass walls.

Looking the other way, the view opens onto a small courtyard with two trees that are typical of this particular forest as well as a nearby lake with mountains in the background. Around the back of the complex, the association between the imposing concrete walls and the water evokes an intimate and secluded atmosphere.

One of the primary objectives here was to create a structure in which it was possible to enjoy the natural surroundings from the inside and the outside of the building. To do this, a classic element of Japanese architecture known as the *engawa* was used – a veranda or terrace that surrounds the house.

In the course of the project the boundary between the buildings and the environment was in effect removed so that it was open to the water, the sky and the forest. A walkway along the perimeter of the structure was laid out in the traditional style of Japanese gardens. This provides visitors with views of the lake and the densely forested mountains while allowing them to enjoy the birds singing in the woods. Water features were positioned along the entrance way so children could come into direct contact with nature.

The pleasant surroundings are rich in natural beauty and work to create a positive atmosphere, which in turn leads to good relationships between the people who work in the park and within the wider community. The centre has since become an important and popular meeting place.

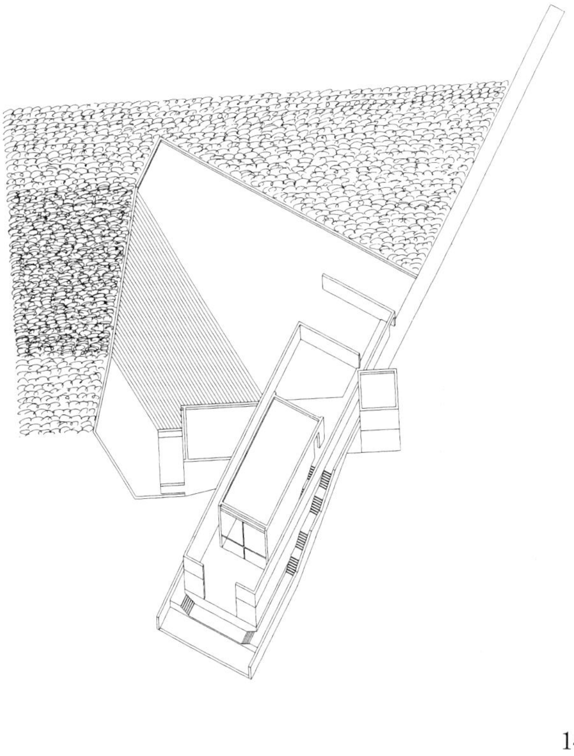

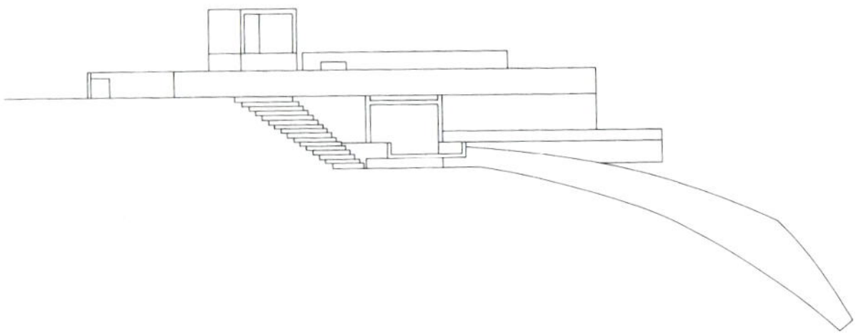

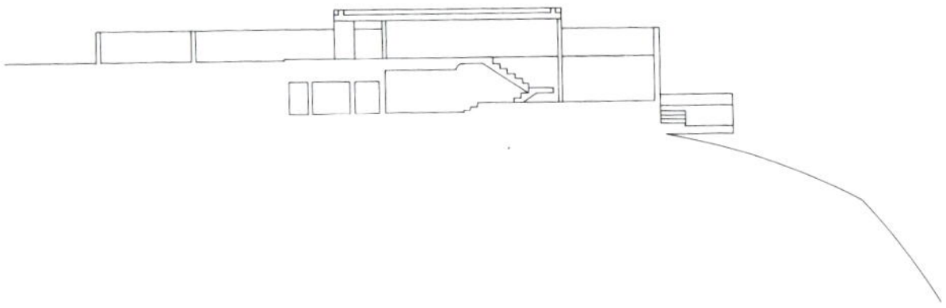

Previous pages: View of the lake plus planimetric drawings of the centre, general and axonometric.

Left: Section plans and a view of the man-made lake.

Floor plans of first and ground floors and a view of the courtyard with trees.

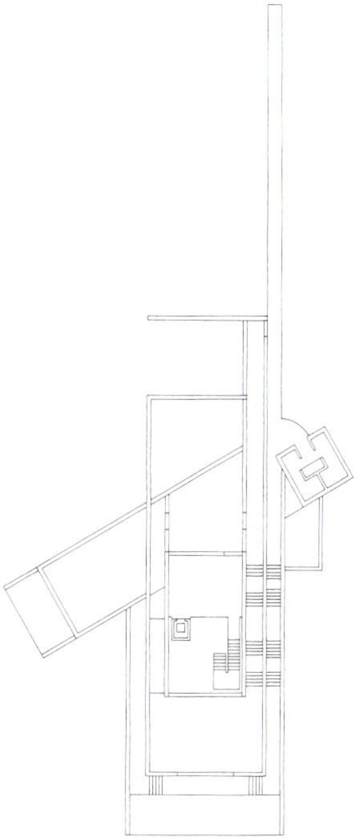

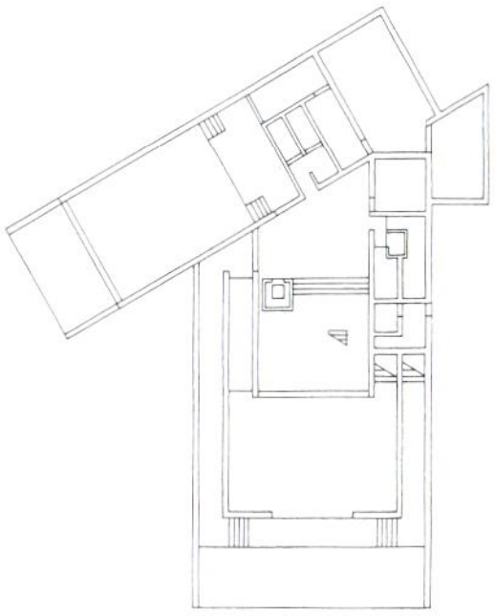

Location Awaji, Hyogo, Japan
Design 1993–1994 (before the earthquake); 1995–1996 (after the earthquake)
Construction 1997-99
Site area 213,930 sq m
Building area 38,429 sq m
Total area 95,078 sq m

On January 17, 1995, the island of Awaji off the coast of Kobe in the Bay of Osaka became the epicentre of a major earthquake that devastated the entire region around the city. The quake took more than 6,000 lives. The design for Yumebutai was nearly finished when the disaster struck, which resulted in an inevitable postponement of the building plans as well as a radical revision of the project.

Elaborate drawings had to be prepared twice for the same work – before and after the earthquake. Yumebutai was to represent a symbol of both the physical and spiritual reconstruction of the city – it was to be born again.

Yumebutai commemorates the fatalities and devastation that occurred by celebrating their opposites: life and beauty. It is a place in which visitors find themselves surrounded by the treasures of nature and where they can appreciate the physical pleasures of our existence.

Yumebutai is a complex of spaces running in multiple directions – circular, linear and irregular – that superimpose and intersect each other. They combine to provide a series of structures that include rooms for international conferences, a hotel, a beach made up of a hundred thousand shells, various gardens and plazas, a hothouse and an open theatre. One specific modification made in the

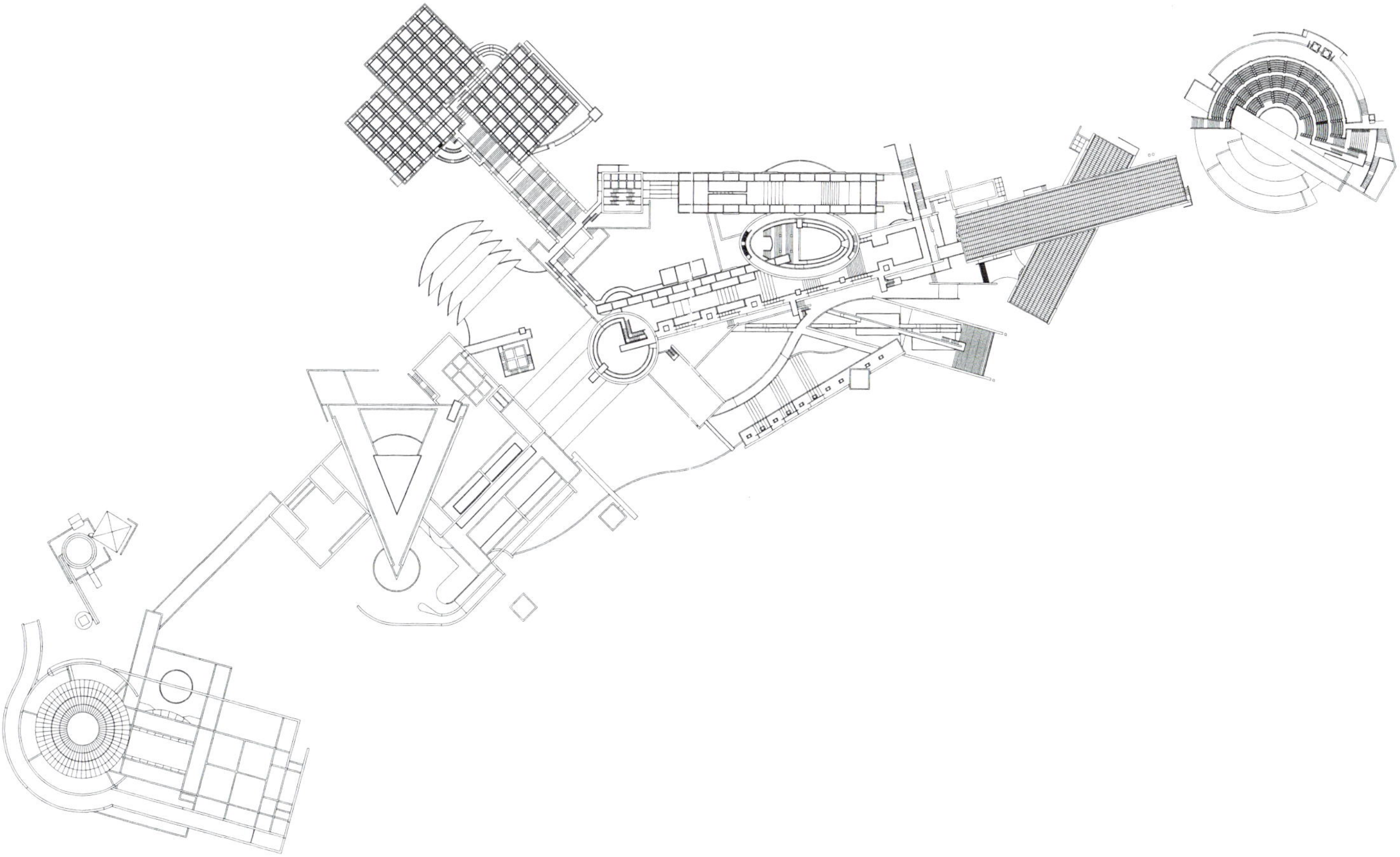

Sketches for the scale drawing and aerial views of the complex from the south and the north.

Design sketch and view of the terraces in the centre of the complex.

Right: The forum, hotel and open-air theatre.

Following pages: The Garden of a Hundred Steps.

"post-earthquake" version was that of an enormous terraced garden called the Garden of a Hundred Steps. Set behind the hotel, it incorporated elaborate planting schemes that varied according to the season as a tribute to those who had lost their lives in the catastrophe.

The first idea for the project came in 1989. The selected site was in a locality that had been torn apart and defaced by more than thirty years (since the 1950s) of massive soil and rock excavation, the results of which were used as landfill in the Bay of Osaka to make space for the rapid population growth in post-war Japan. During this period more than 106 million cubic metres of earth were taken from the area. Virtually an entire mountainside had disappeared, exposing a bed of reddish rock in a steep slope.

The plan for Yumebutai was to take an area that had been devastated by human intervention and bring it back to life, in an act of redemption, through a programme of improvements and reforestation. Starting in 1994, 250,000 young trees of about ten centimetres in height have been planted on a stony slope with a 30-degree incline.

Indeed, before proceeding with the architectural intervention, the creation of a wooded area was the first step in achieving the principal objective of restoring to nature an area defaced by past development – and in turn creating a place for people to meet and relax.

The vegetation and natural environment are the key elements at Yumebutai. Working to protect and make the most of this marine and forest landscape was an exciting project. Our actions in the twenty-first century will hopefully bring about healthy regeneration here and, over the course of the project, satisfy a number of functional needs while melding the various structures and gardens with nature and developing the overall potential of the region.

The great challenge lies in persuading visitors to pay attention to certain important but often neglected aspects of the environment, leading them to make new discoveries on their own. These days we cannot leave it to nature alone to create or preserve our environment.

The moment has come in which each of us has a duty to make an active contribution to the protection of the environment by leading a life that is in harmony with it. The hope that accompanies the project is that Yumebutai, surrounded as it is by the sea and lush vegetation, will become a place that will continue giving us courage and hope for centuries to come.

Sketch of the circular plaza and the vista terraces.

Opposite page: The oval plaza for open-air events.

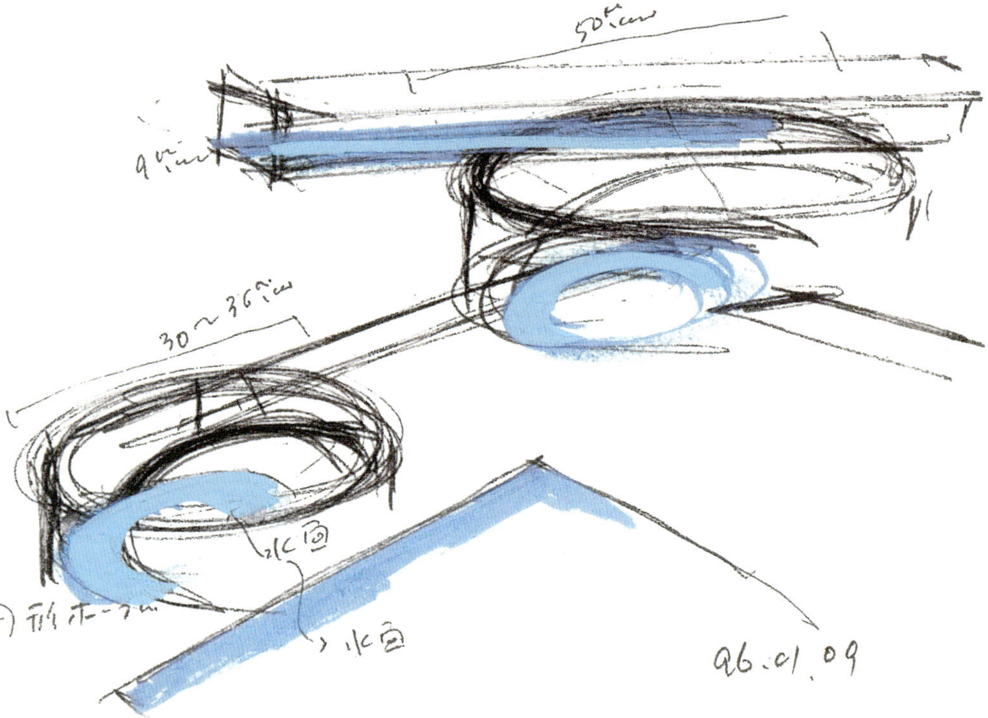

Left: View of the partly sunken level and section.

Opposite page: Living area on three levels.

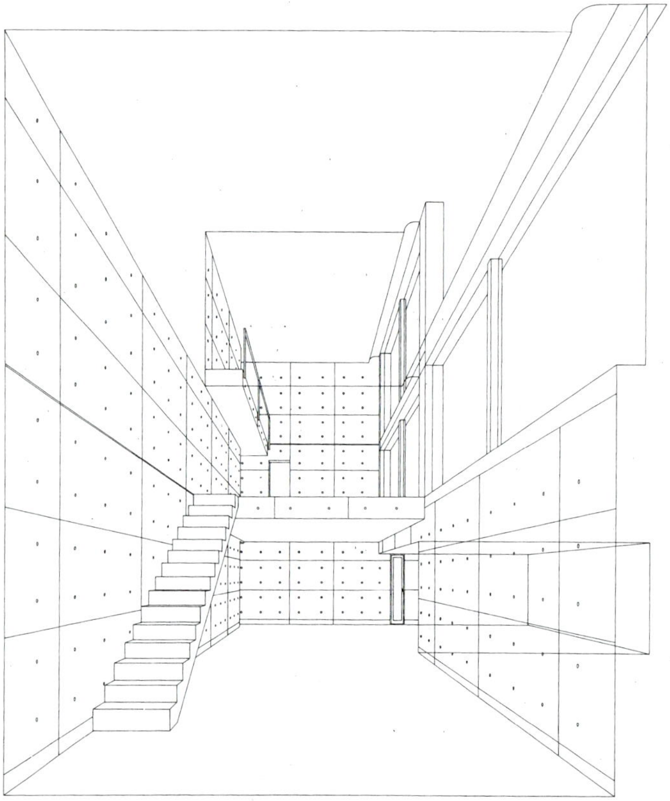

Location Paris, France
Design 1994–1995
Construction 1995
Site area 350 sq m
Building area 33 sq m
Total area 33 sq m

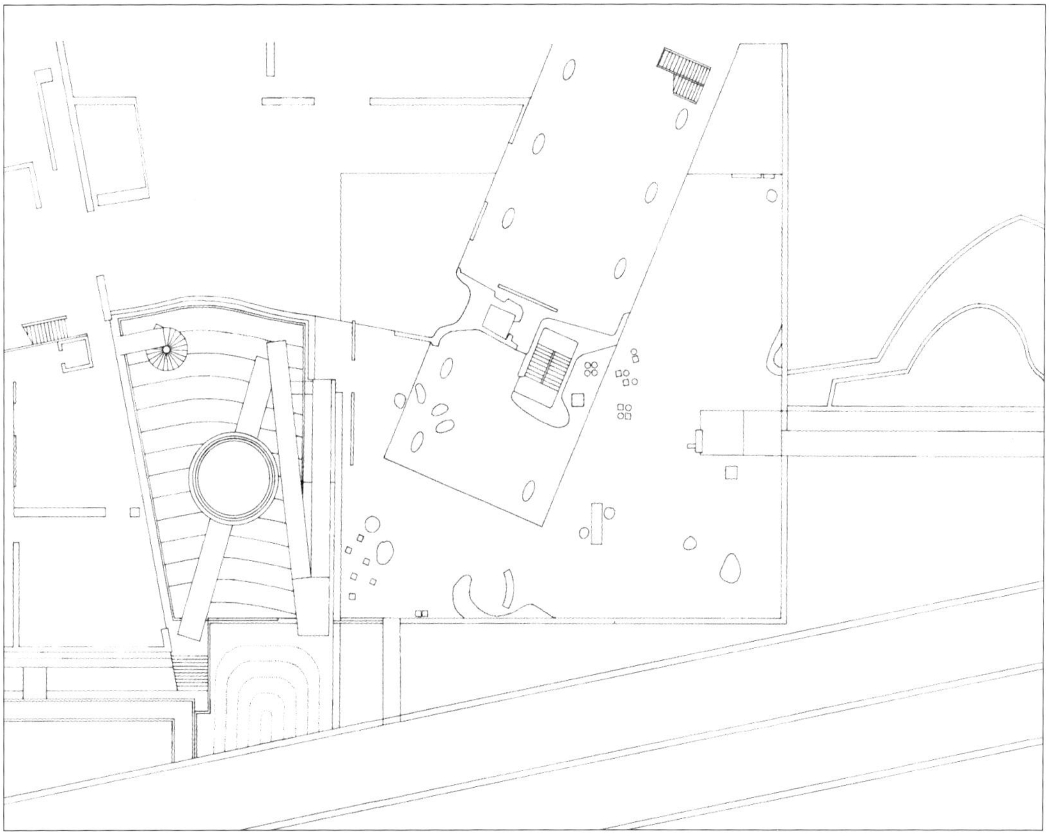

The United Nations Educational Scientific and Cultural Organization was founded in 1946, at the end of World War II, with the aim of promoting peace, scientific co-operation and cultural exchange. In 1995, UNESCO celebrated its 50th anniversary.

On recommendation from the Director General Federico Mayor it was decided to commemorate the milestone anniversary by creating a space for meditation at the organisation's headquarters in Paris. It would be a place to contemplate a world without conflict and with lasting peace between nations regardless of religious, ethnic, cultural or historical differences.

The structure consists of a cylinder of reinforced concrete with a floor area all on one level measuring about 350 square metres at a height of 6.5 metres. In keeping with its name and purpose, the space communicates a sense of solemnity and serenity.

An integral part of the building was to be a chilling reminder of the atomic bomb that was dropped on Hiroshima. With the co-operation of the city, granite slabs that had been exposed to radiation were reclaimed and then used for the flooring and the base of the pool.

To this day, ethnic and religious conflict feeds war in all regions of the globe. According to the wishes of those that commissioned this work, this area for contemplation would be a symbol of peace and a place in which visitors were able to feel at one with the world.

Skylight viewed from below and a scale drawing.

Section and view of areas inside the complex.

Right: View of the meditation space from the entrance gangway and an interior view looking out.

Left: Articulation of the building along the slope.

Below left: View from the sea with the overhanging entrance area facing towards the Bay of Osaka.

Below: Axonometric plan.

Location Awaji, Hyogo, Japan
Design 1994–1996
Construction 1996–1997
Site area 5,822 sq m
Building area 1,734 sq m
Total area 3,192 sq m

This idyllic site facing the ocean was perfect for a company retreat "at one" with the sea. However, it was set in a seismically unstable region west of the epicentre of the Hanshin earthquake of January 1995. The hilltop location looks 30 metres down to the sea on a 45-degree slope facing south-east.

Overlooking Osaka Bay, the new international airport at Kansai can be seen over the east and the magnificent 180-degree views of the ocean from the top of this richly forested coastline are truly special. This charming locality is now a seminar centre that can accommodate up to 70 people.

In order to ensure all the rooms would enjoy ocean views, the building is split over eight levels that mirror the profile of the mountain. The atrium on the highest level extends the full length of the building from east to west and provides spectacular views of the island and the bay. An exposed footbridge gives the impression of walking across the bay and even the pool has panoramic views, like bathing in the very waters of the sea. The entire complex transmits an intimate connection between land and sea.

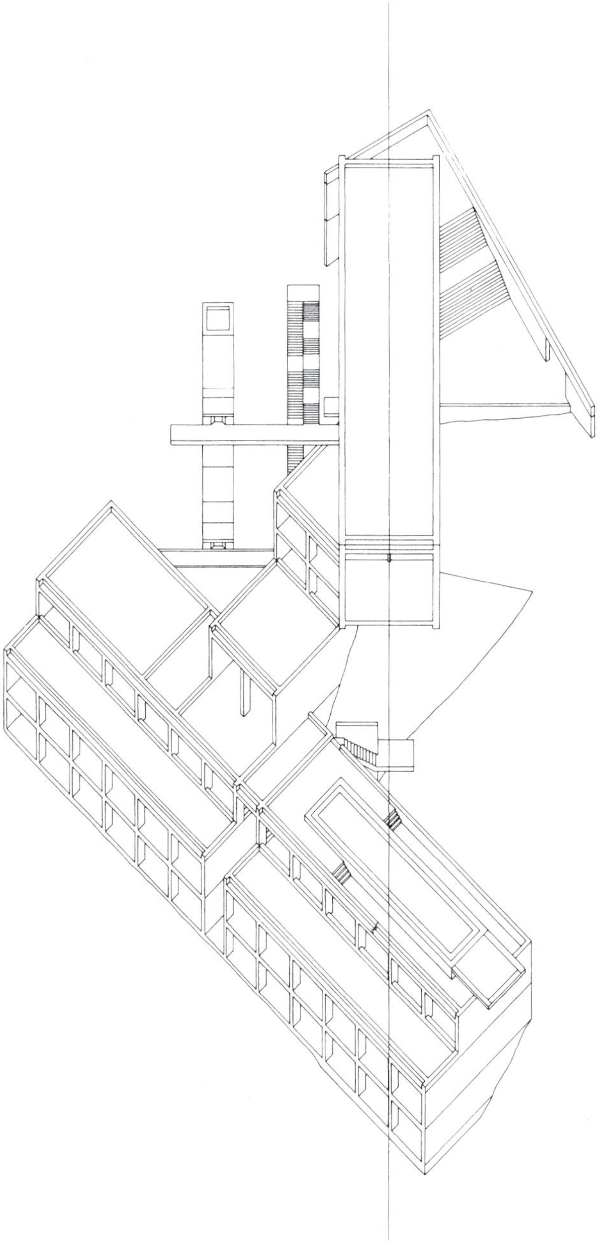

Left: Roof gardens and the swimming pool facing the sea.

Right: Floor plans for the seventh, third and first floors; an image of the swimming pool on the roof terrace for guests.

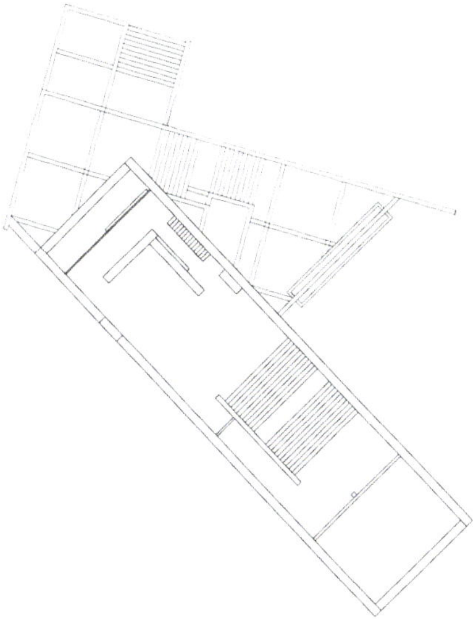

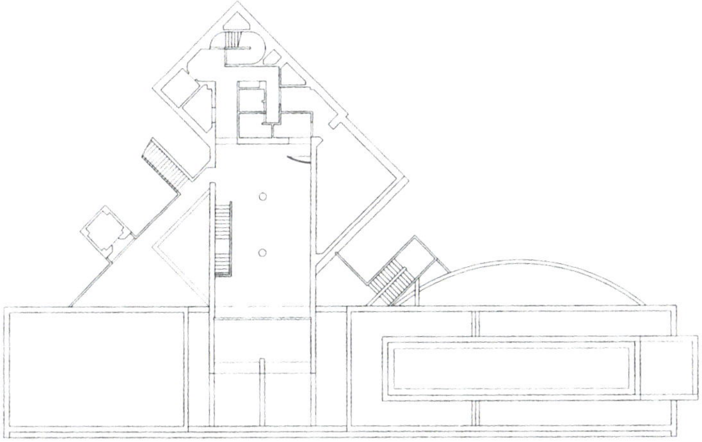

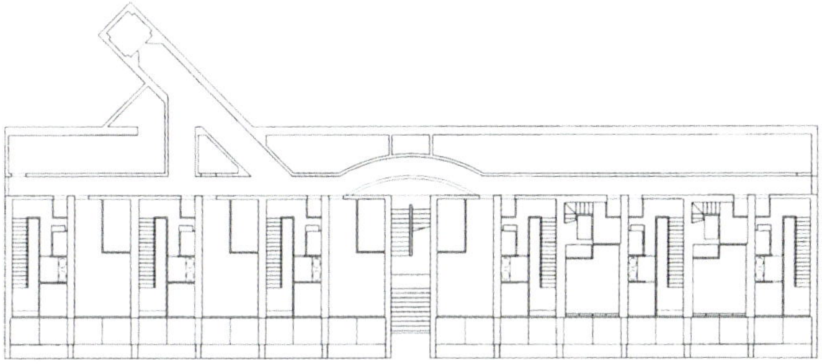

Section and view of the sea from the centre of the entrance area.

Right: Facing east and an interior view of the atrium.

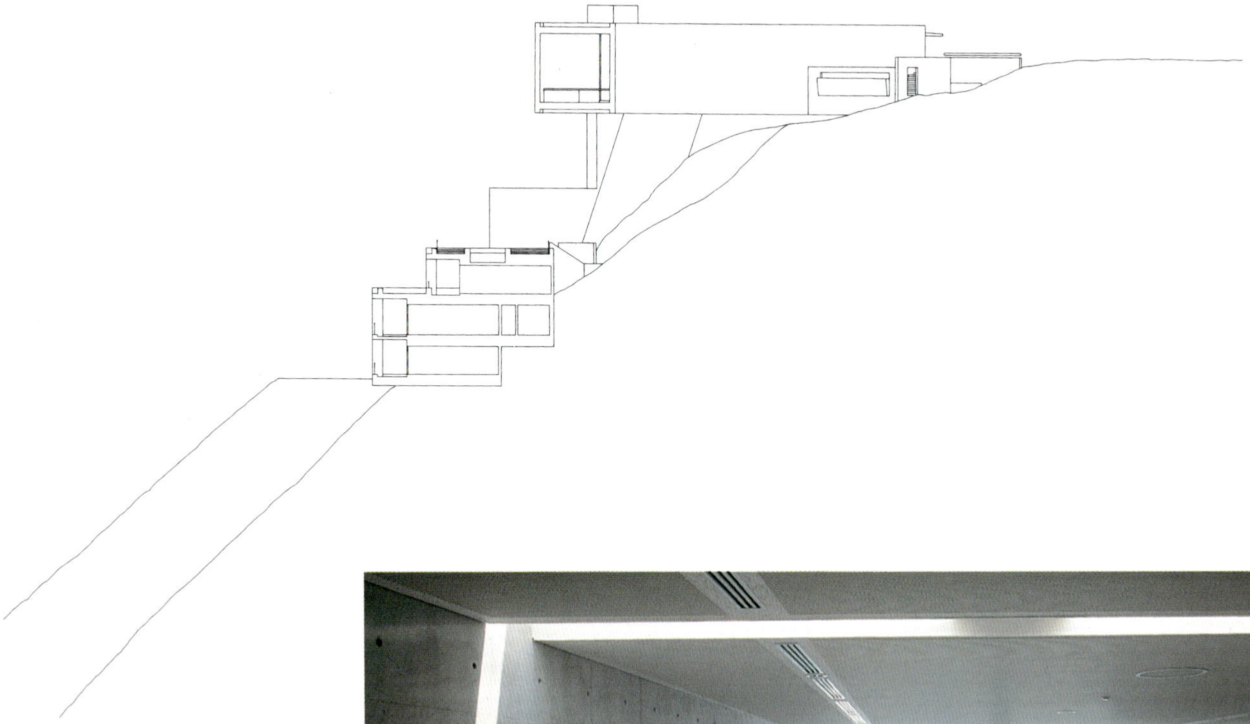

Left: The museum's forest setting.

Scale drawing of the museum.

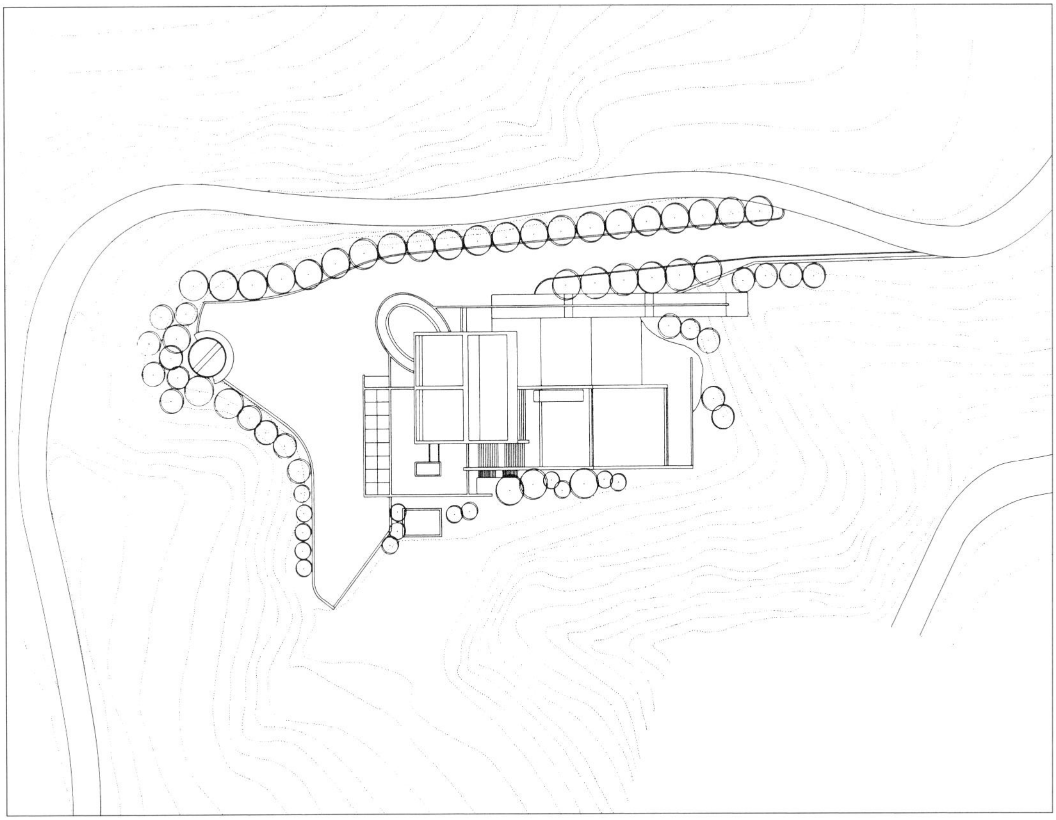

Location Takaoka, Kochi, Japan
Design 1994–1996
Construction 1996–1997
Site area 7,284 sq m
Building area 1,163 sq m
Total area 2,094 sq m

The small town of Ochi in the centre of Kochi Prefecture is known as the Town of the Cosmos and features a dahlia-like flower that grows along the river Niyodo. The museum, set within Yokogurayama Natural Forest, is on the scenic route leading to Mount Yokogura, right in the heart of a marvelous area that is rich in vegetation.

It is here on this mountain, a geological formation dating from the Palaeozoic era, that some of the oldest fossils in Japan have been found, making it one of the most important sites in the country. In addition, the area has a rich history connecting it to the legendary 81st Emperor Antoku (1178–1185).

The exceptionally diverse flora in the region led to its selection as an important research site by the father of Japanese botany, Tamitaro Makino. In fact, several plants that he discovered growing here in their original natural habitat have been named after him.

The museum was intended to inform visitors about the Mount Yokogura region and help them appreciate its wealth of natural treasures. The uphill entrance ramp leads directly to the first floor, with views over the surrounding landscape and a series of water features. The verdant green woodlands can be admired through the glass screen that frames the winding path and

Floor plans for roof area, second, first and ground floors.

Opposite Page: View of the roof garden on the second floor and the water courtyard.

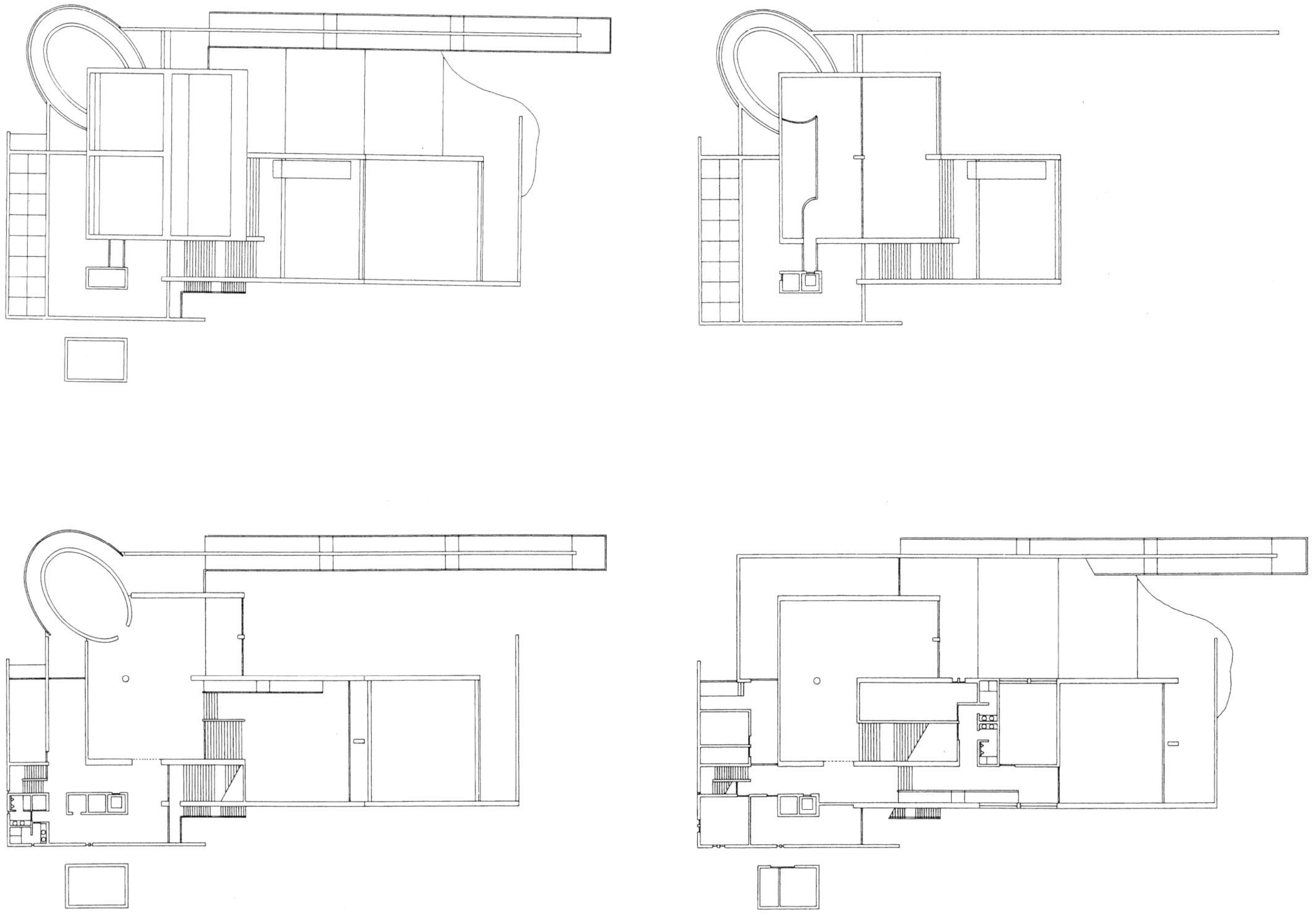

helps draw the visitor's attention to a natural world that is too often overlooked.

The extensive use of glass and the numerous skylights in the atrium and exhibition areas allow the collections to be displayed under natural light. The building was in fact planned with the intention of re-creating conditions that would be appropriate for the exhibition of relics from the natural world.

Through the glass walls on the front of the building, visitors are brought into contact with the landscaped gardens around the museum and given the chance to admire the planting schemes, a hanging garden and a water courtyard. Among the items on display are several of the discoveries made by Tamitaro Makino. Inside, where the architecture was designed to blur the boundary between indoors and outdoors, an illusion is created whereby the items on display seem to still be immersed in their natural surroundings.

From the courtyard on the second floor, outside the lobby, one can look down on the river Niyodo and beyond to the town centre. When autumn arrives, the cosmos flower, symbol of Ochi, grows wildly along the banks of the river.

The treasures of this little known place have been exhibited in a systematic and analytical way in the museum while the architecture allows the town and its many charming elements to be integrated into the building in a way that highlights important elements that might otherwise be overlooked.

Section and detail of the pedestrian ramp along the water court.

Right: Axonometric plan and view of the water court, plus the area behind the water court.

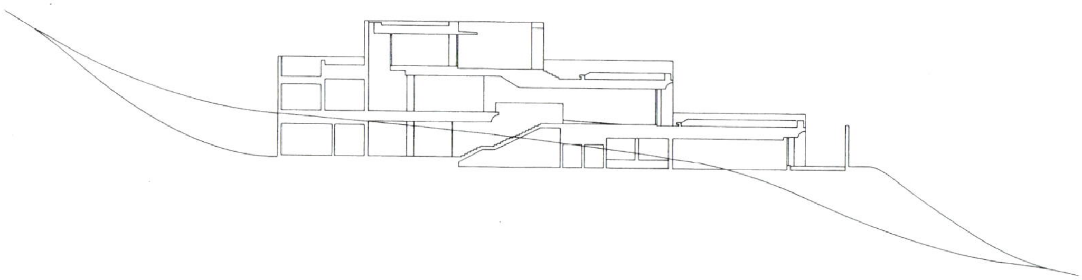

Cross-section plan and interior views of the main gallery and atrium.

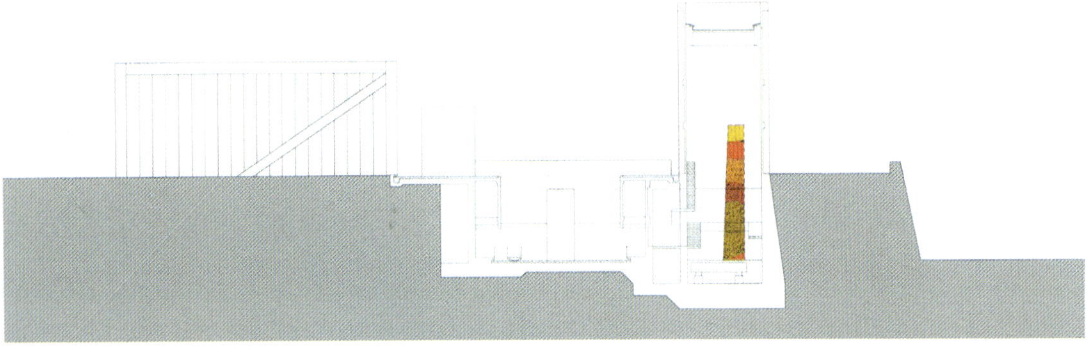

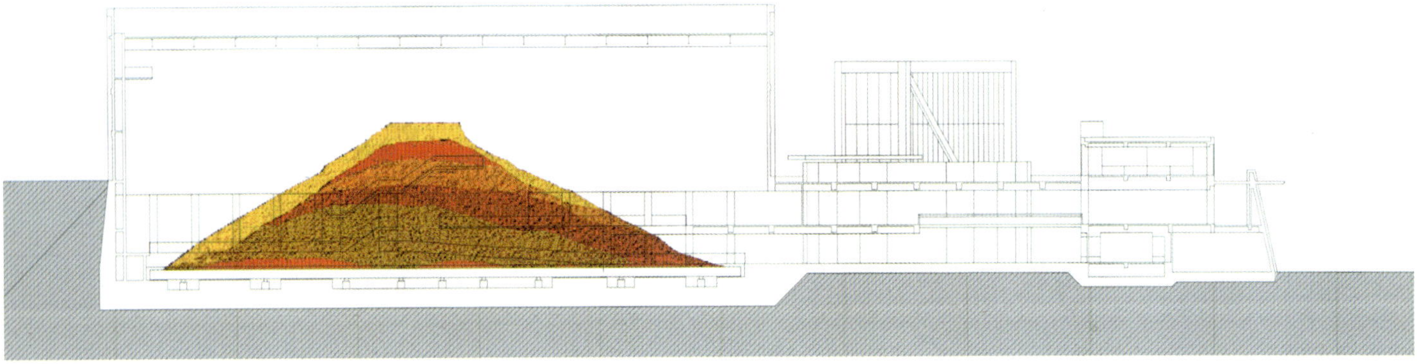

Langen Foundation

Left: The cement wing that screens the platform from the park and the artificial lake that parallels the entrance way.

Design sketch.

Location Neuss, Germany
Design 1994–2002
Construction 2002–2004
Site area 120,220 sq m
Building area 1,860 sq m
Total area 3,050 sq m

On the banks of the river Erft, on the outskirts of Dusseldorf, is an art museum known as Insel Hombroich. As indicated by the name (Insel in German means "island") the entire site is an island in the middle of a vast marsh area, a nature park museum that is a rarity in today's world.

The area of 200,000 square metres accommodates a series of sculptures scattered amongst lush vegetation and a number of elegant exhibition pavilions that are themselves works of art by the sculptor Erwin Heerich. Both the sculptures and the pavilions are scattered randomly between the trees.

Since coming into ownership of the land, proprietor Karl-Heinrich Müller has invested considerable resources and time transforming the topography of the place and restoring the natural environment through a programme of reforestation that will eventually return the area to something like it was several centuries ago.

About a kilometre north-west of the Insel Hombroich, on an site occupied by a former NATO missile silo, Müller has opened a new museum for which he himself designed one of the galleries and other architectural features. This was the point of departure for the Langen/Hombroich Foundation project.

We visited the area for the first time in 1994, but because of financial issues, much time was lost between the presentation of the plans and the work actually starting. Further delays were caused by the distance between Japan and Germany. In 2000, Muller's project was approved by the then 90-year-old Marian Langen, who had allocated the funds for the art museum project, and the building started at the end of 2002. During this long period, however, ideas had progressively gained force and depth. In this sense, although it was exhausting, the delays in getting the project started turned out to be a boon.

The museum housed collections of oriental and modern art belonging to the Langens. The setting for the oriental art is a space of "immobility" pervaded by a suffused light. The other space for the modern art, by contrast, uses a variety of light

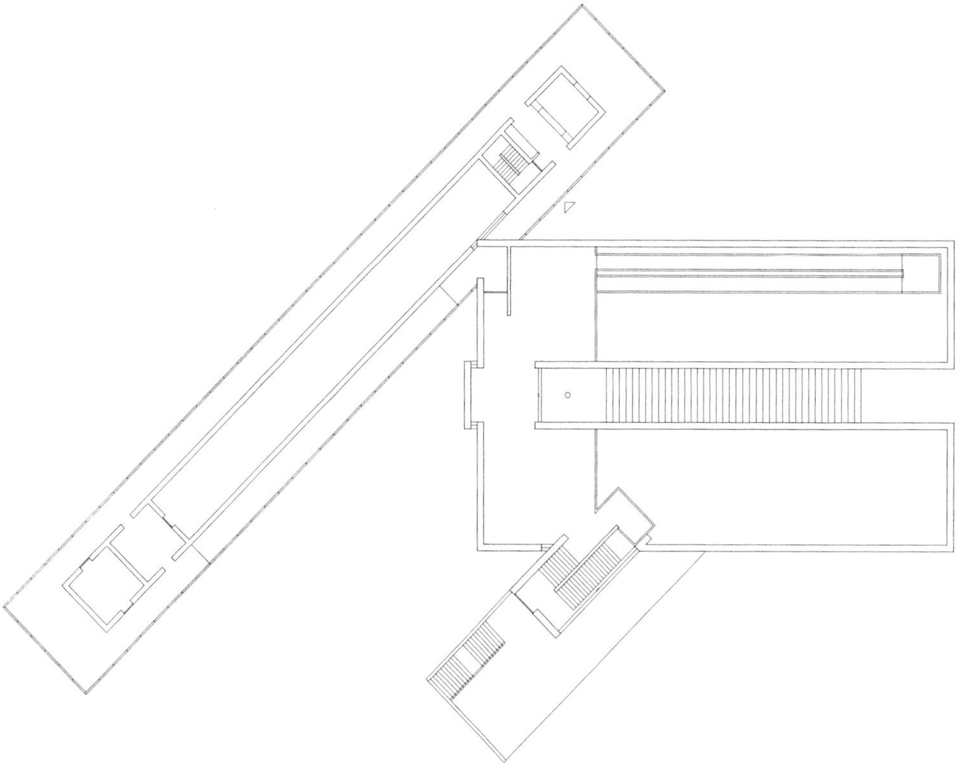

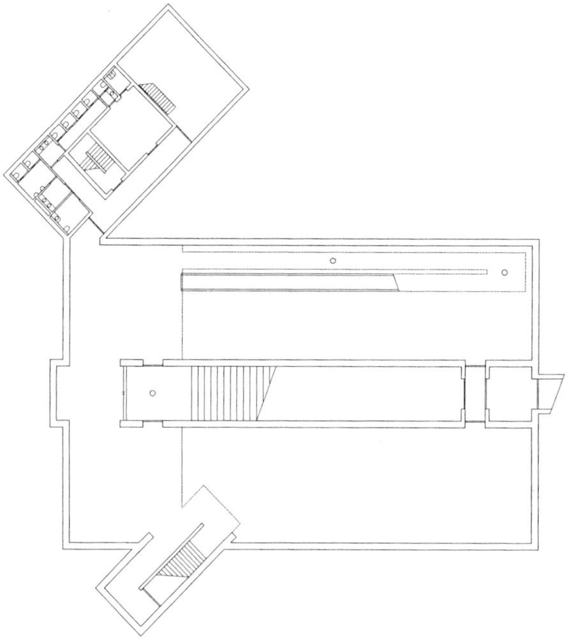

Floor plans of the first floor and underground section.

Right: Views of the glass pavilion for temporary exhibitions and the semi-buried block for the permanent collection from the west, south-east and east.

sources. Recalling the philosophy of Insel Hombroich, where the environment itself has been transformed into a stage for art, the two spaces were inserted into the greenery as discreetly as possible.

The "immobility" of the permanent exhibition is echoed in a concrete structure within a glass enclosure so that running alongside the perimeter is an area similar to the traditional Japanese *engawa*, or veranda, which blurs the boundary between the indoors and outdoors. Visitors inside the museum feel like they are walking in the woods. The "dynamic" space for temporary exhibitions, on the other hand, is in an entirely underground section where a series of skylights create a spectacle within this sealed box.

Immersed in a splendid natural context, the works of art are not isolated from the visitors: they can be touched. When you see the Insel Hombroich for the first time you are blown away. "This is an art paradise," you will think. And it was from this that the impulse came to create a museum fully integrated with nature.

The dreams of these two passionate patrons of the arts are incarnated here in this idyllic setting. Sadly, Marian Langen died before it was completed, but perhaps her spirit will continue to live on here.

Tadao Ando

Details of the perimeter engawa in the pavilion for temporary exhibitions, and of the semi-sunken block for the permanent exhibition.

Following pages: Frontal view from the east.

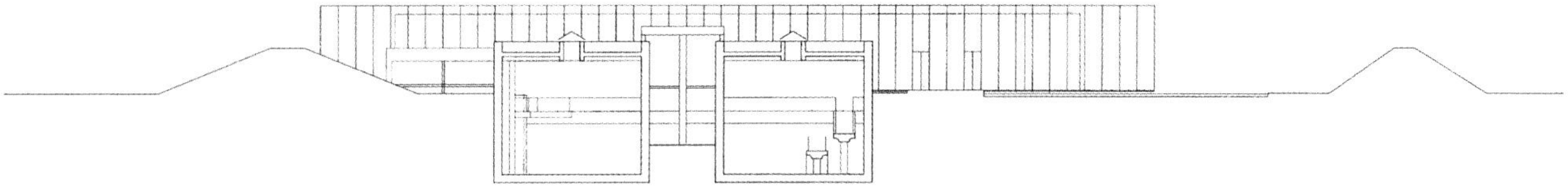

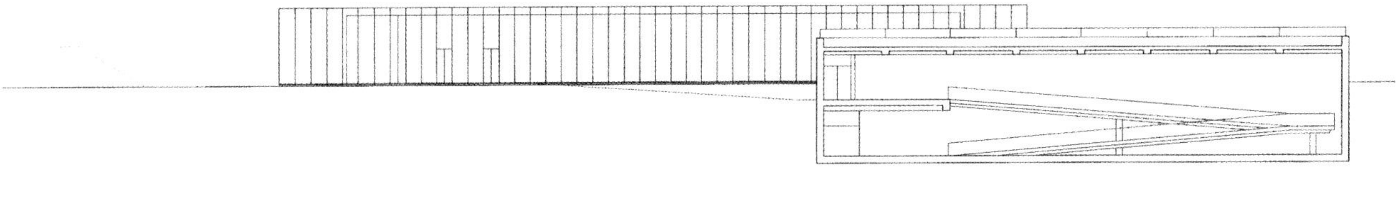

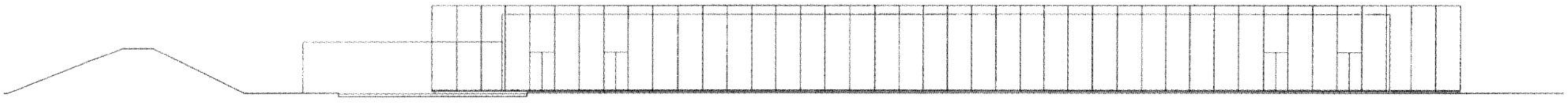

Interior views of the underground galleries and of the link areas between the aboveground and underground floors.

Location London, England
Design 1995
Site area 35,610 sq m
Building area 13,660 sq m
Total area 25,200 sq m

This project was presented to the panel of an international competition announced in 1994. The idea was to come up with a redevelopment plan for a power station on the left bank of the Thames for the Tate Gallery, opposite St. Paul's Cathedral.

The proposed development had the theme of "collision". Rather than try an adaptation of the historic architecture, it played with the concept of a collision between "pure form" and the existing context, confident that the energy and tension would inspire a new panorama.

A large space of more than 40 square metres is enclosed by old walls in brick. Two concrete volumes that house the galleries are suspended inside, pierced by two obelisks of glass that stretch towards St. Paul's.

Natural light enters the building through skylights in the roof, illuminating the public areas of the lower floor. The radical contrast between the brick and the glass instil a sense of vivacity into the place. In an urban context as rich in history as that of London, the obelisks of glass reach up like the cathedral, thereby establishing a dialogue between old and the new.

The Thames can be reached on foot from the building by means of a stepped plaza. The galleries of glass appear to float on the river, fusing into a single entity with the cathedral and the water.

Left: Design sketch and the model of St. Paul's Cathedral.

Plans for the first and the second floors.

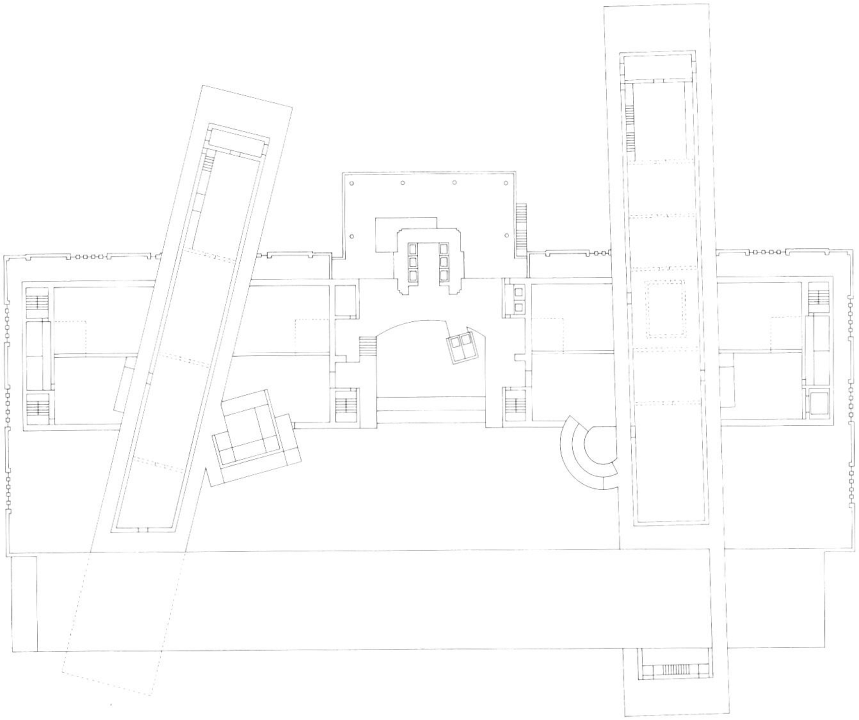

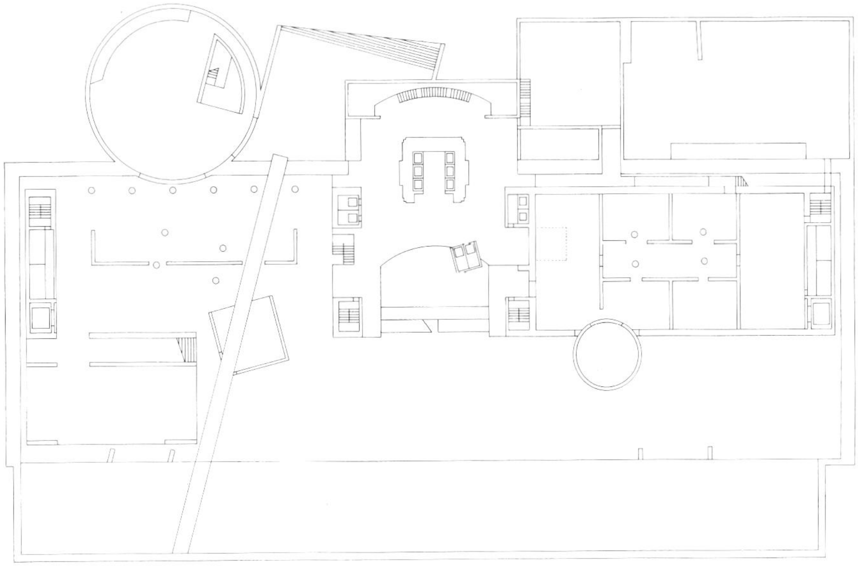

Views of the model and transverse section.

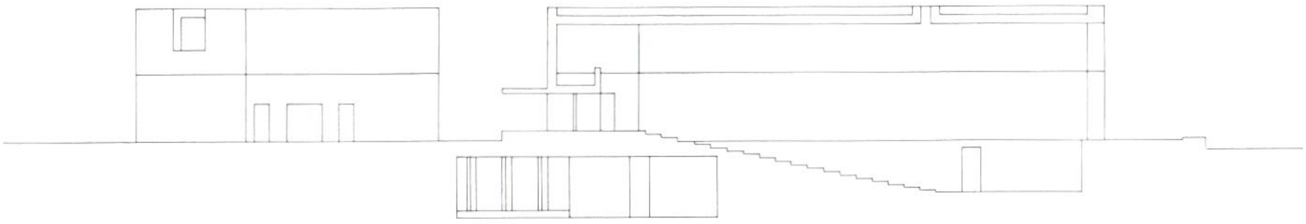

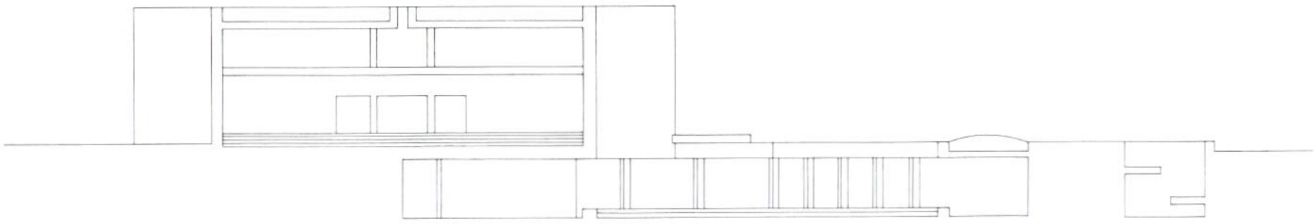

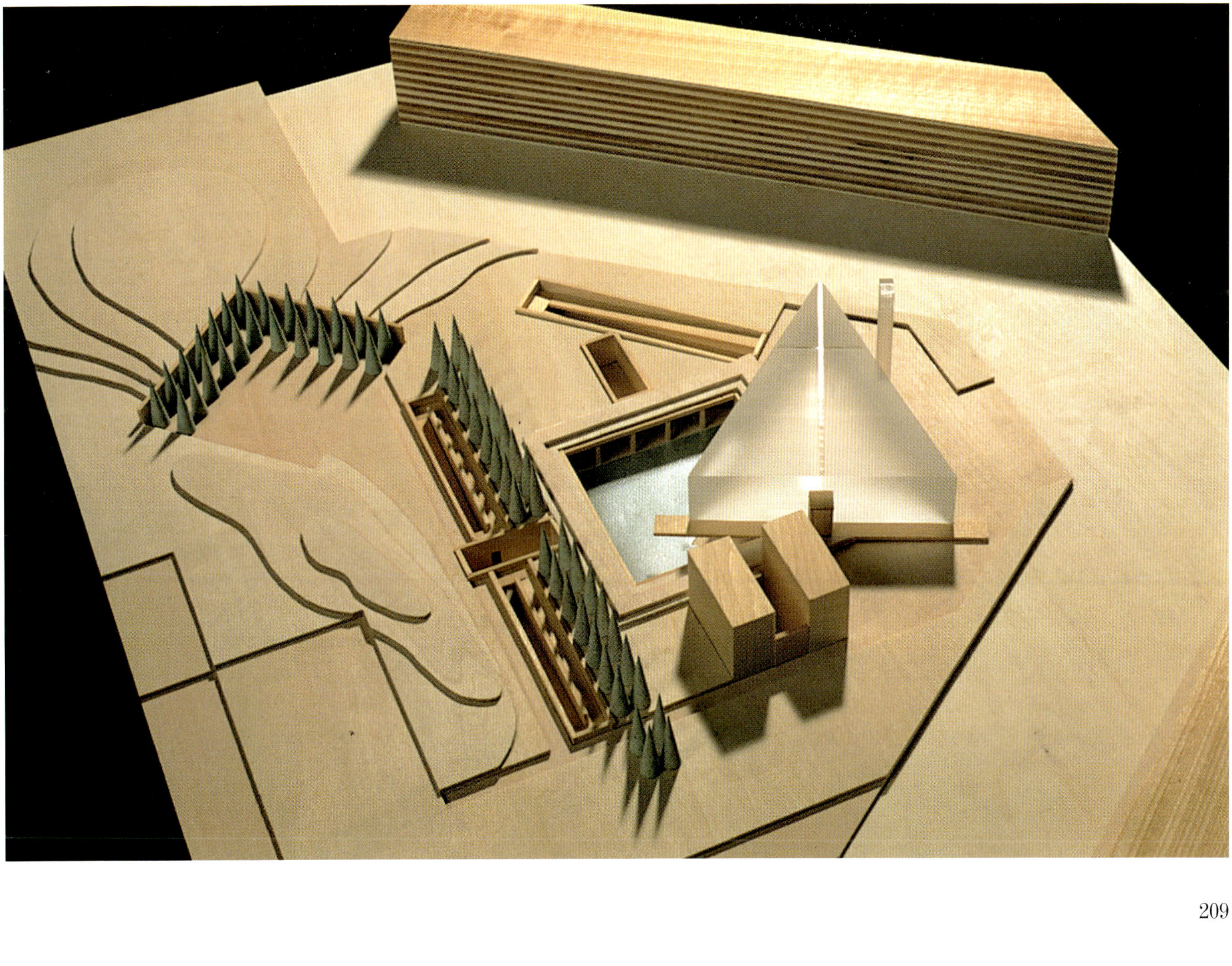

Townhouse in Hirano (Nomi House)

Location Hirano, Osaka, Japan
Design 1995
Construction 1996
Site area 121 sq m
Building area 72 sq m
Total area 92 sq m

This house is in the centre of Osaka where there are still many traditional Japanese terraced homes from before World War II. With their characteristic tiled roofs on a wooden frame they are humble but retain a considerable sentimental value for the community.

In recent years, the common theme has been to carry out extensive renovations, but this townhouse was built in an area that has managed to preserve many of its historical features. Designed for a young couple and one of their mothers, the house is completely protected from the surrounding environment by a two-storey stone wall. Within that, the volume is divided into two distinct, separate areas so that the interior and exterior living spaces occupy footprints of more or less the same size.

The living room, dining area and communal terrace are all on the upper level while the two bedrooms are on the ground floor. Each bedroom opens onto its own courtyard so that all of the family members can enjoy a little privacy.

Nestled in this sea of traditional terraced houses, each yard becomes its own tranquil microcosm. Shards of light and the elements such as wind and rain play in these spaces, displaying the charm and energy of the passing of the seasons and times of day. A sizable Japanese

The building in its urban context and an interior perspective.

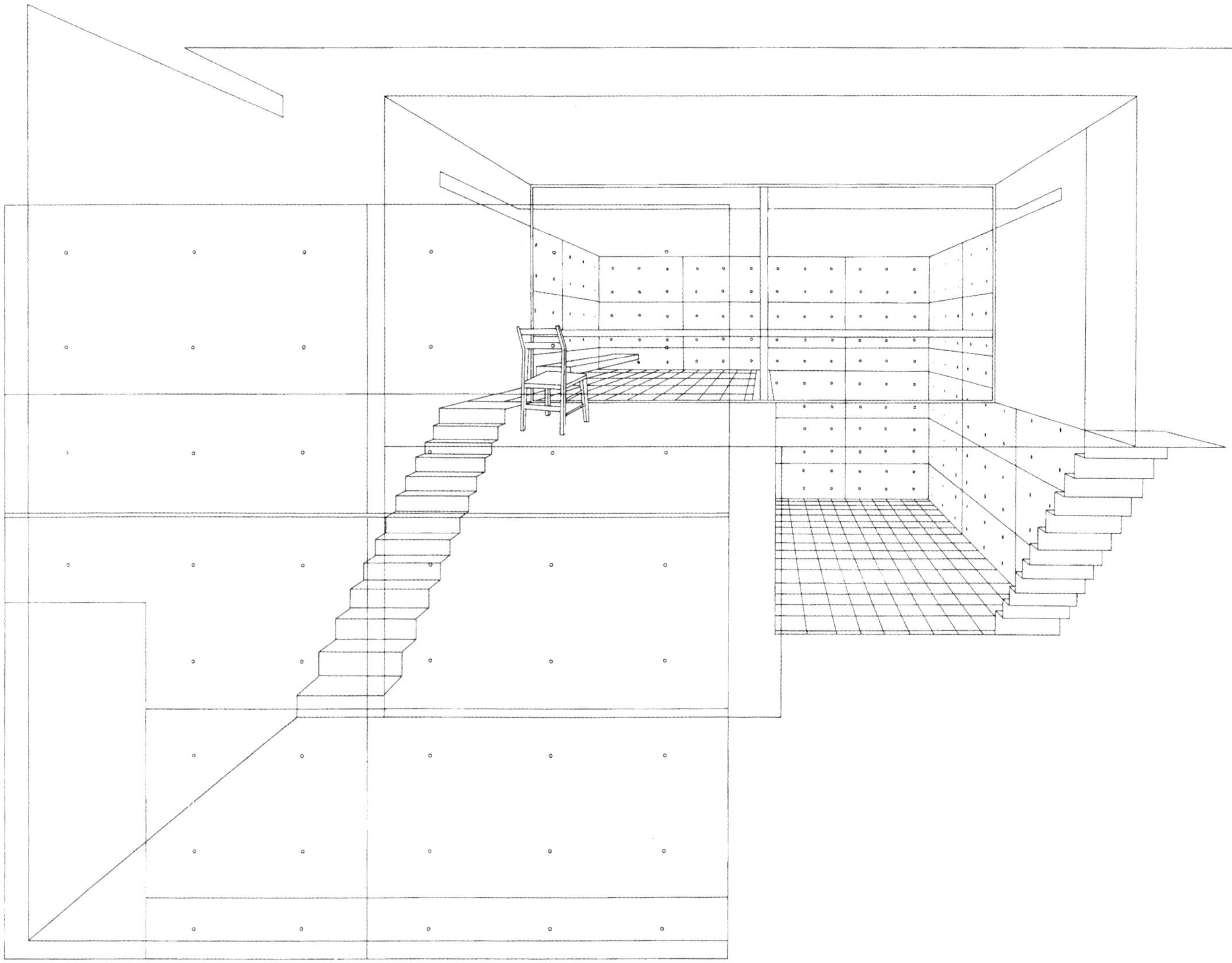

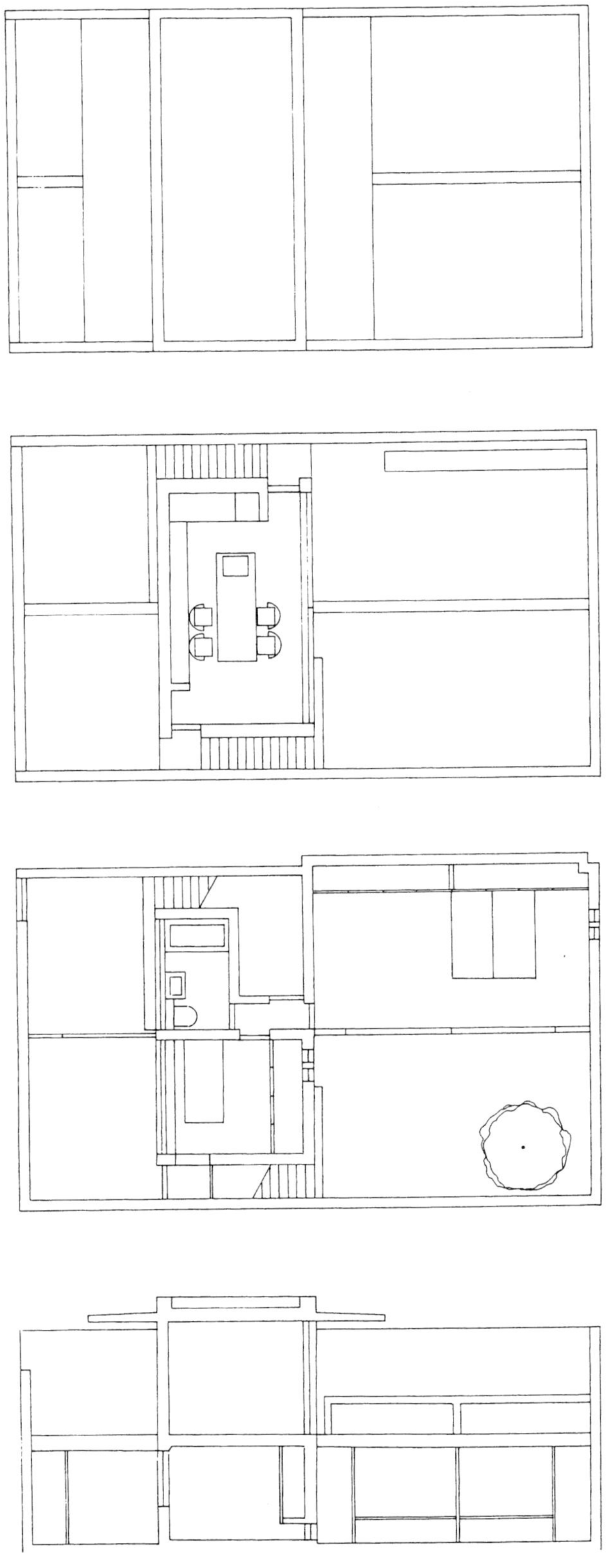

Plans of the roof terrace, first and ground floors and a longitudinal cross-section.

Opposite page: Views of the courtyard entrance and the rear courtyard.

elm in the master bedroom courtyard watches over the inhabitants of the house, creating a dialogue with the other gardens in the neighbourhood.

The dwelling is accessed by a single door cut into the perimeter wall and a flight of stairs leads directly to the upper floor of the residence. The building is designed so that to reach the private areas it is necessary to cross the common areas first.

In contrast to the open, light-filled living room, the bedrooms downstairs are tucked away in the shadows and express a sense of serenity and tranquillity. The two areas are linked, but since they open in opposite directions one cannot be seen from the other, giving them complete autonomy.

Each of these semi-private courtyards is configured as an extension of the adjoining bedroom, creating a larger spatial feel despite the obvious limitations imposed on the house by the small size of the lot. Moreover, although there is a close physical connection between the individual spaces, the presence of the courtyards ensures that the sense of spaciousness is far greater than we would instinctively suspect.

Because of the use of stairways and courtyards, the house is not necessarily an inherently functional building. The primary goal of the project was a different one. Some people might think it would be difficult to live in a place where nature's harshness is so present, especially on cold and rainy winter days, but the building perfectly matches the lifestyle of its inhabitants.

The rear courtyard.

Right: Axonometric diagram and views of the roof terrace over the master bedroom.

Yagi House

Location Nishinomiya, Hyogo, Japan
Design 1995–1996
Construction 1996–1997
Site area 1,757 sq m
Building area 362 sq m
Total area 501 sq m

This site is located on top of a hill overlooking Mount Rokko in the quiet residential area of Shukugawa. The great Hanshin Awaji earthquake of 1995 totally destroyed the original house that occupied the site, a historic building designed by William Vories Meiji (1868–1912).

In its place, a new residential structure to accommodate a family consisting of two different generations was proposed. The only request was that the house be "safe". In addition to that, the project was to enhance the home's relationship with its natural surroundings.

The structure consists of two rectangular volumes organised on a 5.4-metre grid and rotated at an angle of 60° to each other. To reduce the environmental impact, one level was placed underground and opens onto a large sunken courtyard, while the height of the building above ground is limited to only two storeys.

The angle and the distance between the volumes have been carefully calculated in order to safeguard the privacy of both family units. In each wing, openings have been made to complement the functions of the home and provide a living space that is devoid of areas where internal and external spaces merge. Each wing is also designed in such a way that it offers a unique panoramic view.

Unlike many of the projects in the past for small residences in densely populated Shitamachi (in central Tokyo), where the idea was always to set the outdoor spaces toward the inside spaces and close the building off, this project tried where possible to open the building up to its natural surroundings. We wanted to create a home that stands alone in its singularity and yet blends in with the surrounding landscape.

Opposite Page: The sunken courtyard from the southeast.

The terrace from the living space and the final steps of the staircase down to the sunken courtyard.

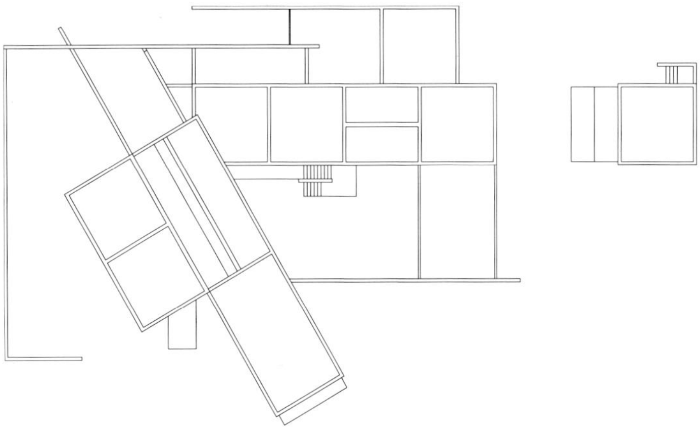

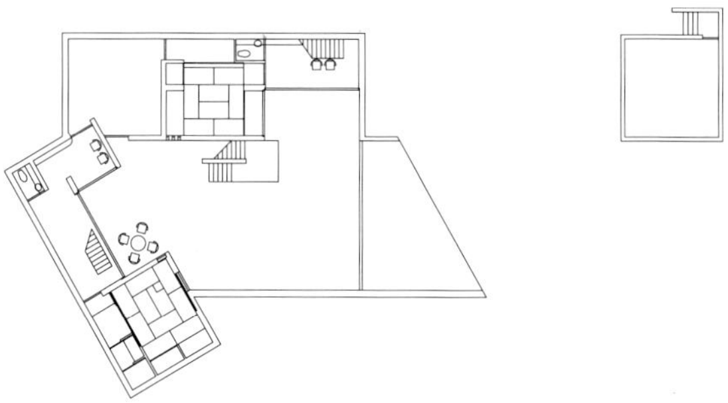

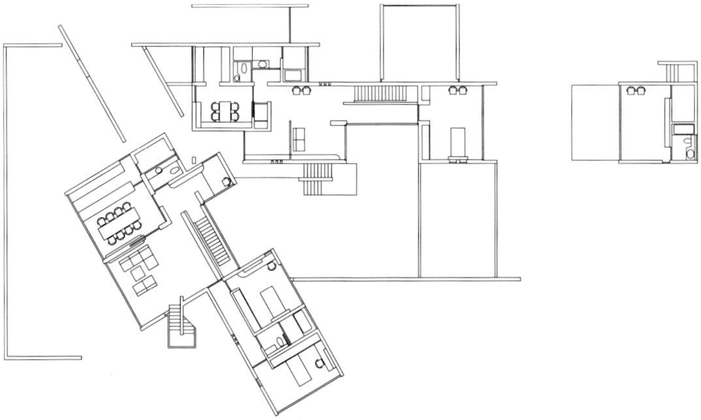

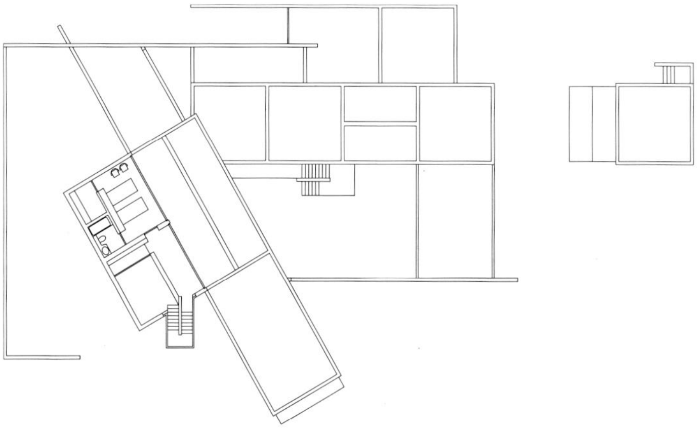

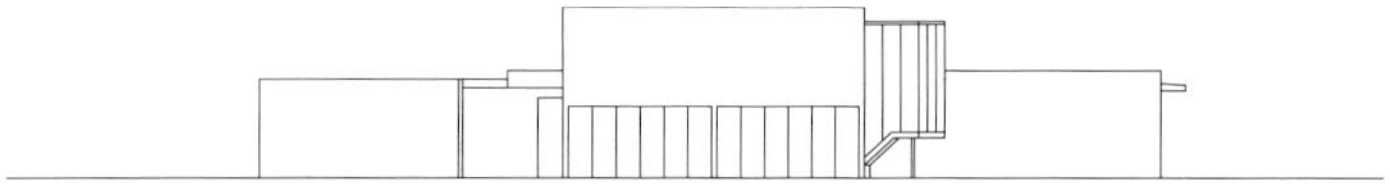

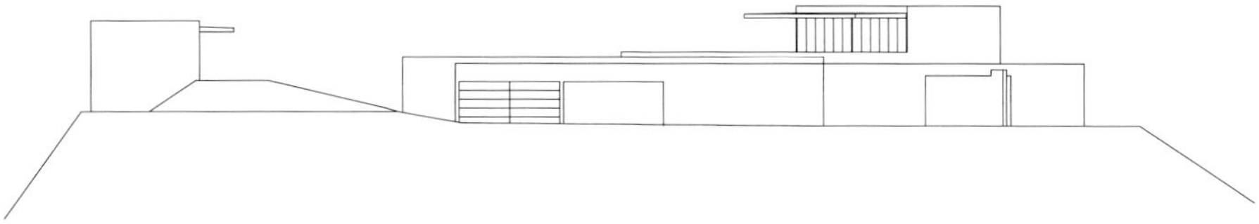

Left: Site plan.

Views of the tower and the pool facing away from the ocean from the northwest and southwest.

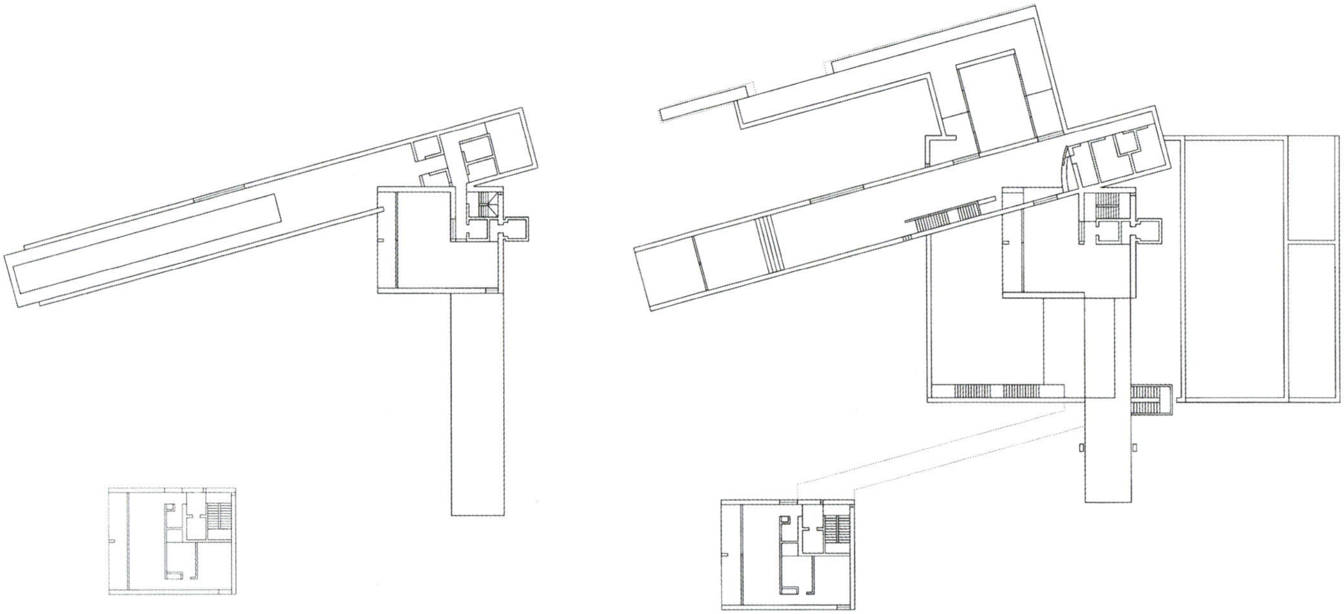

Left: Plans of the ground and first floors, and a photo of the end of the south wing.

The sunken courtyard and a seascape from one of the rooms.

a second volume, some distance from this that was connected by a partially underground corridor; and two wings constructed at right angles at the foot of the tower, each with a swimming pool, a gallery, a lounge and a cafeteria.

The hotel was given spaces that have their own specific individuality, including outdoor pools overlooking the sea and sunken courtyards surrounded by greenery. From the rooms guests can enjoy water, sky, and magnificent views of the Inland Sea of Japan. And yet the various spaces do not give an impression of individual elements divorced from each other, but elements in harmony within a unique complex.

Detail of the glass entrance volume and a studio sketch.

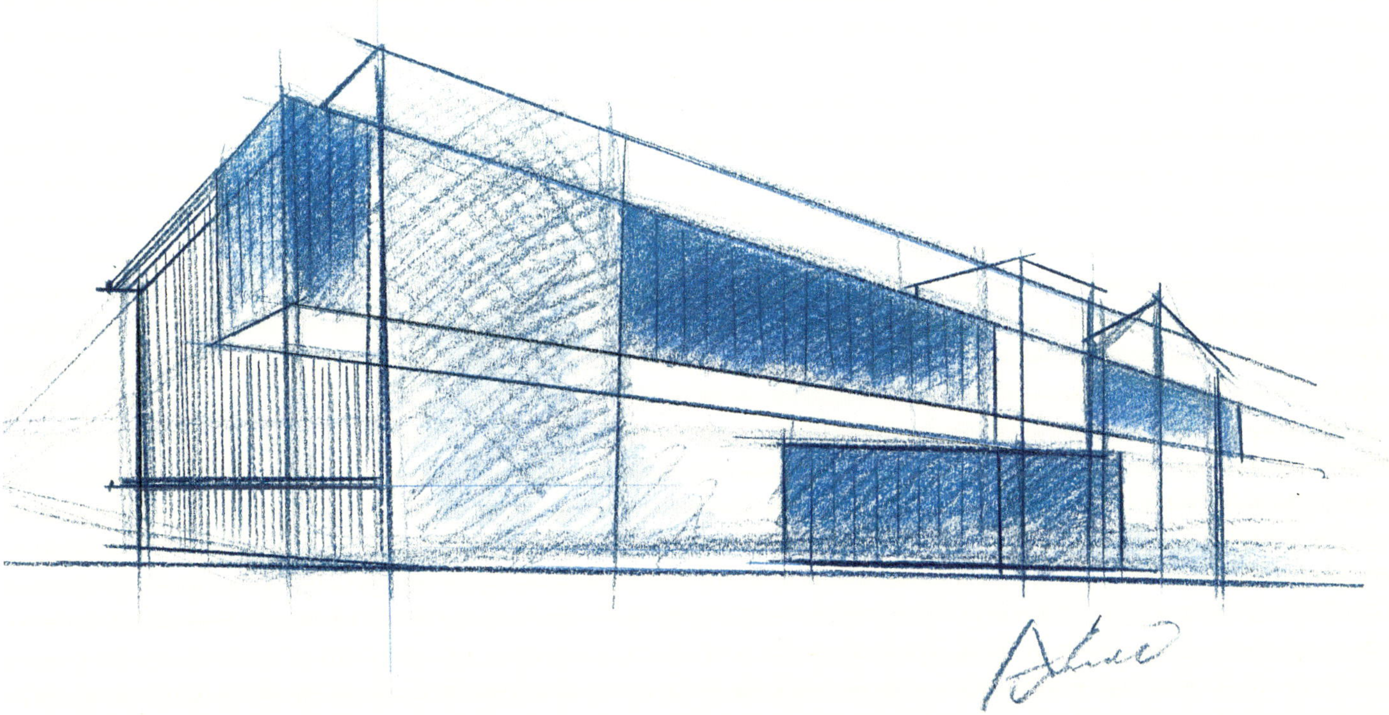

Location Taito, Tokyo, Japan
Design 1996–2000
Construction 1998–2002
Site area 5,434 sq m
Building area 2,018 sq m
Total area 6,672 sq m

During the Meiji era, Japan had already begun its transition to a more Westernized society. This building, which now houses the International Library of Children's Literature, was built during that time (1906) and was originally the headquarters and national library of the Diet (parliament) in Ueno.

Together with other cultural institutions in the area, the building's obviously Western, or at least "pseudo-Western", character contributes greatly to the evocative atmosphere of Ueno Park in Tokyo.

Responding to expectations from the client asking for a "regeneration" of the old library, Tadao Ando & Associates were commissioned to design the project taking into account the "conflict" between old and new, while respecting the historic building and its cultural value. This collision between the past and present was achieved by inserting two glass blocks into the existing body of the carefully restored building.

The glass element on the ground floor, which contains the entrance hall and the cafeteria, forms an angle of roughly 60° with the longitudinal axis of the structure, while the other

Plans of the second, first and ground floors.

Opposite page: Site plan and view of the front from the main road.

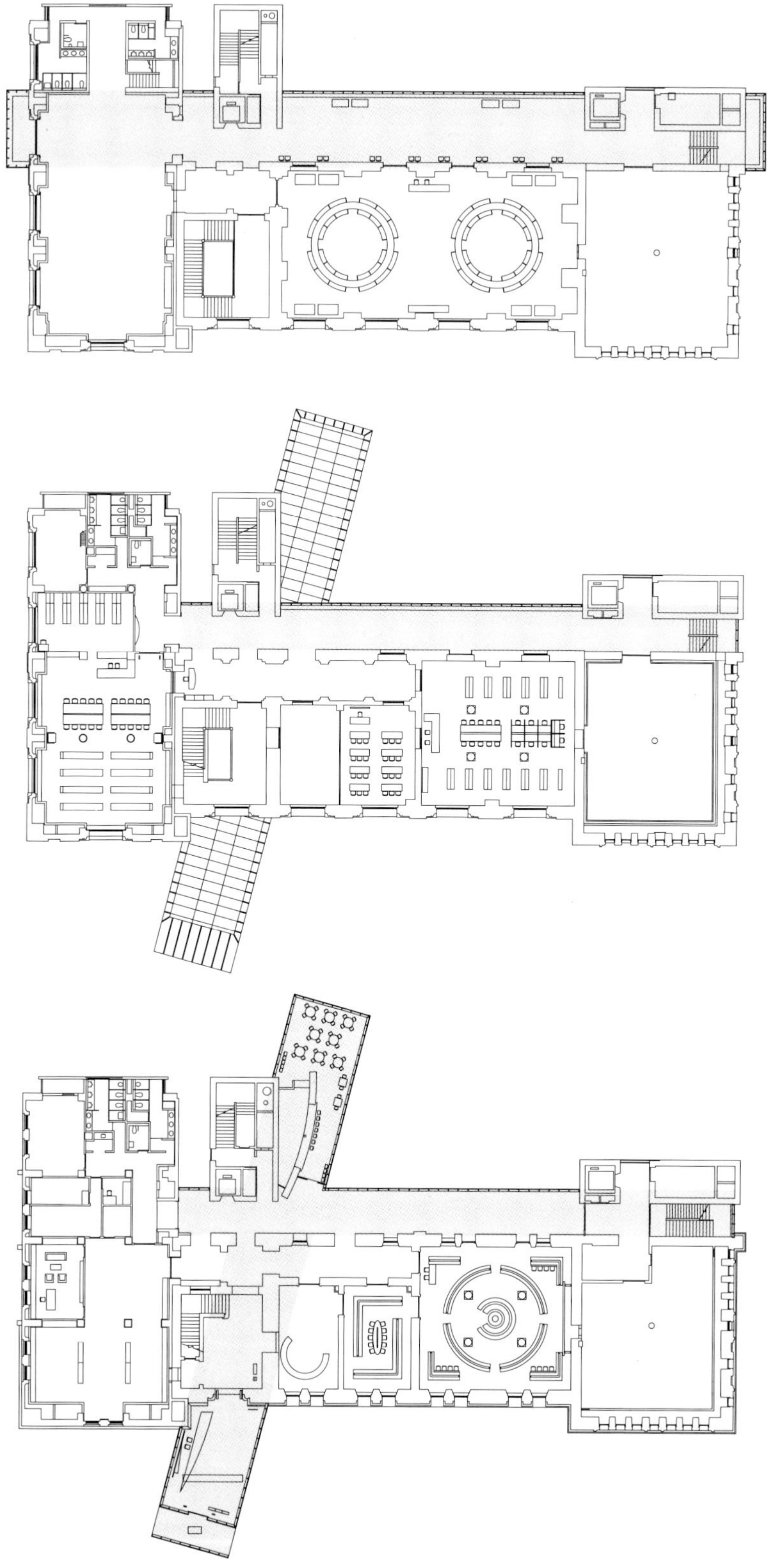

Left: Detail of the front façade towards the garden.

Interior view of the gallery on the second floor.

The reading room for children on the ground floor.

Right: The cylindrical, wood veneer exhibition halls on the second floor.

Views of the model and studio sketch.

Location New York, USA
Design 1996
Total area 712 sq m

This design involved the expansion of a penthouse apartment and a guest apartment on the top floors of a 1920s Manhattan skyscraper.

For a home in a city like New York, where the mixture of old and new is a source of seemingly endless fascination, this project brought with it a direct clash between the stylistic elements of the historic building, designed for its height, and contemporary architecture, which tends to feature steel, concrete and glass.

The resulting penthouse was a concrete box wrapped in a glass membrane that seems to float on top of the building. A body of water on the roof reflects the city's skyscrapers and other elements of this "borrowed" urban landscape.

Five floors below, another volume, identical in shape and materials, is wedged into a corner of the building, completely disrupting its symmetry. The presence of a house suspended in the air outside the building communicates a strong message concerning the intentions of its inhabitants.

The goal is that this modest design addition, included as a sort of stab at the urban landscape, may provide further stimulus to a place as dynamic and desirable as Manhattan.

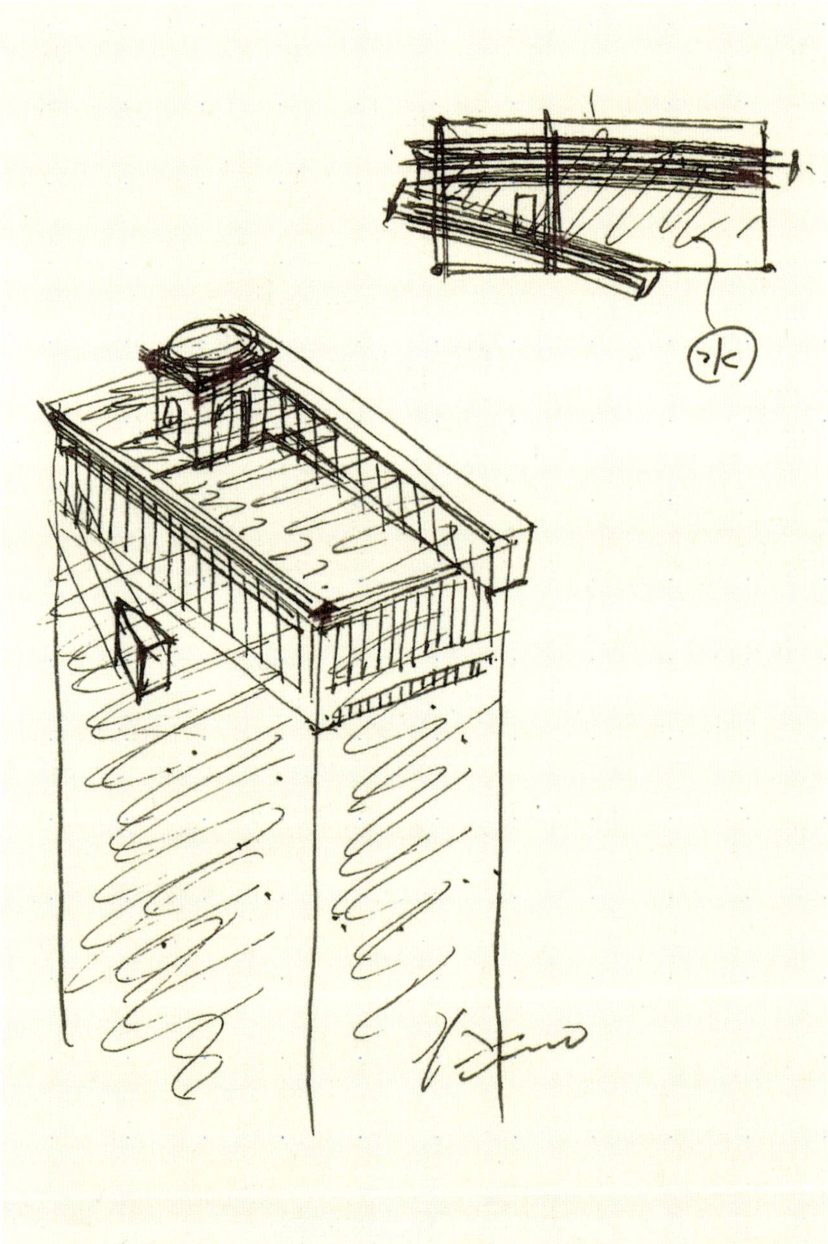

Studio sketch, perspective and the plans of the upper and lower floors.

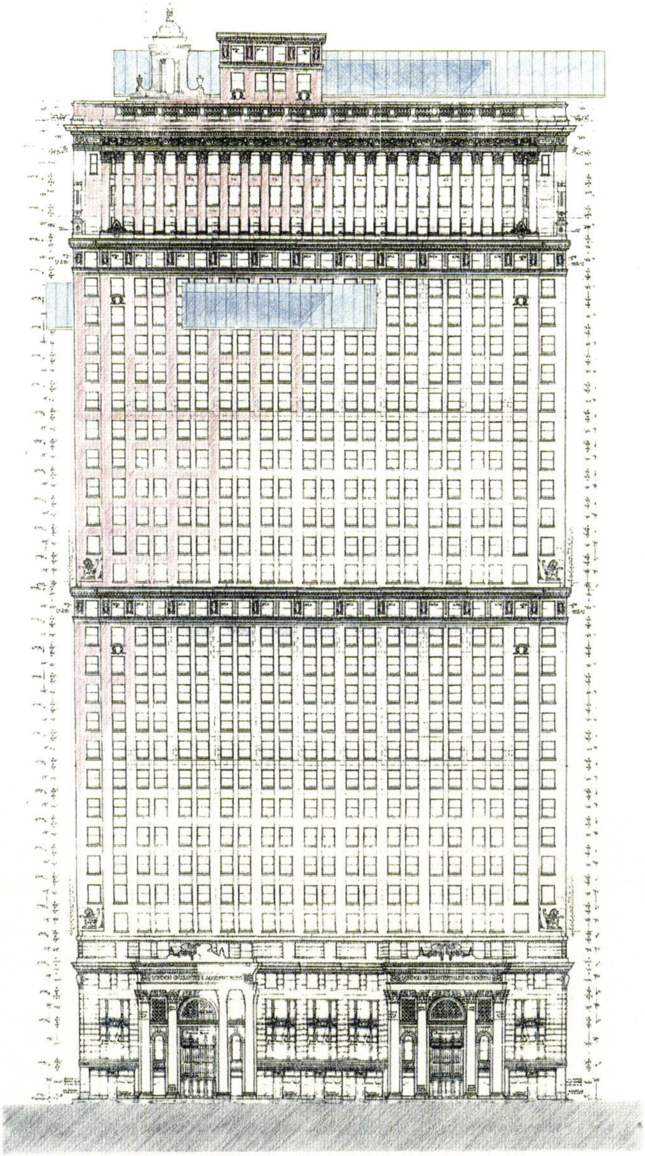

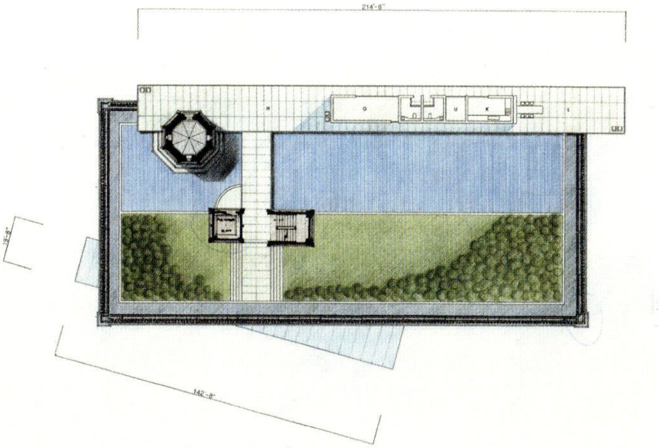

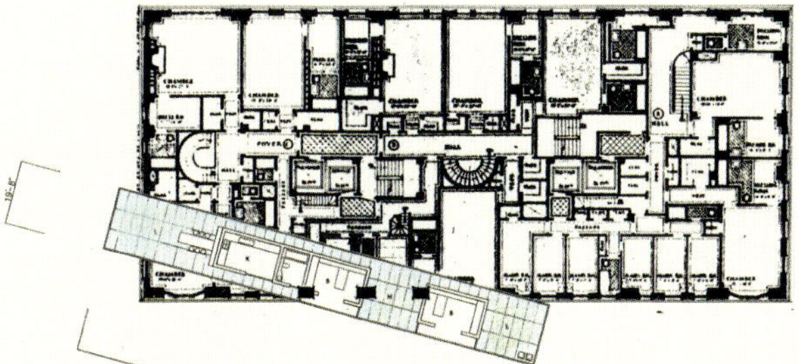

Views of the model and a photo montage.

Location Bad Munster am Stein, Germany
Design 1996–2010
Site area 6,034 sq m
Building area 130 sq m
Total area 221 sq m

This is a modest museum housing the works of German artist Wolfgang Kubach and his wife Anne-Marie Kubach-Wimsen. Kubach is famous for his sculptures carved directly into stone in the shape of books or stacks of books.

The museum is located in a hilly region near Baden-Baden, Germany. First, an 18th-century barn typical of the region with a gabled roof was moved to the middle of the lot, restored and transformed into the main exhibition space.

In addition, a number of concrete walls were designed to follow the natural topography of the property and delimit the courtyards and water features where the sculptures are on display. They also divided the interior and exterior spaces and defined a set of new areas.

The old shell of the barn was removed, with only the warping wooden roof of the former barn kept intact. By renovating it in this manner, natural light could filter through the cracks in the two-storey space, animating the works arranged inside.

New concrete walls created a striking contrast with the existing rafters. The image of the old barn is reflected on the surface of the water in the central courtyard pool, moving with the wind and representing yet another fusion of old and new.

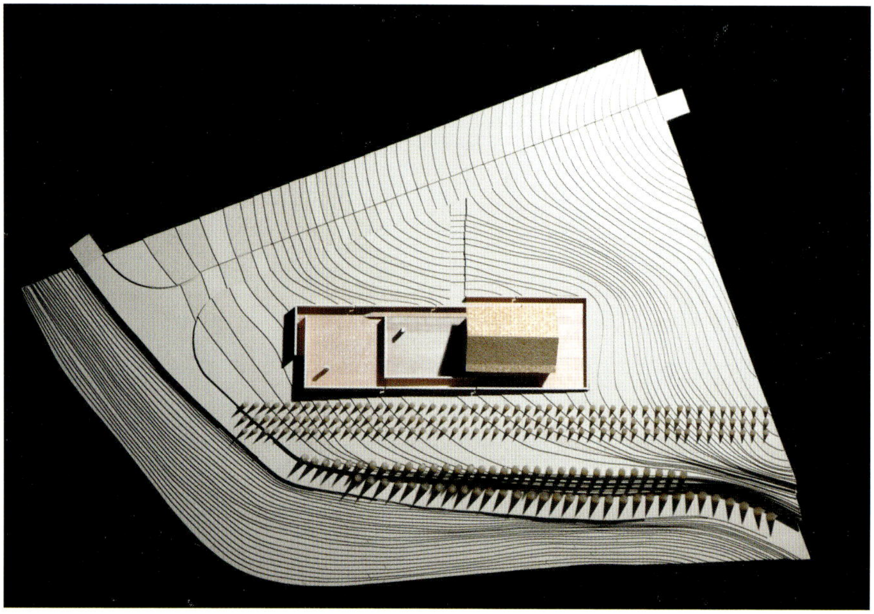

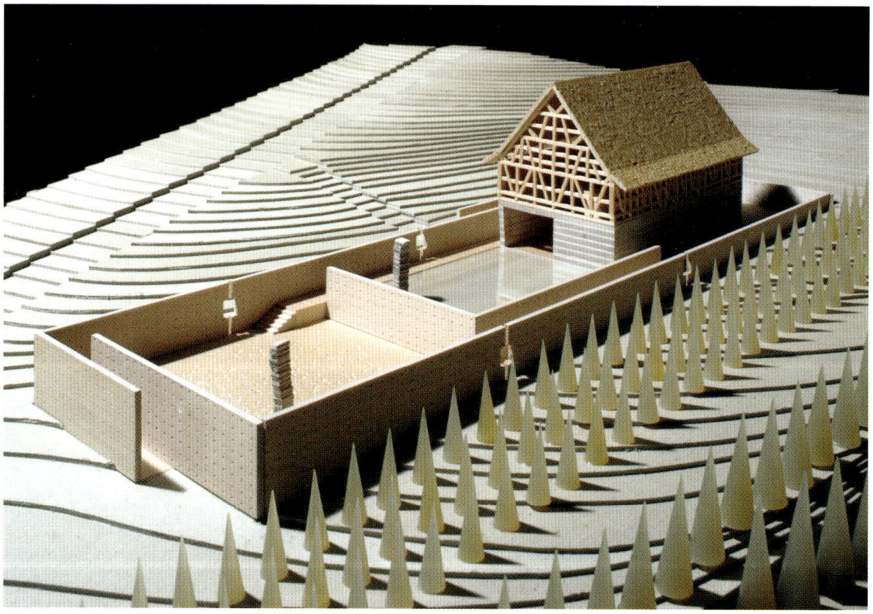

Model views, a perspective of the courtyard entrance and a split perspective.

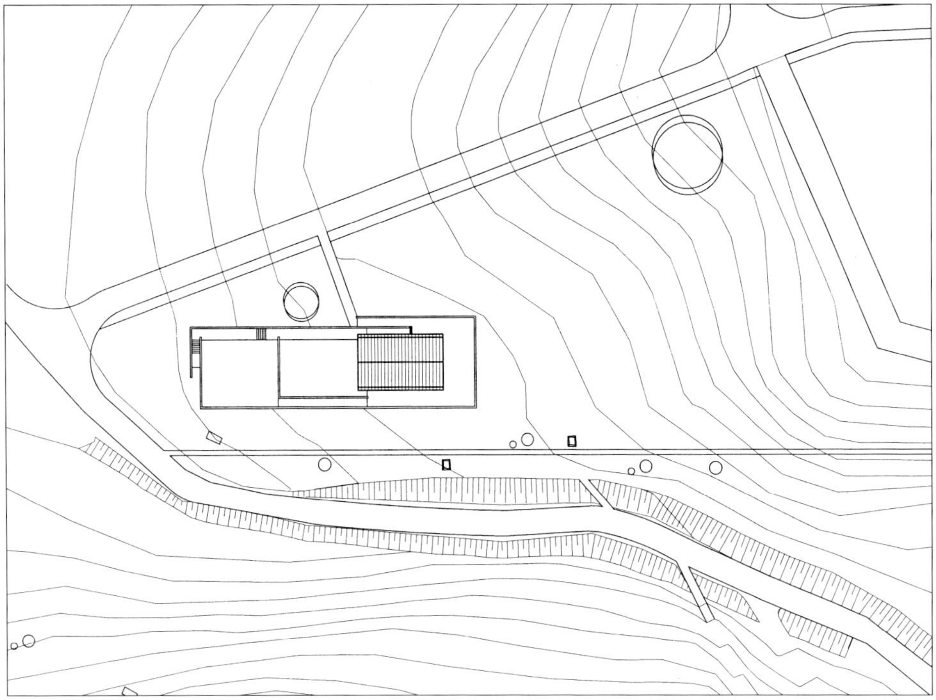

Site plan and plans of the first and ground floors.

Right: Cross-sections and elevations.

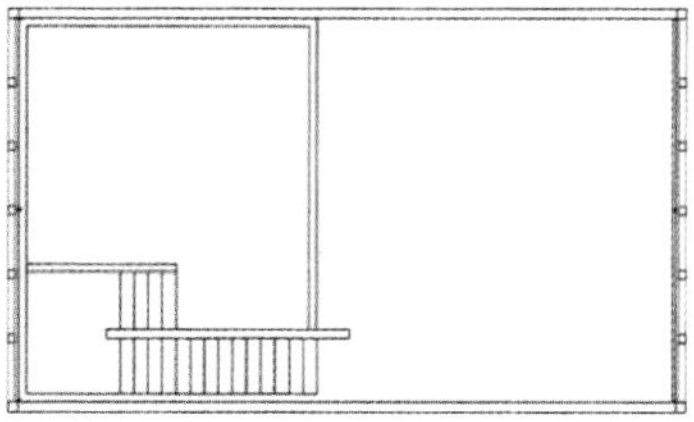

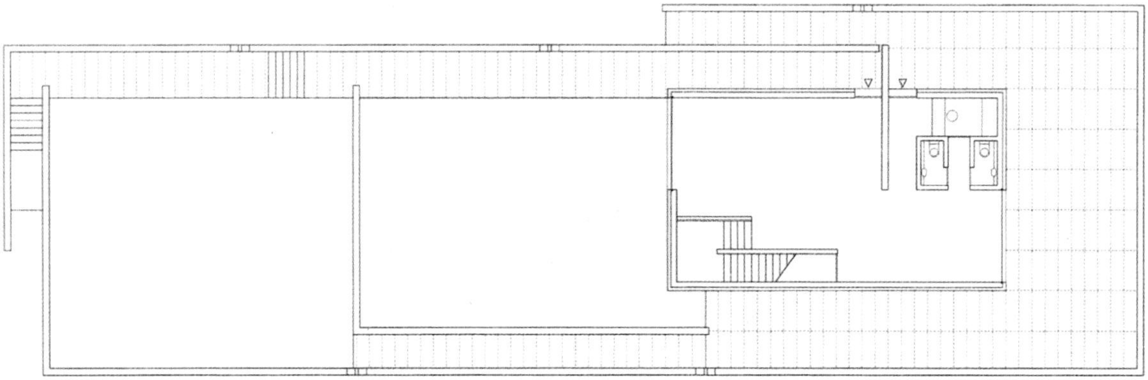

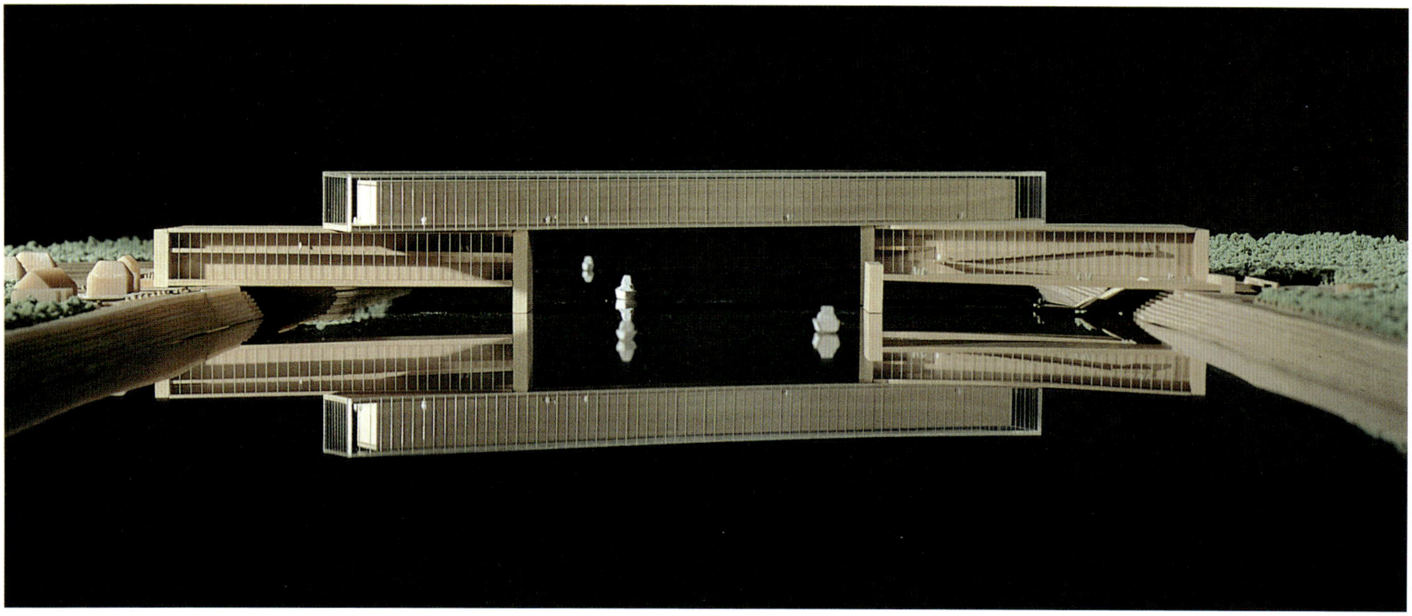

Location Between Karlsruhe, Germany, and Strasbourg, France
Design 1997
Total area 15,739 sq m

This structure, in addition to housing a museum on the history of world cultures and a foundation for the creation of a "new culture", is also meant to represent a symbolic bridge between Germany and France and a monument to world peace.

The project was to mark the end of the 20th century, with its unique mixture of creation and destruction, and enter the new millennium by calling for the formation of a new culture. This culture is one that springs from the gradual removal of barriers separating the people of the world, and accepts the fact that the driving force of human evolution lies in our intercultural encounters.

The new force in humanity will not just result from a recognition of differences and mutual compromise, but derive from a confrontation between these differences and the dialogue that follows. At the same time, the process of building a "new culture" will be an opportunity to assess our current cultures to the full. The negative aspects of war and aggression are also part of our civilization.

To build a Museum of World Culture on the border dividing two nations like France and Germany, involved as they have been in so many bloody wars with each other, is a significant gesture in promoting a new sense of reconciliation in a world still torn apart by conflict.

The two base blocks, which extend along opposite sides of the Rhine, were designed to symbolise the many different cultures that have developed throughout human history. At the beginning of a new era, the objective awareness of disparities and the inherent differences between different cultures can transform this diversity from a source of discord into an inspiration of further development.

These elements, designed as two separate blocks of cement, will offer visitors the opportunity to retrace history and reassess their own societies while understanding and appreciating the cultures of others without prejudice. It will also act as a space to contemplate, meditate and reflect on the genesis of a new "world culture" represented by the museum, which is supported above the two base blocks.

Firmly combining existing cultures, the bridge structure will become a meeting place and a point of contact for dialogue between the cultures of all peoples. Formed by a glass prism and a concrete casing, it will allow for a relatively open view of the building's surroundings, creating a sense of hope and expectation in the future for the visitors.

Because of the way it was designed, the museum will be a stage for all kinds of cultural activities as well as a centre for the synthesis of all the different cultures and a venue to nourish creativity, free expression and optimism in the future.

Views of the model.

Location Butwal, Nepal
Design 1997
Construction 1997–1998
Total area 1073 sq m

This project came into being as a tribute to all those countries in Africa and Asia that had provided aid to Japan in the aftermath of the Kobe earthquake in 1995. A decision was taken to build a paediatric hospital run by the Association of Medical Doctors of Asia, AMDA, with finances donated through a fundraiser that was launched in the media.

The chosen site was Butwal, Nepal, in the Lussi region of Lambini, an area sacred to the Buddha near the border with India. Land for the project was set aside by the city, which also put the necessary infrastructure in place.

Before this building was constructed, there had been only one paediatric hospital in Nepal, in Katmandu, a situation that contributed to the dismal mortality rate for children under five years of age: 20 times higher than that in Japan. For this reason, a top priority for the local population was to build a new hospital.

In the face of very difficult building conditions, the project ultimately became a meaningful example of how successful partnerships can be formed between architecture and communities. The building was modelled on a simple rectangular form, with a design and appearance dictated by the limited building materials available and the project's overall financial and technological constraints.

Locally manufactured red bricks were used for the exterior walls while inside the plastered walls were painted white to create a bright and clean feel. The south elevation of the building is fronted by a colonnade behind which there are windows designed to of course let in light but also shade the interior from the blinding rays of the sun and ensure consistently pleasant and cool temperatures.

The main spaces of the hospital, the children's rooms and the wards all look out over the colonnade with the idea of creating a sense of openness and light that was in tune with the local climate. All construction, from the brick laying to the finish work and including the building of the main concrete structure, was carried out exclusively by human hands.

Since the day it was completed, the hospital has received more than 200 patients a day and the hope is that it can in every possible way become a growing part of the community.

Left: Plan of the ground floor.

View from the south.

Detail of east and west elevations.

Right: Views of interior ramp.

Daylight Museum

Studio sketch and general planimetric drawing.

Right: Front of the building with view of lake and mountains above a drawing of a planned extension – not yet constructed.

Location Gamo, Shiga, Japan
Design 1997
Construction 1997–1998
Site area 178,225 sq m
Building area 210 sq m
Total area 196 sq m

Many years ago, I came across an old photograph that made a profound impression on me. The image was of a painter and his family taken just after World War II.

The artist's studio was a wooden hut that he had built with his own hands. It didn't have electricity, gas or running water. He would paint during the daylight hours and retire to bed just after sunset.

Many years later, when by chance I was given the opportunity to design a museum to commemorate the work of this artist, I took inspiration from the fact that he had typically painted in natural light. In a departure from my tendency to design museums that are lit totally by artificial light, in this case I felt that a space based solely on natural light would be more appropriate as a platform for paintings that were essentially a reflection of the life of this artist.

This way, visitors would be able to appreciate the paintings in lighting conditions similar to those in which they were produced. They would thus be able to share the creative world of the artist.

The one-storey structure is made of reinforced concrete exposed on both the outside and on the inside. Natural lighting enters the gallery space through a skylight while the circulation area on the west side of the building receives light through a curtain wall in frosted glass.

The interior of the museum is completely devoid of artificial light. As a result, the quality and quantity of light entering the gallery area changes with the time of day and the seasons, thereby altering the perception of the works of art and of the space that displays them. Needless to say, the museum closes at sunset.

Tadao Ando

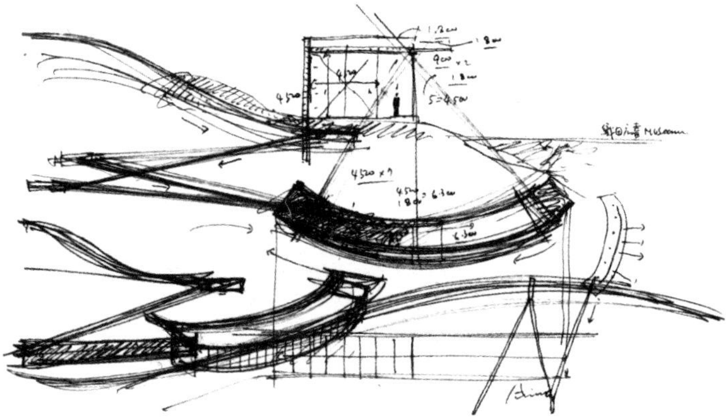

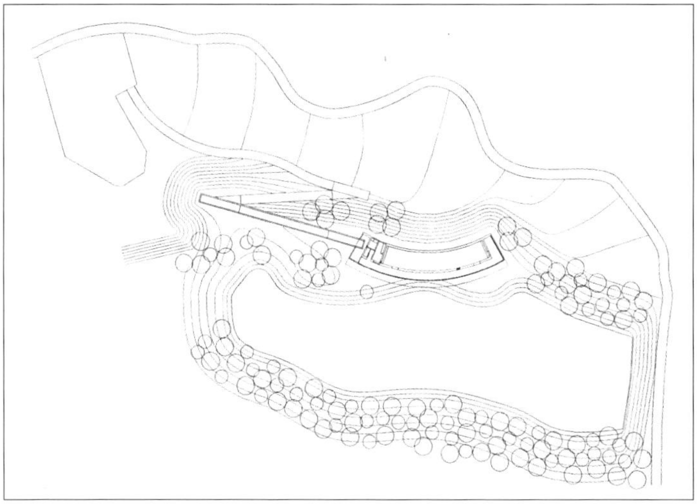

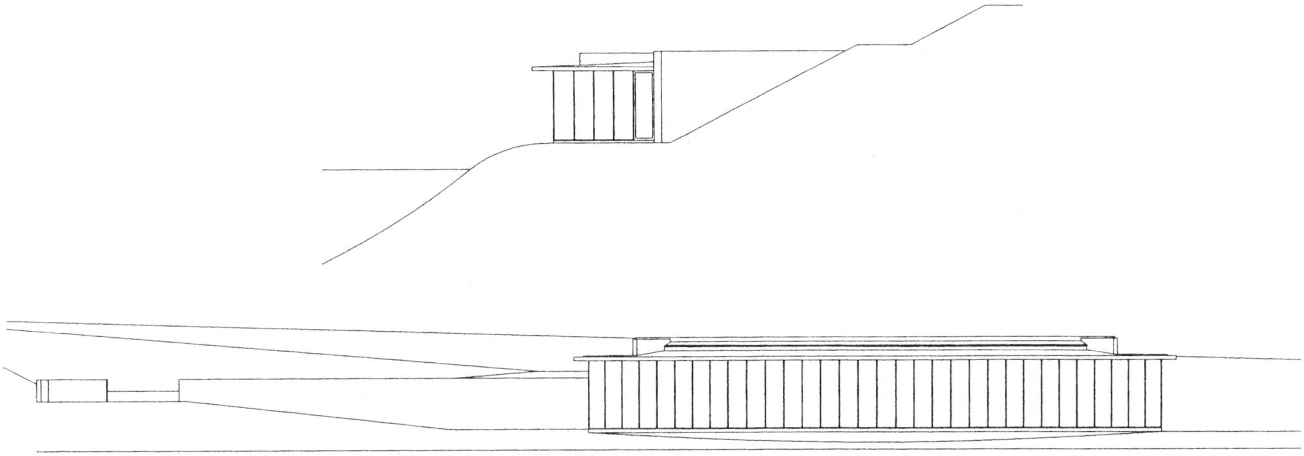

The main hall.

Right: The exterior walls that separate the school from the church, and the entrance to the main hall.

systems including frequent and abundant snowfall, which helps explain the choices that were made here.

In addition, the new library is located on land formerly occupied by a park and a school. It is right in the centre of the city and bordered on the north side by trees. Their presence was respected and provided a starting point for the design of the building, which moved Ando to go with a tried and tested approach wherein the dynamic conditions were matched with appropriate structural and spatial solutions and materials. In this case it was reinforced concrete, a superb choice that has become the signature of his architectural style.

Jean-Marie Martin

Studio sketch and view of the main entrance.

Exterior views of the main cylindrical volume from the northeast and northwest and a studio sketch.

Opposite page: Interior view of the children's reading room.

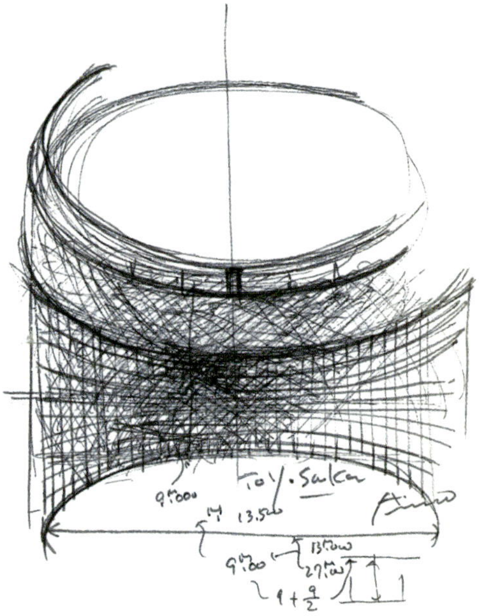

2
1

Main reading area.

Right: Detail of the understair shelving and a view of the main reading area from the hall.

Left: Rampway linking the underground parking area to the open-air exhibition space.

Atrium and a stairway from one of the galleries.

Modern Art Museum of Fort Worth

Location Fort Worth, Texas, USA
Design 1997–1999
Construction 1999–2002
Site area 45,570 sq m
Building area 9,240 sq m
Total area 14,280 sq m

The place destined for the new Museum of Modern Art in Fort Worth has been called "the tree of art", indicating the spiritual reverence with which this site was to be approached.

The museum consists of five rectangular volumes of reinforced concrete arranged parallel to one each other. The orientation of the structures acknowledges the architecture of the Kimbell Museum just opposite, a building designed by Louis I. Kahn and a direct point of reference for Ando.

High walls of glass surround the concrete casing that forms the gallery containing the works of art. The austere linear character of the design is offset by its natural setting and the fact that it is partially surrounded by a large expanse of water. To the east, the project has a dense line of trees between the museum and the road to the Cultural District of Fort Worth. In addition to protecting the environment of the museum, the area also incorporates "silent spaces" that feature outdoor works of art that double as pieces for ceremonies or special exhibitions.

Inside the parallel structures, the circulation areas feature a succession of high-ceiling spaces that function as viewing platforms. Concrete and glass are the primary materials used and they reinforce the themes

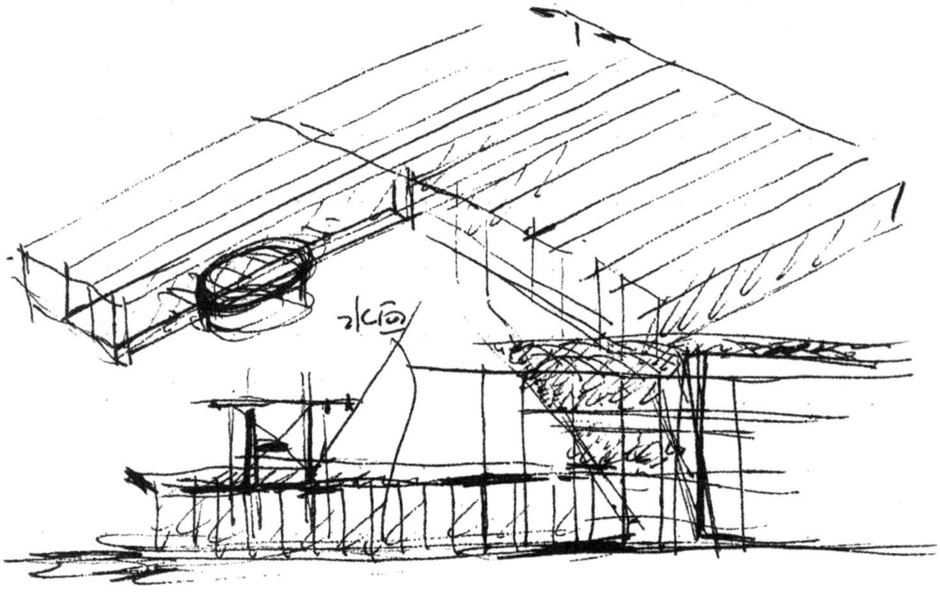

of reciprocity and ambivalence that are so prevalent in the design of the project. A dynamic is created between the two materials, with the qualities of large expanses of glass working to soften the impact that the concrete volumes make on the surrounding environment.

Form is forced to follow function here, with concrete given the task of protecting the works of art from the elements outside and to secure the structural safety of the whole museum. But the extensive use of glass around the galleries establishes a link between the works of art and the surroundings outside.

Despite the fact that the museum is based on a pretty simple plan, it houses a wide variety of exhibition spaces inside, not only in terms of their size but also with regard to the types of natural lighting they feature. The exhibition rooms are in fact divided into rooms lit from above by angled skylights, and rooms that receive light through 40-foot-high glass walls that create very tangible transition zones between the interior and the outside. Beyond serving as spaces that are able to combine the elements of light, water and verdant nature, they are also integral parts of the main exhibition areas.

View of the entrance from the south.

Right: West, east, south and north elevations and cross sections.

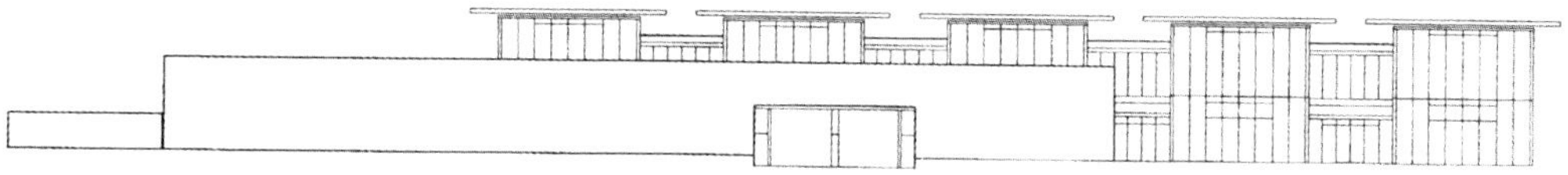

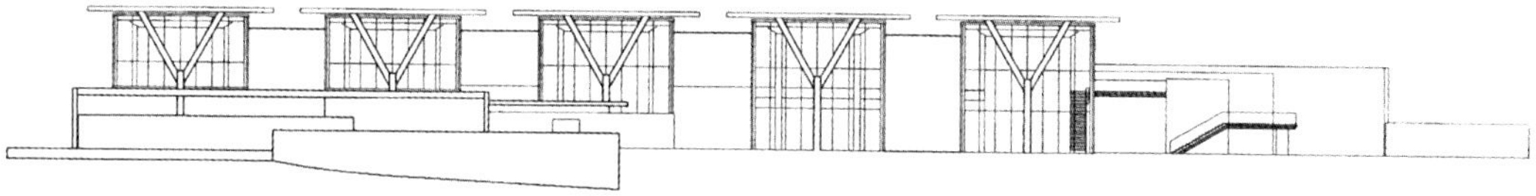

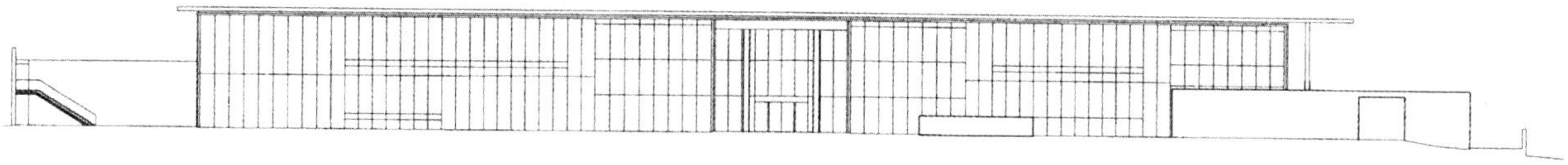

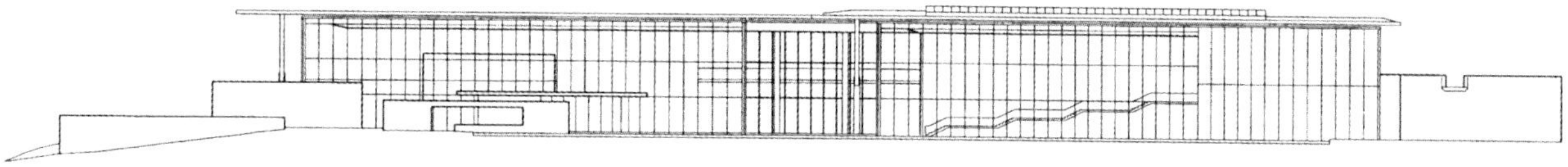

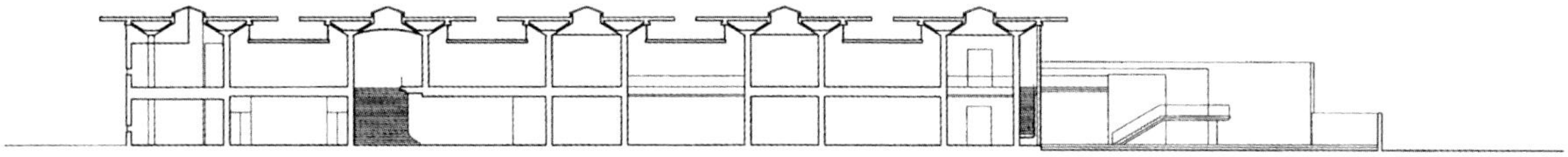

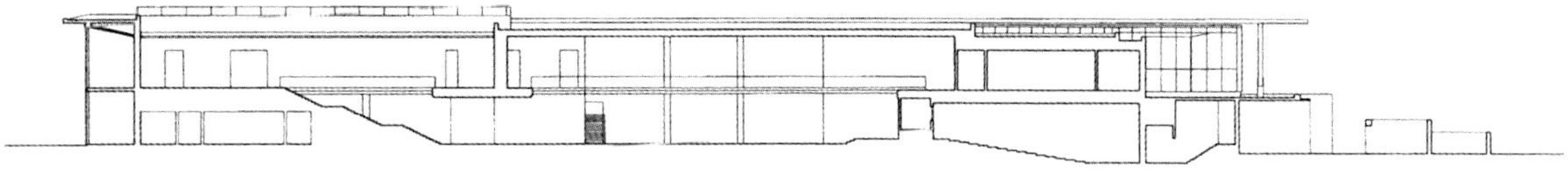

Left: Interior views of the main entrance and of two galleries for permanent collections on the first and ground floors.

Studio sketch.

The main staircase and two spaces for temporary installations.

Left: Views of the entrance and atrium.

The installation "Backside of the Moon" staged by James Turrell, inside the pavilion.

Komyo-ji Temple

Location Saijo, Ehime, Japan
Design 1998–1999
Construction 1999–2000
Site area 3,222 sq m
Building area 1,224 sq m
Total area 1,284 sq m

This project dealt with the reconstruction of a temple of the Pure Land Buddhist sect. Situated on the eastern side of the city of Saijo, in Ehime Prefecture, the site dates back to the Edo period.

A small city favoured by an extraordinarily mild climate, Saijo is well known as a place from which to approach Mount Ishizuchi. The zone is rich in natural springs and the city is crossed by a network of canals carrying mountain streams.

The main temple, built over 250 years ago, was no longer sound and needed major repairs and reconstruction. An adjacent plot was also to be built up for guests and rooms for the monks. The abbot of the temple did not stipulate conditions with regard to the new structure. He simply explained his ideas in general terms, expressing a desire to construct "a temple in which people can meet, that is open to the community".

We conceived the new temple as a wooden building, cloaked in delicate light and appearing to float on an expanse of water fed by a spring. Such a design emphasises the importance of water as a feature of the landscape and, above all, the choice of wood as a material of construction.

Our primary aim was to explore all of the possibilities that wood offered. We were not constrained by the existing architectural style of the temple, but we wanted to incorporate building styles from over the centuries.

As I saw it, traditional Japanese wooden architecture was essentially one of assembly. Building involved cutting all the pieces of wood and, bit by bit, the construction took form as the various parts came together. Such a technique had been perfected to achieve works of power and beauty such as the Nandaimon temple Todai-ji and the Jodo-ji Temple by Chogen, a medieval monk. I wanted to create a space that represented a return to the origins of wooden architecture, a unique structure composed of diverse parts, each one rich in tension.

Studio sketch and the new temple in its urban setting.

View and detail of the south elevation.

Right: Plans of the first and ground floors.

After considering a number of alternatives, the main building was planned as a large space covered by three layers of cross beams supported by 16 columns and divided into four groups. The main area was enclosed by a frosted glass screen next to a corridor that was in turn surrounded by an external wall of softwood joists.

The corridor is formed by poles of 15 by 21 centimetres set at regular intervals of 15 centimetres, with inserts of glass between them that create an indeterminate line of separation between the inside and the outside. Natural light filters through into the main area, the floor of which is covered by a hundred straw mats to create an open, luminous space with an air of solemnity.

From the outside it is possible to perceive vaguely what takes place inside. At night the main building, with light coming from its interior, creates a mystical reflection on the surface of the water. Excluding the fact that the roof turns up at the corners, the work does not have much in common with traditional Japanese wooden architecture. It consists entirely of laminated wood, a choice that came from our research into a structural method that, to keep in step with the spirit of traditional "assembly", resulted in a simple, logical style that also reflected contemporary building technology.

Laminated wood is an extremely versatile material from which a high degree of uniformity can be obtained with very little waste. Since the material consists of layers made up of

much smaller parts this seemed particularly appropriate.

We looked for ways to leave the walls of stone intact and to keep the existing trees on the site, but although permission was obtained to demolish the entrance and the belltower, we decided to leave them in their original position. It was a choice intended to retain the original geometric form of the approach to the entrance.

In the end, it was decided to abandon the pure symmetry and to create a walkway that wound around the pavilion. In the final version, we accepted that unforeseen elements should be integrated into the perfection of the context. They gave depth to the architectural space and performed an important function.

Rather than following a uniform logic from the beginning to the end, thanks to this project I had the opportunity to acquire something intangible and mystical. I was able to return a memory to the place and enter into a dialogue with the site while defining the architecture. Building Komyo-ji Temple allowed me to rediscover and gain a new awareness of the origins of my architectural methods.

Tadao Ando

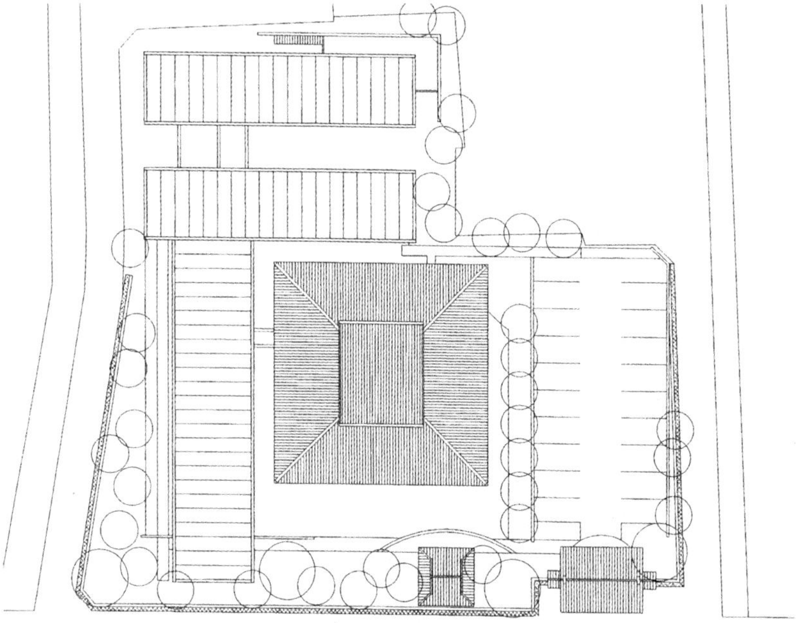

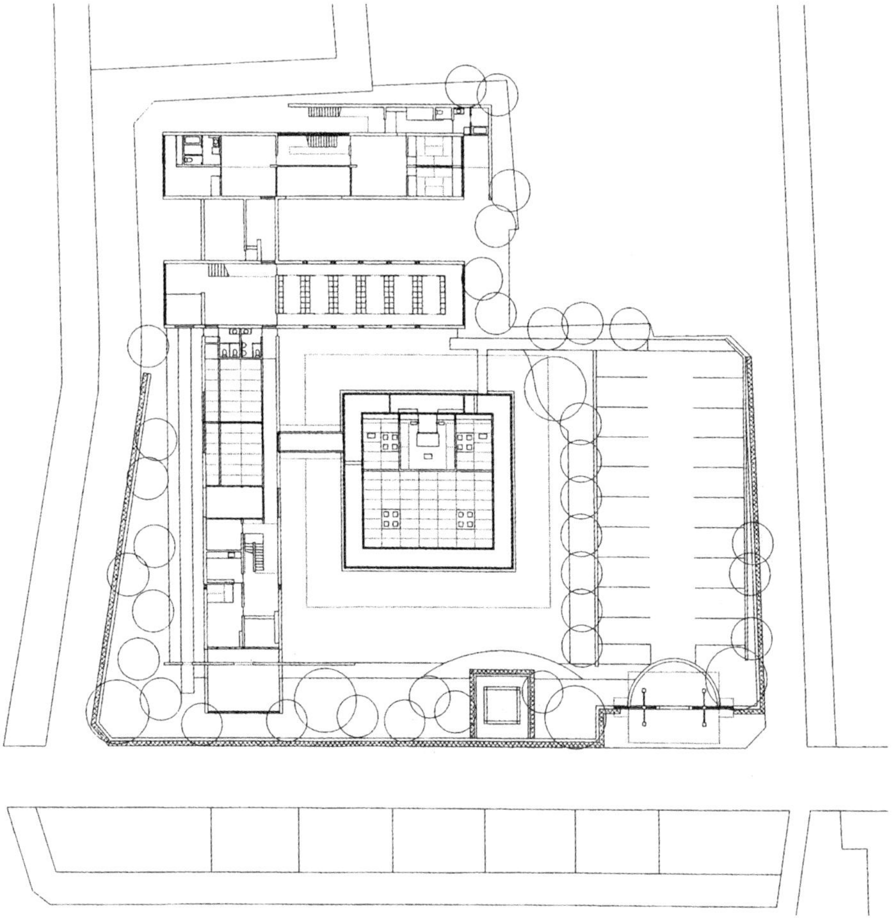

Studio sketch and a foreshortened view of the south elevation with the existing pavilions on the right.

Opposite page: South elevation, cross-section and views of the circulation area and hall.

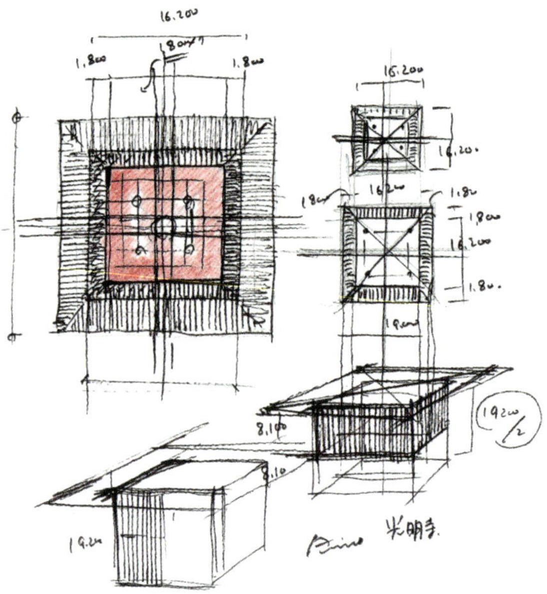

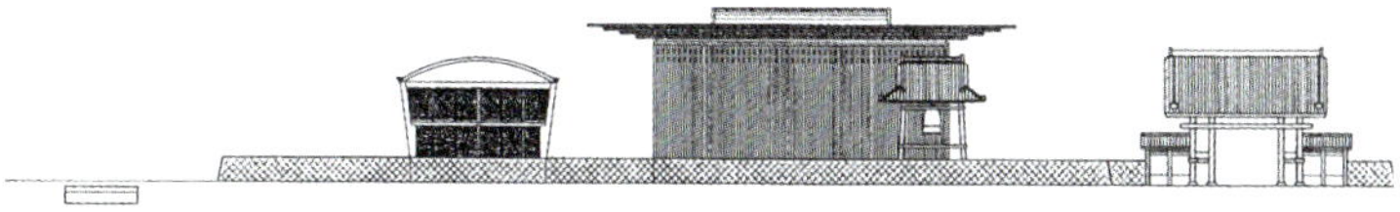
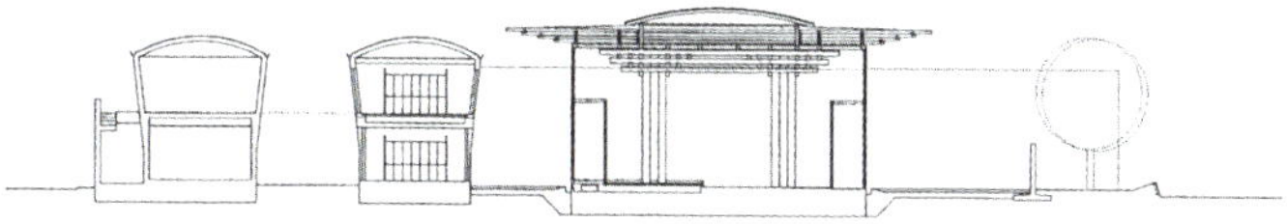

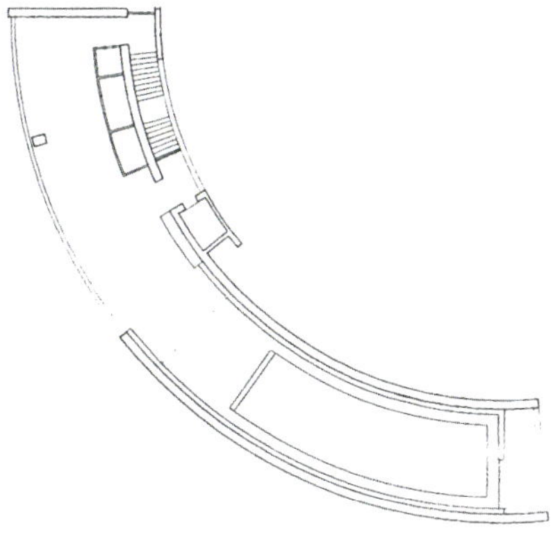

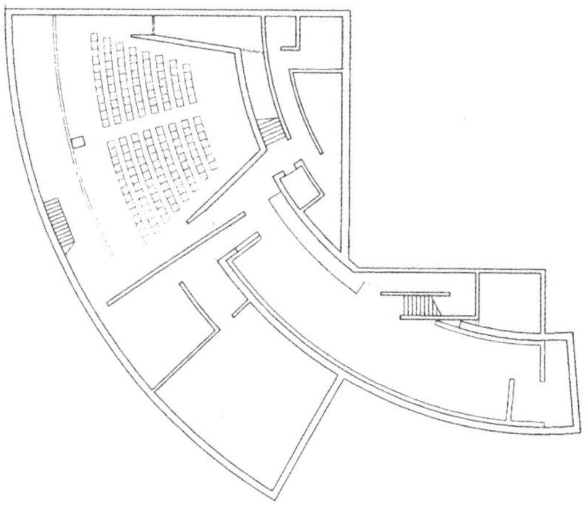

Studio sketch and a view of the space that houses the collection.

Location London, England
Design 2000

The subject of this project, presented at an international competition held in 2000, was a new baptismal font to be erected in St Paul's Cathedral. The cathedral is situated opposite the Tate Gallery on the Thames.

A year earlier we had presented our proposal for a new art gallery on the site as part of an international competition. Our design had been very much based on the contrast between the old and the new, employing materials such as glass.

In the proposal for the baptismal font we were aiming for a well constructed design with "movement" based on a limited number of simple geometric forms, essentially squares and circles. Thin squares of glass one metre wide and five millimetres thick with circular holes at the centre were mounted together in an ascending rotated progression to suggest a spiral appearance. At the top was a basin for consecrated water.

In this way, the intended effect to bring out the aesthetic properties of glass would be achieved, and the winding of the material into a helix form would give rise to an ethereal architecture of glass and water.

Tadao Ando

Left: A computer-generated simulation of the new font in the cathedral nave.

Close-up view of digital image.

Fukuoka Camera Museum

Location Nishitonami, Japan
Design 1999
Construction 1999–2000
Site area 2,708 sq m
Building area 791 sq m
Total area 1,035 sq m

Fukuoka-machi is a small provincial town with just 13,000 inhabitants located in the very northwest of Toyama Prefecture. It is home to the famous Tateyama mountain range and the climate is typical of the coastal region on the Sea of Japan: very high precipitation and snow levels of over a metre during winter.

These particular features of the climate led Tadao Ando to adopt a distinctive roofing solution for this project, which was completed in 2000. The profile of the building is "folded", becoming gradually smaller towards the top, as shown in these pages. Set within a primeval woodland, it houses an historic collection of over 3,000 cameras and photographic equipment donated by a local collector.

The structure consists of two volumes, arranged on an east-west axis. One forms an exhibition pavilion with an area of roughly 61 by 6 metres where the curved roof rises nearly ten metres from the ground. The second contains a room almost 22 by 11 metres and runs parallel to the south elevation of the former show pavilion. The roof is configured like an inverted L, with the two volumes linked by two wedge-shaped walls.

In relation to the main axis, the walls are inclined at an angle of 30 degrees and 60 degrees, respectively. The internal circulation area is made up of a series of stairways and ramps along these walls. A lively series of spaces leads from them into a characteristic form that Ando has worked on in recent years, and the "movement" of the ramps gives drama and depth to the surroundings.

In working on a museum designed to contain an unusual collection, Ando paid particular attention to the layout of the exhibition areas, and great care was also given to the design of the showcases and how the contents are displayed. This gave

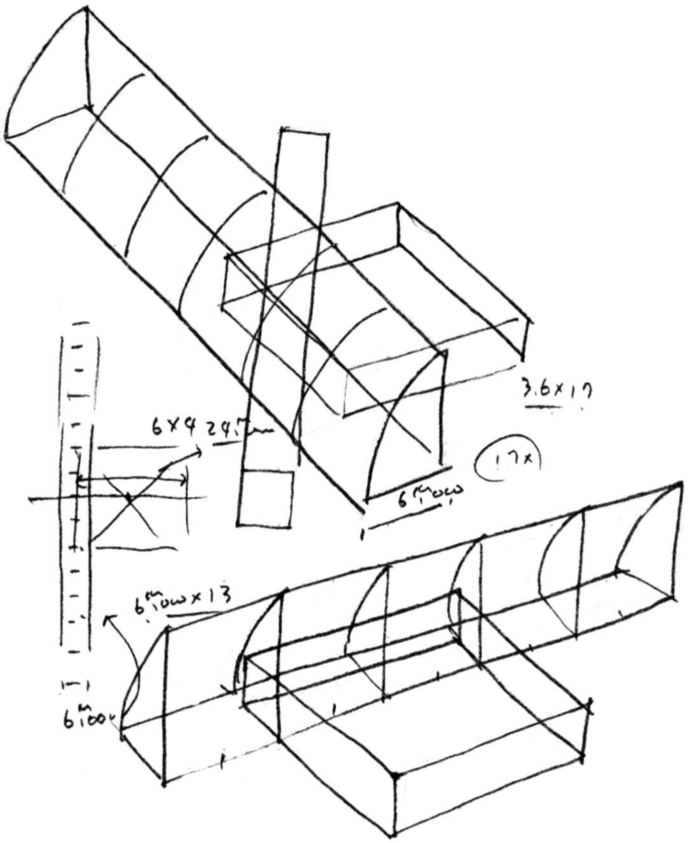

Studio sketch, vertical section and foreshortened view of the entrance way.

life to an elegant and restrained staging. Wide expanses of the internal walls (made of exposed concrete and with a treatment that is typical of Ando's style) were created to hold large photographic reproductions.

As typical products of modern technology, Ando has made visual references to the equipment on display by using materials and products used in their manufacture. An example of this is the metallic treatment of the bowed roof, a style that is difficult to locate in his past works.

Functionality also played an important part in the layout of the spaces, forcing the architect to plan flexible surroundings that would meet the requirements of the various events, conventions and seminars held at the complex and leave separate areas dedicated exclusively to the permanent collection.

Jean-Marie Martin

Glass volume seen from ramp in south facing hall and detail of front section of building, facing south.

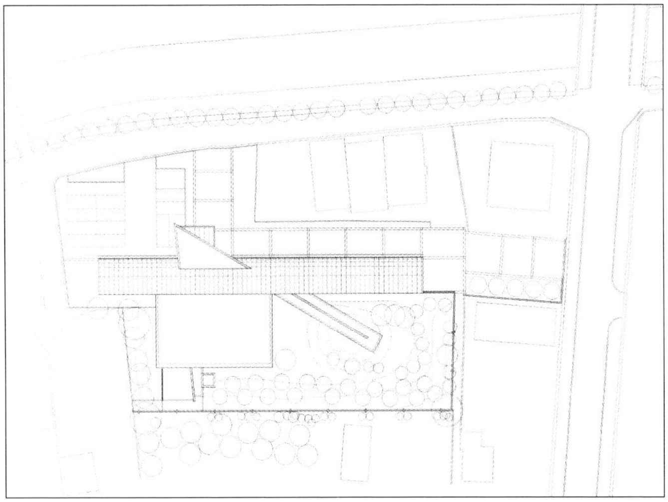

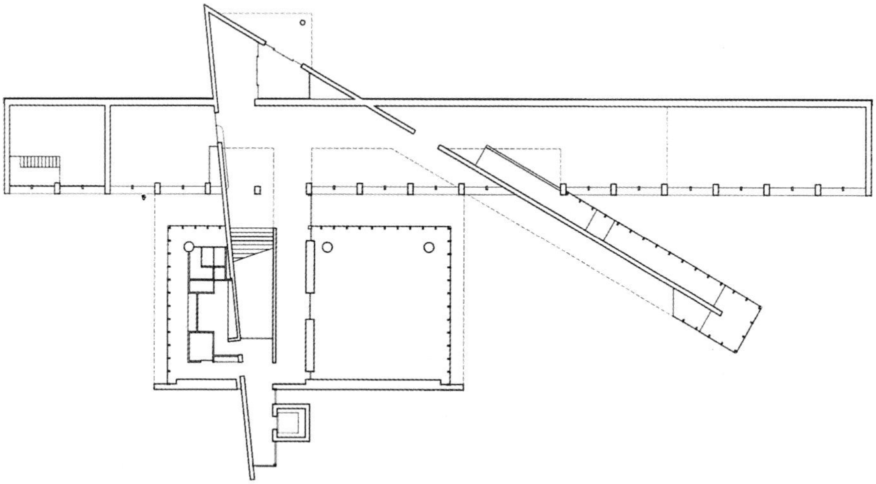

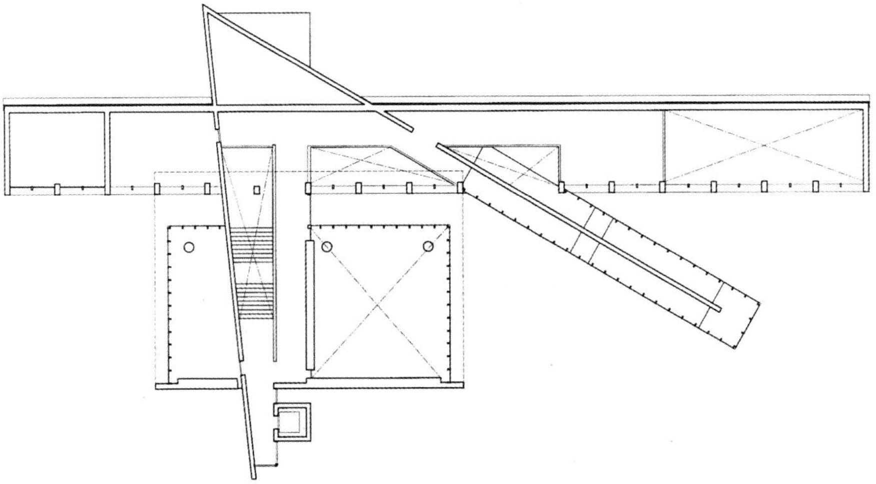

Left: General planimetric drawing and plans of first and ground floors.

East elevation, cross-section, shot of main exhibition gallery and a reverse shot.

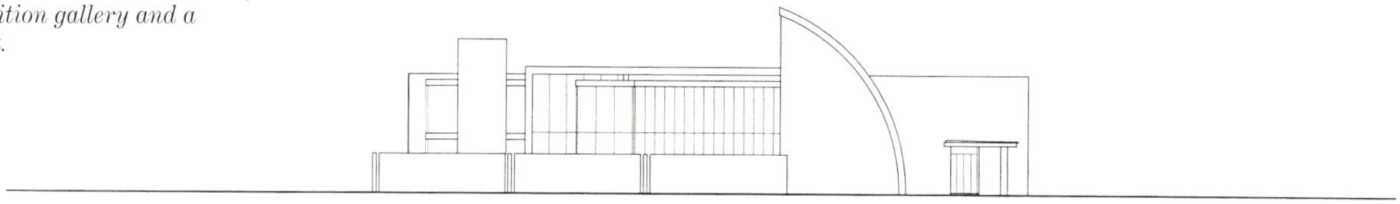

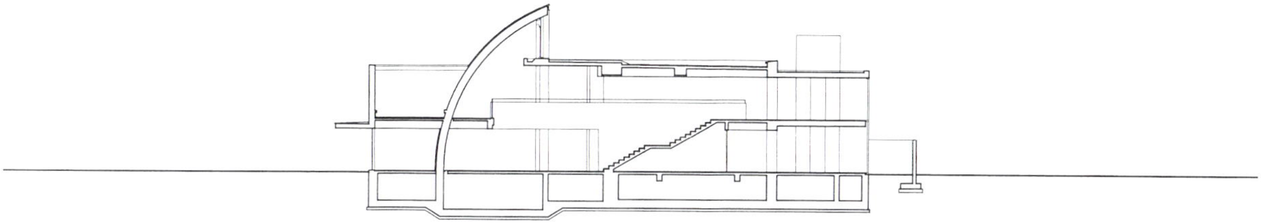

View of model from above.

Right: General planimetric drawing.

Location Manchester, England
Design 1999–2000
Construction 2000–2002
Site area 80,000 sq m
Total area 500 sq m

The area around Piccadilly Gardens in the heart of Manchester is rather gloomy and uninviting. This urban green space features a number of historical monuments it and had once been an important gathering place for the people of Manchester.

The aim of the redesign was to inject new life back into the site, which had long been neglected and underused. The project provided for an oval plaza with a fountain (the Water Plaza), a multifunctional barycentric grass area (the Central Lawn), an information pavilion for the city with a curvilinear profile (the Garden Pavilion) and a new tree-planting scheme. In the middle of the gardens was a statue of Queen Victoria, one of many monuments to be kept.

In order to safeguard the open spaces, minimal development and a simple design were sought. The entire grass area was enclosed by a wall that could be used as a framework for other structures. As a 24-hour park, top priority was placed on the comfort, functionality, accessibility, security, and adaptability of all the architectural elements.

Construction of the project, elaborated in partnership with Ove Arup & Partners and EDAW, was completed during the spring of 2002.

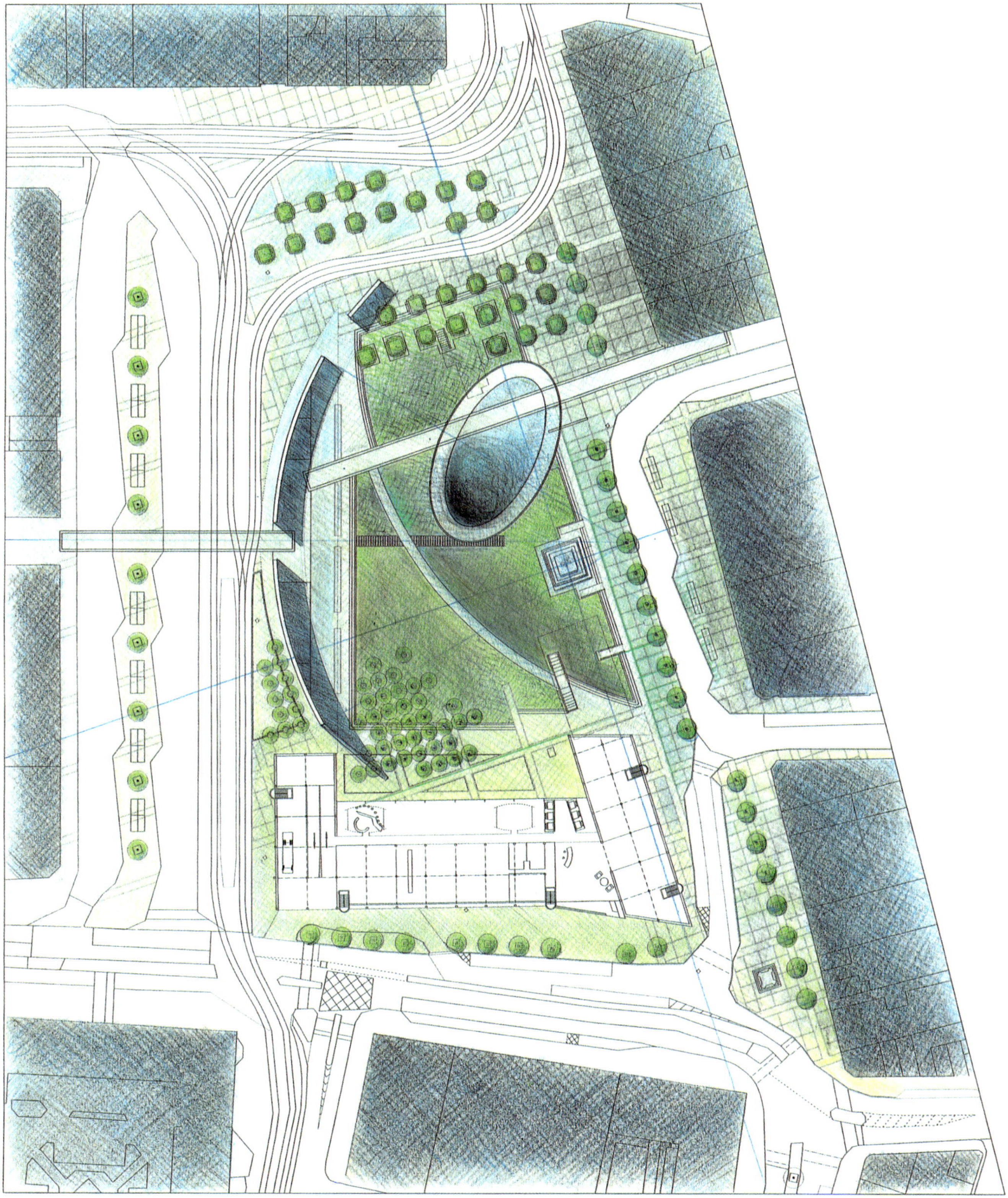

Aerial view and the fountain with water feature and footbridge looking towards Oldham Street.

Invisible House

Location Treviso, Italy
Design 1999–2001
Construction 2002–2004
Site area 30,600 sq m
Total area 1,350 sq m (main residence); 100 sq m (lodge house)

This project was for a secluded dwelling set in the beautiful countryside near Treviso. An exceptional degree of freedom and flexibility was granted to the architect, who was able to express his ideas without the typical constraints that often apply to rural architecture and its design.

The only condition imposed by the client was the absolute guarantee of privacy, so the design needed to take into account the position of the building vis-à-vis adjacent roads and the boundaries of the site. With this more than reasonable request in mind, the idea of a house in harmony with nature and its surroundings became the focal point.

A proposal arose for an "Invisible House", a semi-subterranean complex on a 30,600-square-metre site. The problem posed by an "invisible" building constructed underground exists not in the surface forms, but rather in the spatial relationships. The aim of the project was to achieve a labyrinthine underground area full of surprising spatial experiences, all within this "invisible" structure.

The plan was a simple rectangular one based on a 7.2-metre repeat. Within this rigid geometric pattern was a series of extremely varied spaces created through architectural interventions specifically designed to maximize the amount of natural light: the use of skylights, internal courts in different styles that inverted the usual interior/exterior dialogue, and changes in the floor levels. To incorporate the ever-changing play of natural light as a design element, an austere yet detailed geometric style was introduced to the composition at the expense of forms lacking in rigour.

The presence of this "invisible house" is revealed to the outside world only through the continuum of a volume emerging from the ground that contains the studio and integrates the entrance and the upper terrace. Rows of trees common to that area were then planted along the perimeter of that structure. It is envisaged that when the trees mature, the site will give the impression of a natural fortification.

Left: Aerial view of the complex.

General planimetric drawing and the southeast front of the exhibition hall configured as an amphitheatre.

Location Aomori, Japan
Design 2000
Construction 2000–2001
Site area 262,500 sq m
Building area 4,278 sq m
Total area 4,015 sq m

The decision to build a centre for contemporary art in Aomori was not an obvious one. The city is noted for the highest snowfall recorded in any urban area in the world – it is said.

In addition, a number of such centres providing opportunities, support and exhibition locations for "artists in residence" in different phases of their careers already exist in Japan. And typically these complexes occupy more pleasant sites in scenic locations.

The Aomori Centre was conceived by Tadao Ando in 1999 and completed just two years later. The structures that made up the centre were built on separate small plots deep within an area of dense woodland not far from the town centre.

The layout of the planned buildings, which are set apart from one another within the trees, provided for three main spaces: one for exhibitions, the Creative Hall that would allow performers to develop acts, and the Residential Hall.

Ando's design included two parallelepipedons with converging axes of different dimensions and one volume with a circular plan hollowed out for an open-air amphitheatre. In addition to these three areas was another curious construction: a pergola intended to shelter the walkway around the park which, in section, takes the form of a depressed arch.

Particular attention in this construction was given to an unusual solution for a recurring problem. In this site-specific project, Ando's objective was to immerse the volumes in nature. In the design he availed himself of pure geometric forms, or non-representational figures devoid of artifice, whose characteristics stood out against the natural surroundings.

The advantages in renouncing imitation are demonstrated by Ando here. This experiment that he has completed provides an opportunity for the planners to rethink the relationship between architecture and nature, to free themselves from the practices that so often limit them, and to return to the simple forms that are the basis of the co-existence of the natural and the artificial.

Jean-Marie Martin

Left: The amphitheatre looking towards the valley and the gallery space with Sasaki Hiroko's "Space of Blue 1967–2002" exhibition.

Cross-sections, plans and northeast and southeast elevations of the exhibition hall.

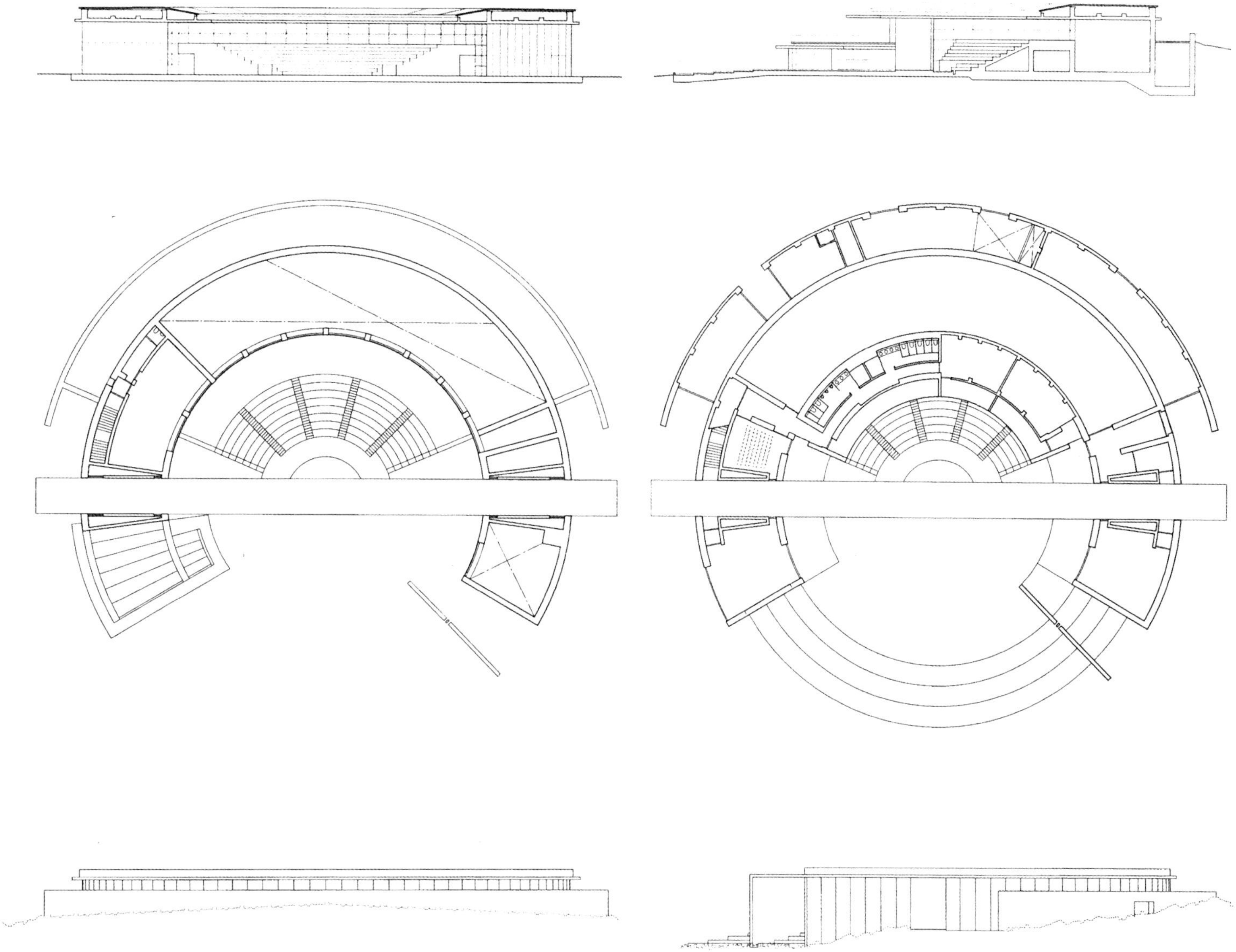

Views of the Creative Hall and guest rooms overlooking the valley.

Right: Plan, sections and elevations of the Creative Hall.

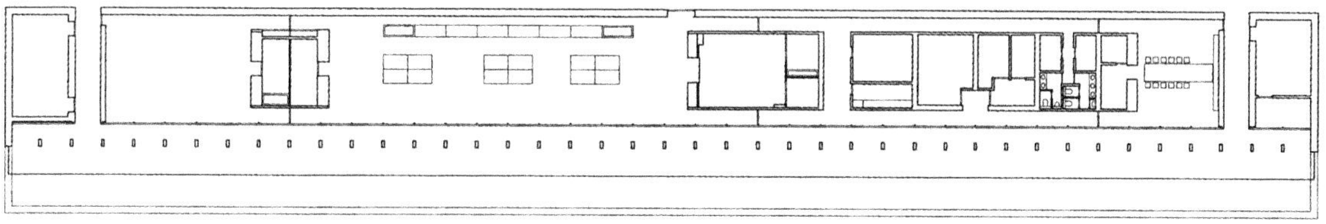

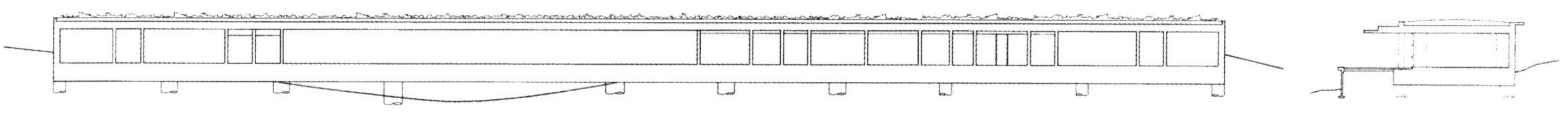

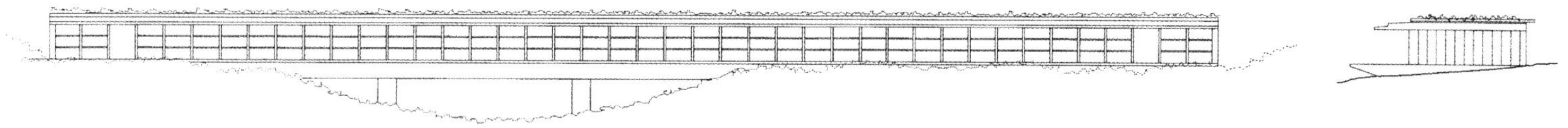

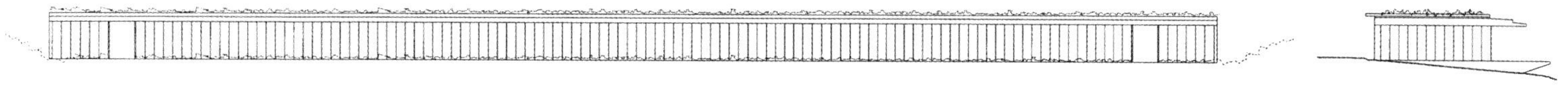

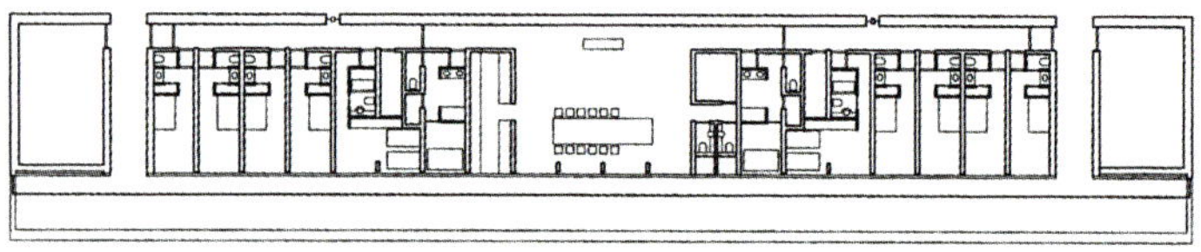

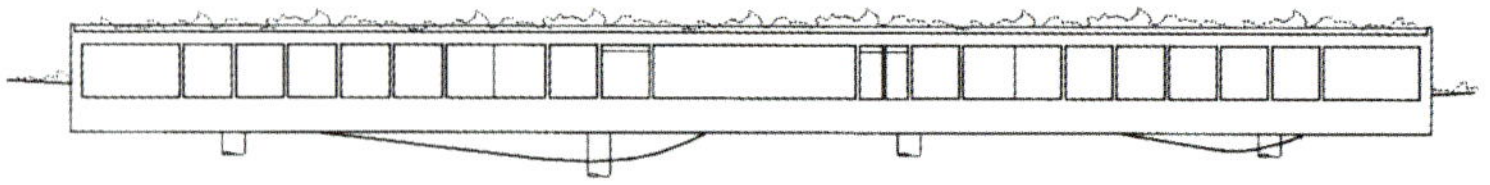

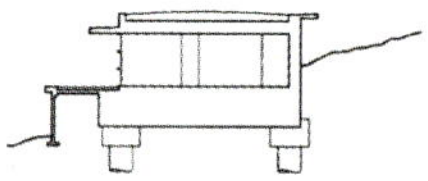

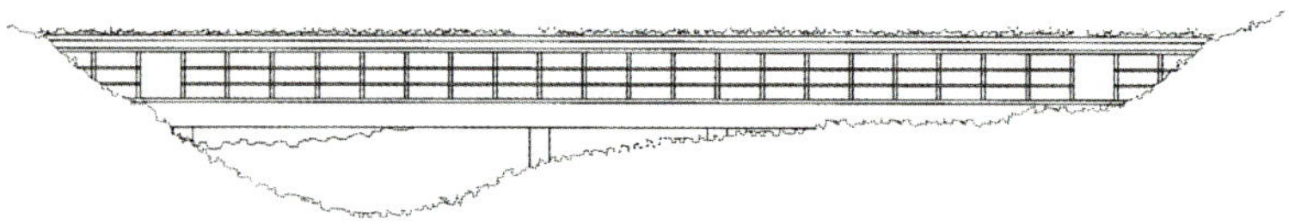

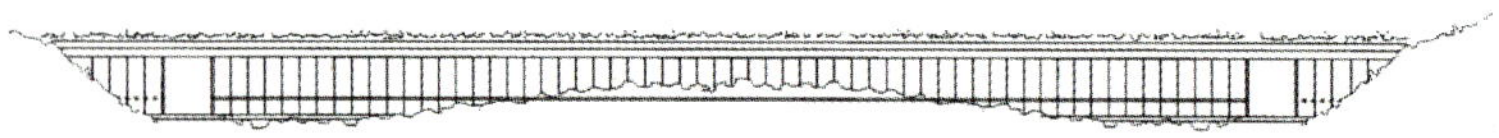

Left: Design for studio and plan, sections and elevations of the Residence Hall.

Views of the pergola protecting the walkway that runs along the edge of the park.

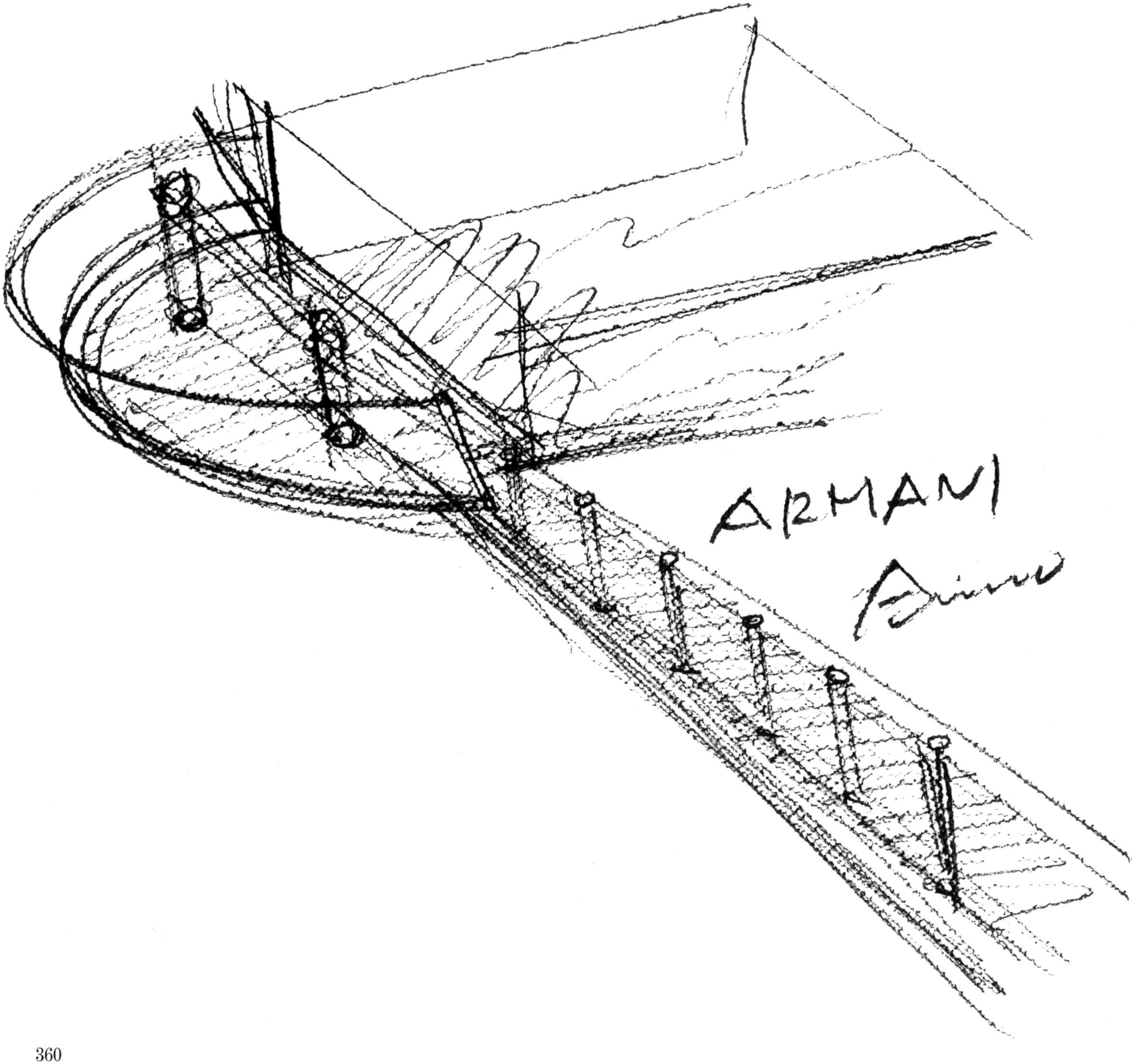
ARMANI

Studio sketch and view of the entrance.

Location Milan, Italy
Design 2000
Construction 2000–2001
Site area 9,700 sq m
Building area 3,400 sq m
Total area 12,300 sq m

In early 1998, I received a personal telephone call from Giorgio Armani, who proceeded to explain that he wanted to renovate an old building on the outskirts of Milan and transform it into a theatre for an audience of 1,000. He asked me if I would be available to work with him on the project.

A week later I was in Italy with the designer visiting the site. The building in question was a disused factory in a poor state of repair that dated back to the mid-19th century. The project called for the conversion of the space into a theatre, but at the same time sought to conserve significant parts of the building's fabric.

Although I didn't personally believe it was worth the effort to preserve the existing structure, I accepted the task because I was won over by the humanity of Armani himself and his wish to realise an "architecture that stands the test of time". Treating it as a showcase project direct from the world of fashion, the main theme was to create a "flexible" and versatile space in which it would be possible to mix art, music and other forms of spectacle and communication.

Italy is a country that is extraordinarily active in preserving its heritage through the restoration of its historic buildings, but rare are the cases that call for a "refunctioning"

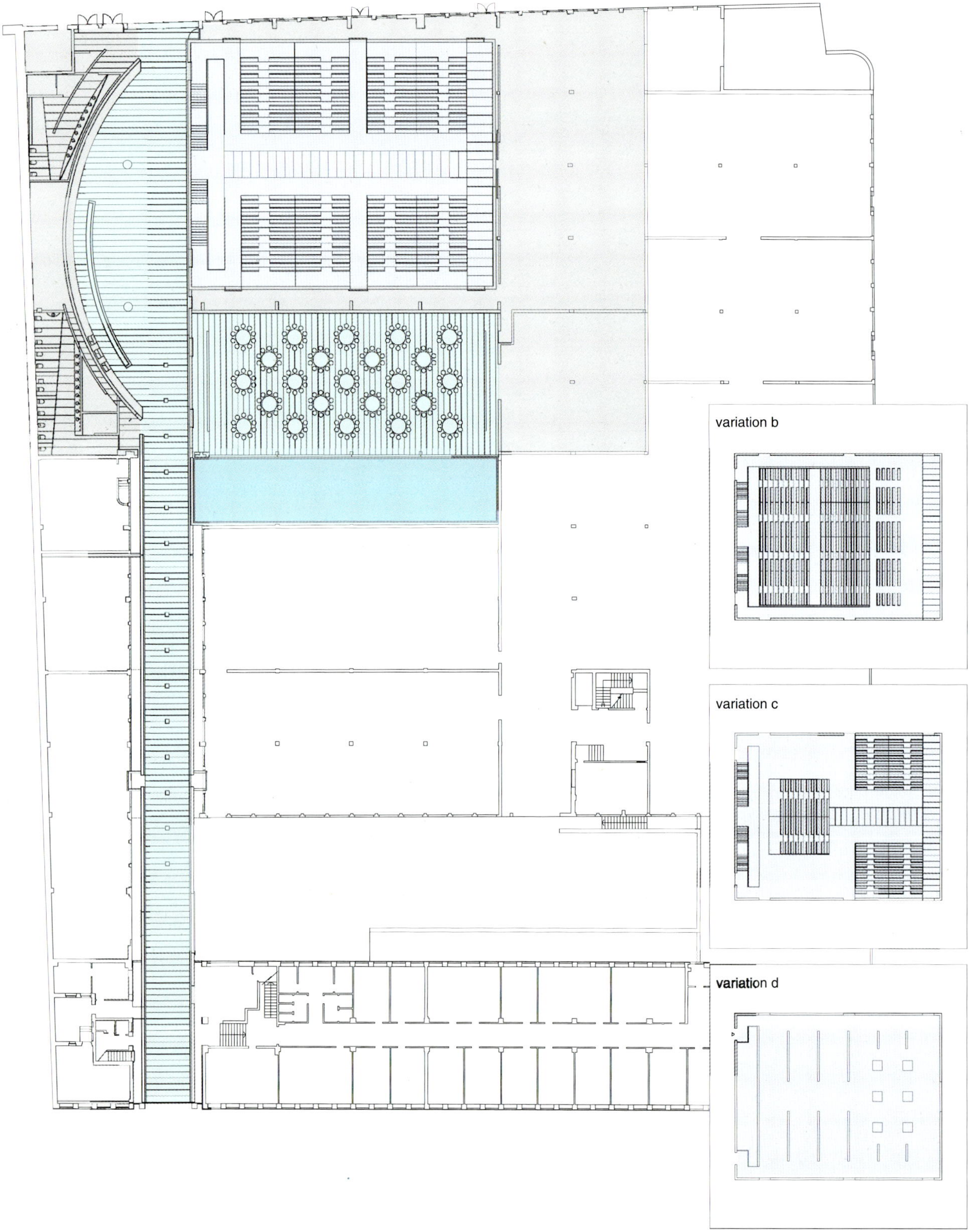
variation b
variation c
variation d

Left: Plan with the different designs for the theatre staging.

Perspective section and views of the entrance gallery and foyer.

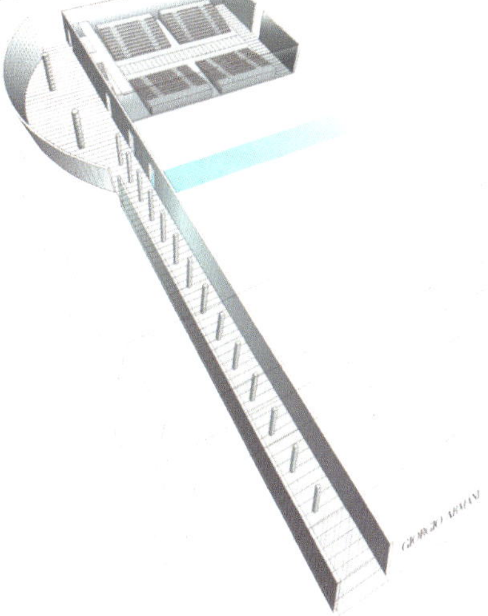

Interior of the theatre and the exhibition space.

of existing buildings by grafting on a new structure. In this way, a project conceived to transform an industrial building into a cultural one could be considered an atypical experiment that contradicts the more typical approach to urban regeneration in Italy.

With that in mind, the solution assumed that the old factory was to be seen as a place in which to introduce new and independent spaces. I would be able to use a methodology that I have already applied in a number of interventions of amplification and restructuring.

The new space now consists of a sequence of elements including a colonnaded entrance concluded by a curved wall, beyond which is the foyer, an exhibition space and a theatre auditorium for 1,000 spectators. The nucleus of the theatre is completely enclosed and separated from the original external casing. Articulating this peripheral space like this in relationship to the show area provided infinite opportunities to redefine and vary the connection between the public and the stage. It's also worth making the point that this is the space where the actual theatrical action takes place.

Tadao Ando

Kinjo Junior High School, Kaga

Location Kaga, Ishikawa, Japan
Design 2000–2001
Construction 2001–2002
Site area 51,102 sq m
Building area 5,615 sq m
Total area 7,515 sq m

Built on the outskirts of Kaga to replace a school that had long been closed, this complex has 17 normal classrooms, nine specialist classrooms as well as a refectory.

Spaces that could also be used for community activities and the public are arranged within a parallelepiped on one floor, over which the body of the main building is partially superimposed. This volume rises over two floors from an oval base whose profile has a very broad diameter on its major axis, but the length of which is defined by the fact that the ellipsis is inscribed in a square grid.

The resulting three-dimensional figure has been used on different occasions by Tadao Ando, who in this case adopted it in order to organise the layout of the school in a vast communal space on an oval plan. The classrooms are arranged on two floors around this space at full height. On the second level, a continuous gallery is supported on free standing columns, set well apart from the uninterrupted interior walls, below which on the ground floor are the entrances to the classrooms.

Corresponding to the shorter diameter of the ellipsis outlining the construction on the ground, suspended bridges formed by a lowered T-shaped girder that follows the curving gallery provide a means of a passage between the classrooms situated along the long curves of the oval. In the main space, which has an open two-storey ceiling, are double-width linked staircases while the major axis of the oval features a long skylight with a screen that lets diffused light into the communal area.

For the classrooms, natural lighting is provided by large windows that also afford good views of the site and beyond. The fenestration and the main entrance area, which has two-storey-high ceilings and is crossed by slender, freestanding columns that support the roof, immediately suggest the purpose of the building, despite its somewhat cryptic form.

Due to local building regulations, Ando was obliged here to make wide use of cedar wood rather than the polished concrete used in his better known works – a versatile material in his hands that performs many functions both decorative as well as structural. Despite this concession, his signature style was clearly visible through the luminous qualities of the exterior, the use of glass, the dressing of the walls and the thin profile of the jutting roof.

The elliptical design of the main building and the mix of geometric figures in the interior of the complex also represent manifestations of Ando's tested repertoire. Smaller professional assignments such as this school can also take advantage of his varied methodologies.

This project is a demonstration of how this Japanese architect succeeds in getting his ideas accepted by adapting them but without making major concessions to the various interest groups. His instantly recognisable style is the proof of this master's genius.

Jean-Marie Martin

Aerial view and study sketches.

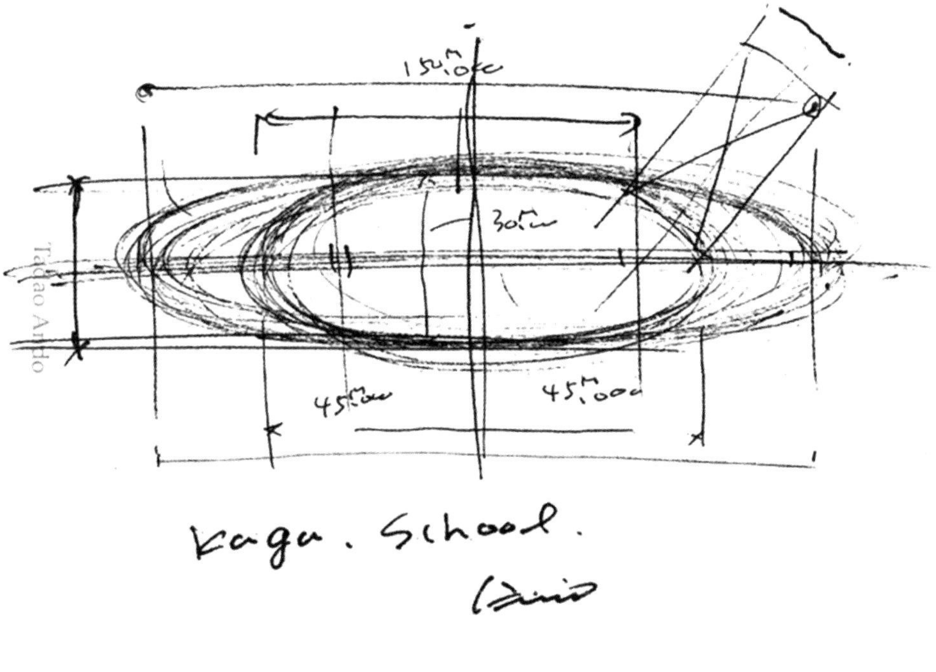

Left: View from the south and from the north side with the main entrance.

General planimetric drawing.

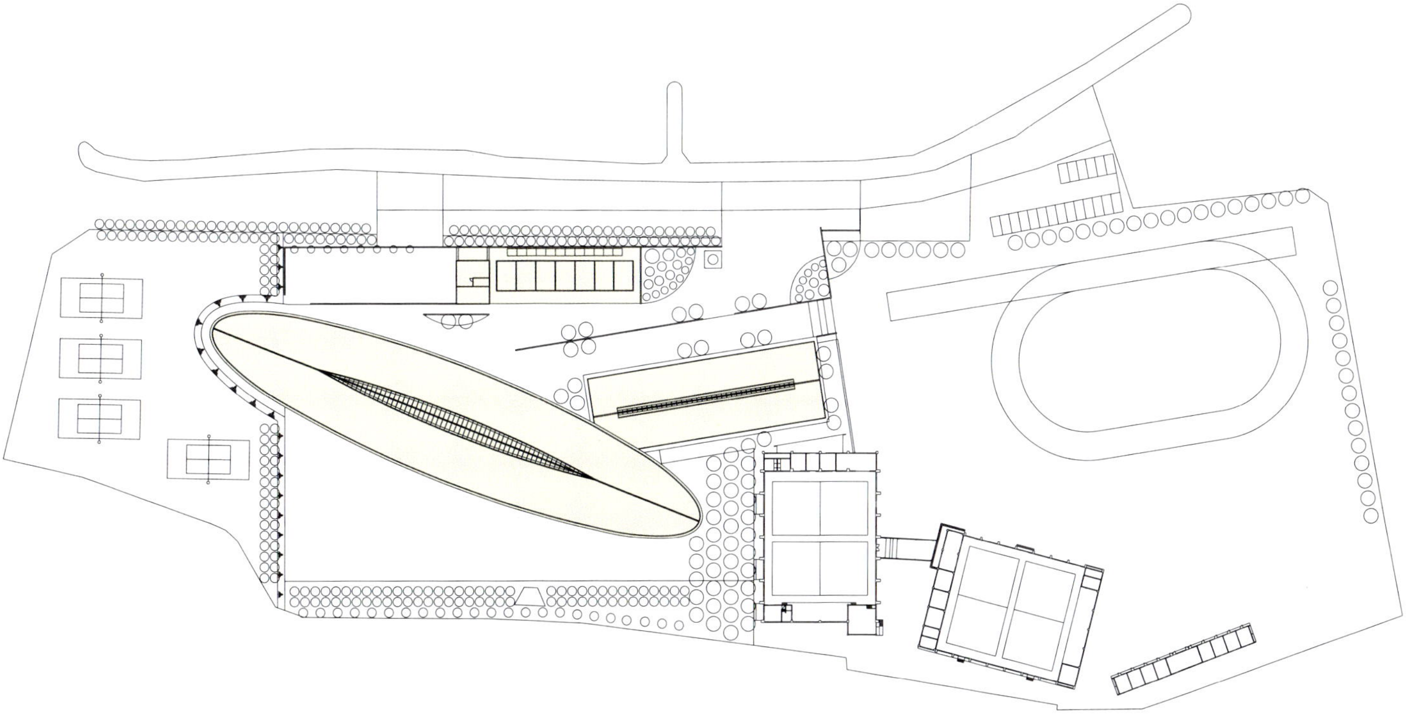

View of the entrance.

Right: Plans of the roof area, first and ground floors.

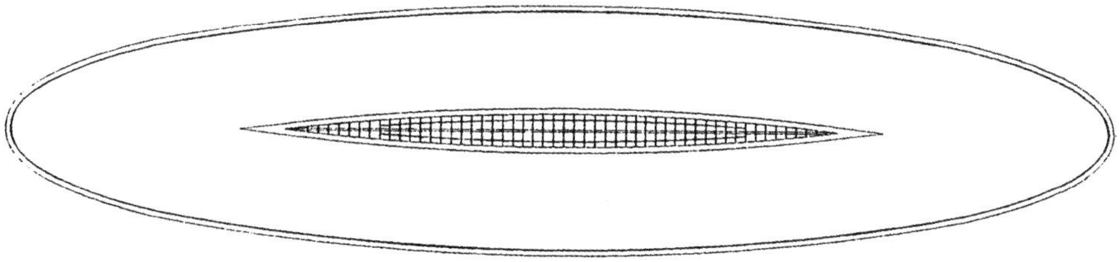

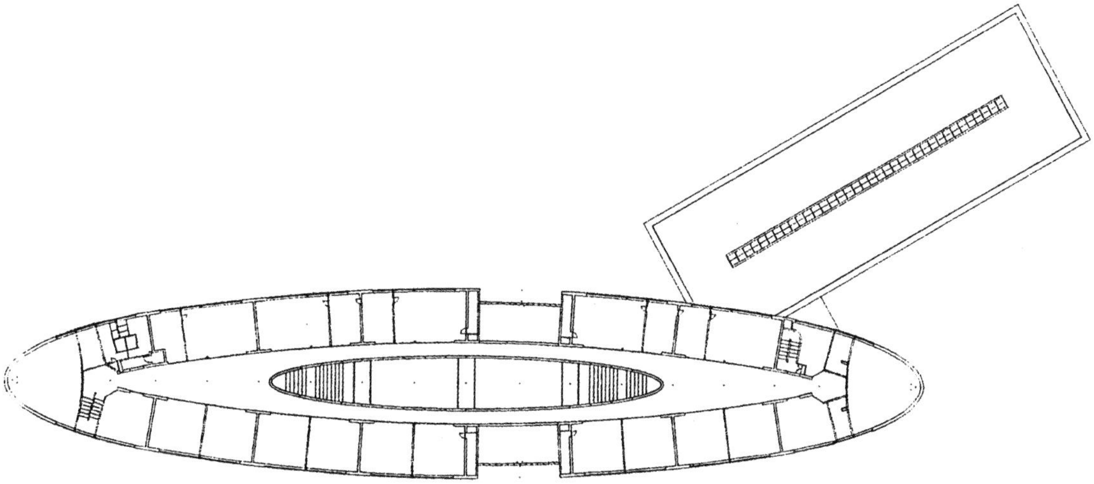

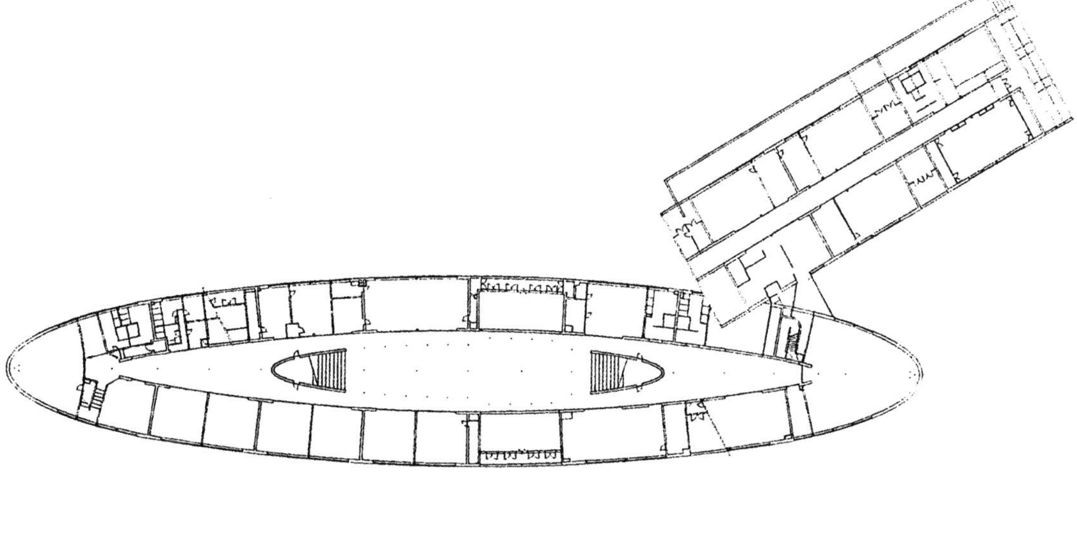

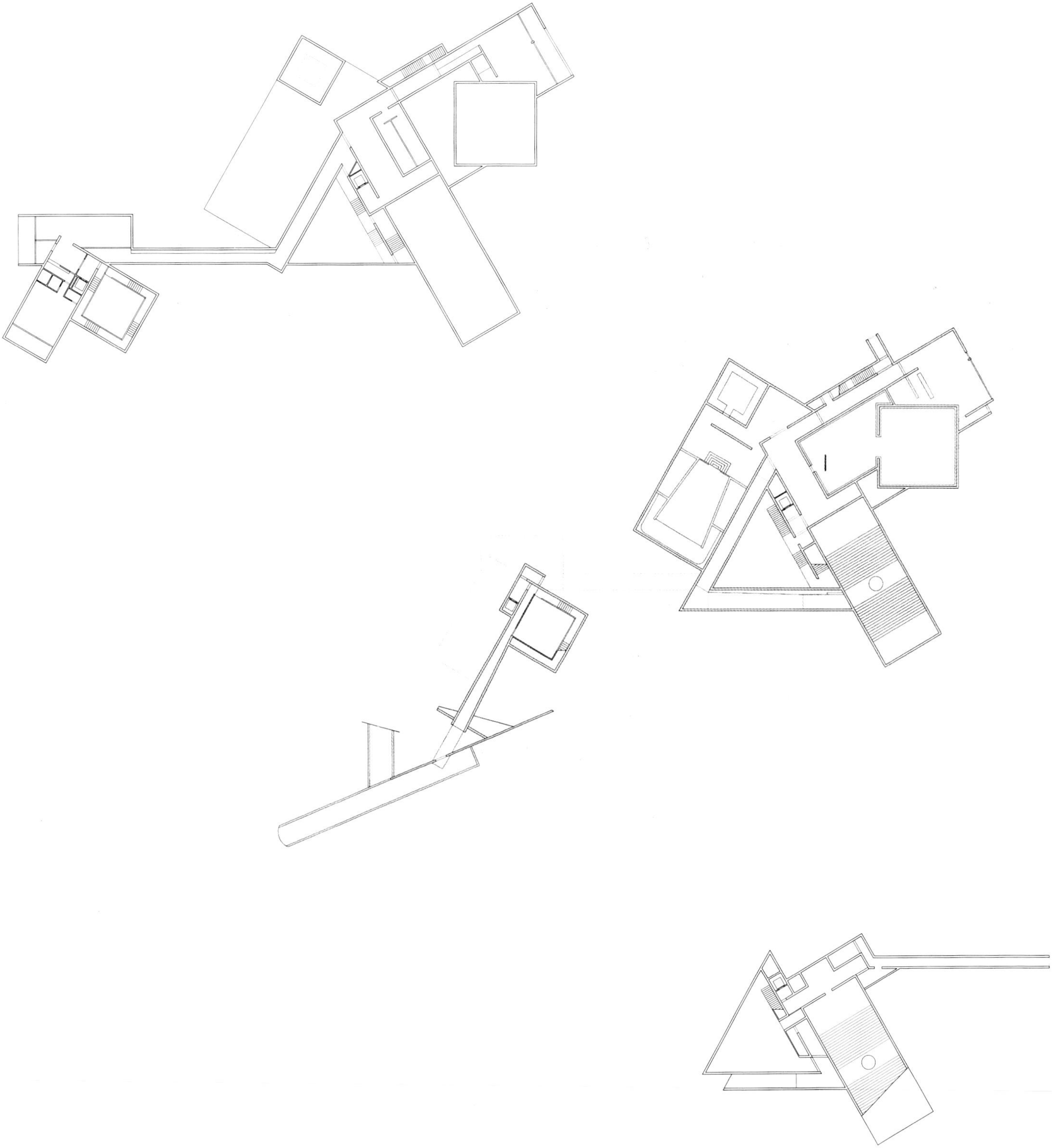

Left and middle: Interior views of the circulation area.

Far right and opposite page: Room dedicated to Walter de Maria with the installation Time/Timeless/No Time in 2004.

Water Lilies by Claude Monet (below) and light installations by James Turrell.

View of model from above and the Benjamin Franklin Parkway.

Location New York City, USA
Project 2001–2002

In addition to the large number of precious human lives lost, the terrorist attacks carried out on New York City at dawn on September 11, 2001, also annihilated in an instant the city's most recognisable icon. The destruction of this symbol of modern New York's prosperity, steadily established over more than 100 years, expressed a total denial of the dominant values of the twentieth century. Barbarism of this kind should never be allowed again, regardless of ideological justification, for nothing pure can ever be born of such violence and retaliation.

Having said that, we need to explain to future generations that a conflict of civilisations is ultimately at the root of this event, a clash between the values represented by American (or Western) standards – a global capitalist economy that breeds opulence and consumerism – and the values of a regional community that wants to preserve their identity and religious principles against a perceived encroachment.

It was an act of resistance from a people who feel their backs are against the wall. But how can people live in peace together if they continue to compete for dominance on this miraculous planet we call home? We need to learn to recognise and respect our differences while giving serious consideration to how we can transform our world into a sustainable, peaceful community.

This monument, which is to be buried in the open wound of the city, should therefore not be a building per se. It must be a place for introspection and reflection, and it must be wholly detached from every aspect of economic activity, a tomb in which the souls of the dead can be laid to rest.

That is what has been proposed for Ground Zero. The monument, a hemisphere with a diameter of 200 metres at its base and a radius calculated in proportion to the equator, could be described as a soft bulge in the earth. It is the desire for a "Unified Earth", engendered not in globalisation but in a dialogue between peoples. The hope is that the memory and meaning of this event and this monument can be passed on to future generations.

The concept of the project and a view of the project model.

Noma Kindergarten

Location Ito, Shizuoka, Japan
Design 2001–2002
Construction 2002–2003
Site area 16,515 sq m
Building area 1,479 sq m
Total area 1,097 sq m

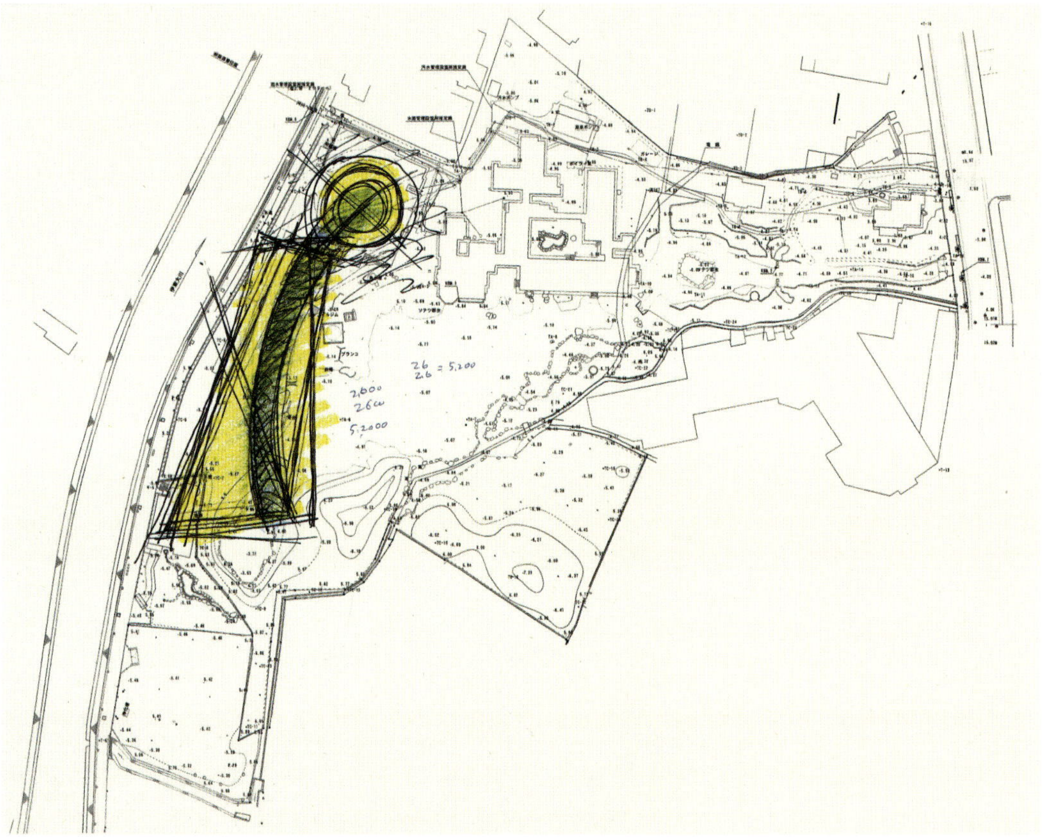

This project involves the reconstruction of the Noma Kindergarten in the centre of Ito in Shizuoka Prefecture. Founded back in 1948, the school covers roughly 16,515 square metres and was integrated superbly into a park where the Western-style villa of internationally acclaimed bacteriologist Shibasaburo Kitazato (1852–1931) had stood.

Due to the dilapidated state of the existing building, built over half a century ago, a decision was made to replace it with a new structure that preserved the charm and atmosphere of the first incarnation. The project aims to enhance the quality of the site's greenery and create an environment in which children "learn and live in contact with nature". This led to the *engawa* component, a traditional Japanese covered veranda that encircles the building as a border between the interior and exterior environments.

The volume extends under a wide covered corridor and the body of the building opens onto a number of egresses and pathways. Light pours in from skylights making each area unique through the different intensities and angles of incidence to the light they receive. The building is on the west side of the site, edging east with a slightly concave face and a broad, 60-metre-long veranda overlooking the garden. This perimeter feature contributes to nearly one-third of the entire complex consisting of partially open spaces.

Certain construction solutions were chosen for the design of the veranda to enhance the sense of lightness, to emphasise continuity between the inside and outside and the horizontal development of the space.

The spatial and tactile qualities of wood made it the most suitable material for the kindergarten. Although the initial project thus called for a wooden structure, fire regulations ultimately required steel. However, elements that children come into contact with are covered in nonflammable cedar wood – in particular the veranda floor – since the children often run about in their bare feet.

A series of carefully studied details helps give consistency and uniformity to the area by emitting a feeling of warmth and lightness typical of wood, all within a dramatically abstracted spatial composition that strays far from traditional Japanese wooden design.

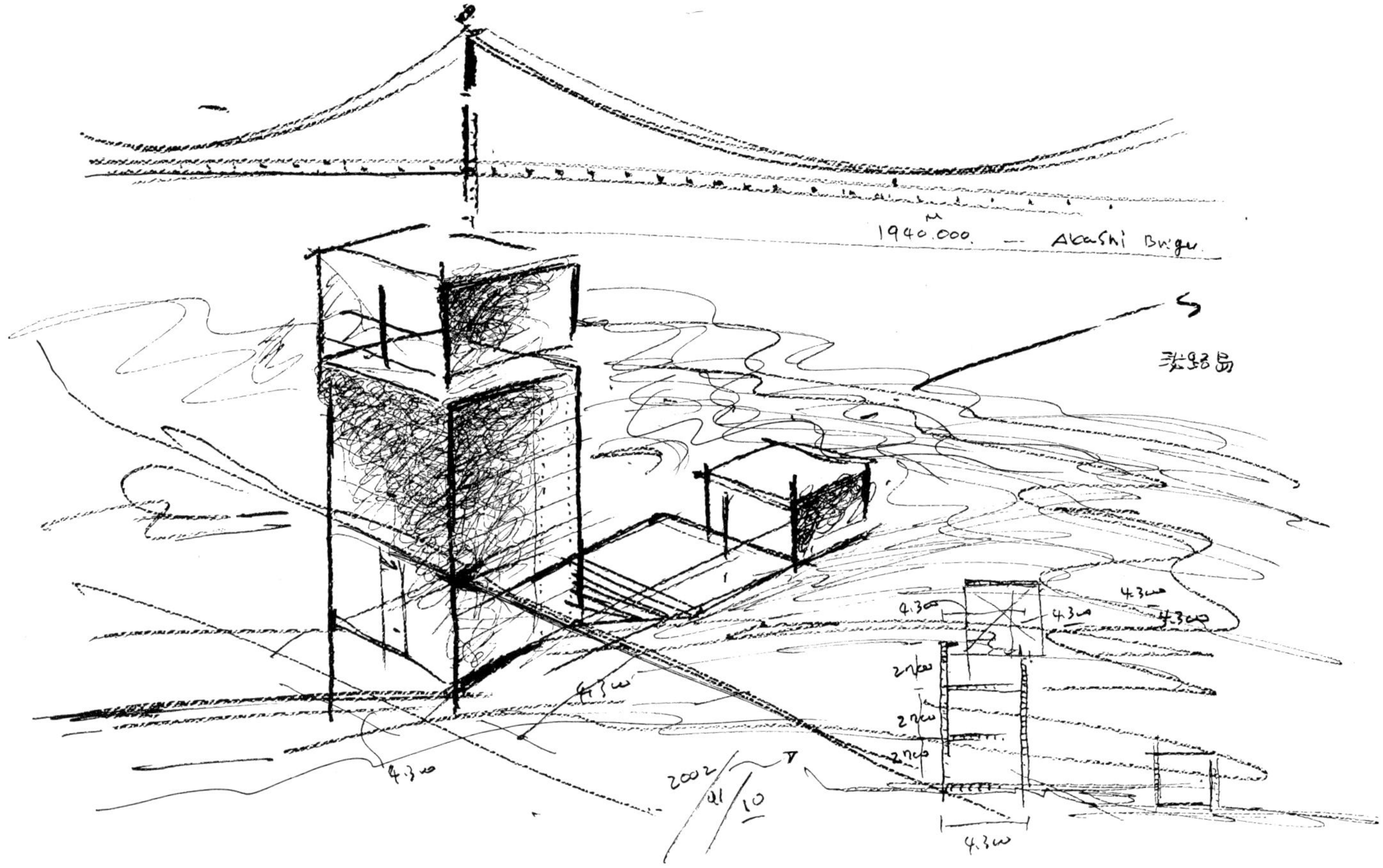

Location Kobe, Hyogo, Japan
Design 2001–2002
Construction 2002–2003
Site area 65 sq m
Building area 23 sq m
Total area 118 sq m

Upon reviewing the techniques that Tadao Ando employed to design this house, the most striking aspect in its appearance is the configuration of the four floors that form the structure.

The taut cement surface, perforated with the anchors of the formwork, envelop the house and represent all that is associated with the way Ando builds. The western façade is interrupted by four thin vertical windows that light up the stairway behind it (the pivot of the building) and are randomly associated with three other smaller openings.

The eastern façade has three smaller square openings, while on the ground floor one can see a vertical window like those included in the western front. To the north is the entrance, above which is a rectangular window, while to the south there are two more windows of different sizes that correspond nicely for the second and third floors. Crowning the whole volume is a cube dominated by glass. This top floor protrudes slightly to the east in contrast to the rest of the building.

The whole building represents a series of surprises, from the entrance, which is on the opposing façade, to the strange yet functional windows that adorn the otherwise somewhat bleak façades. The entire composition is of course dependent on the small plot size of 4 x 4 metres and relies on the glass cube that crowns it to define its distinctive character.

The building moved the stairway from its axis so the four floors (and basement) would lead up to the two-storey living space. This way, the stairwell, after leading up through the first two floors consisting of cement (with the bathroom and bedroom, respectively), leads to the third floor with its generously glazed study and the top floor, a living space with views of the sea.

Ando has created a viewpoint that allows the gaze of anyone in

Studio sketch and the view south-east.

Following pages: The southern façade, the northeast façade overlooking the bay of Kobe, and plans of the third, second, first and ground floors.

Left: Detail of the metal-grid cladding on the façade.

The liaison of the skywalk with the parking area on the western façade.

Location Kobe, Hyogo, Japan
Design 2003
Construction 2003–2005
Site area 24,307 sq m
Building area 9,640 sq m
Total area 30,770 sq m

After constructing the Rockfield Shizuoka factory, I was asked by the same firm to prepare a design for their factory and offices in Kobe. While the project in Shizuoka involved a new building, the Kobe job was a reconstruction of an old warehouse factory (located on the coast) to make it suitable for a food facility.

Moreover, due to the instability of the ground, the pilings of the former building had been damaged since the time of the Hanshin earthquake of 1995. It was therefore necessary to first reinforce the support structure and then completely eliminate the fourth floor of the former warehouse in order to lighten the entire structure.

In allocating the various functions within the building, the factory floor was moved to the lower floors while offices, meeting rooms and common areas for employees were shifted to the top floor. As was the case in Shizuoka, those spaces were designed for rest and relaxation, so attention was given to finding ways of ensuring that the space did not feel enclosed and oppressive. To do this, we repositioned the roof, which expanded the interior space, created the "garden of light", which extends inside the building for 100 metres, and built the "water garden" with the company restaurant.

As for the façade, the 160-metre-long walls were covered with a steel grid tile that is generally used for floors (called Fine Floor) to try to reduce the heavy impression made by the enormous original building and at the same time increase the perception of increased space inside the structure.

Simple repetition of motifs, mostly of industrial products, had given this extensive space a very light rhythm. Now the metal tiles cast a dim light and shadow over those same motifs inside, in the interstitial space between the coating and the pre-existing wall.

It was a meaningful project for me, and at the same time provided an additional personal challenge in the field of architectural reuse. It was not a question of leaving something new for the future, but rebuilding what already existed.

Tadao Ando

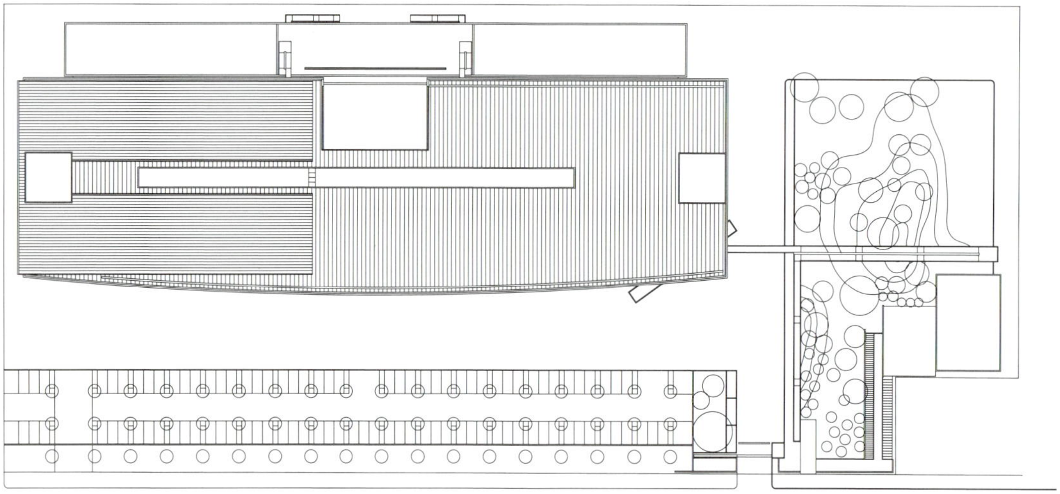

ROCK FIELD

Left: Plan and view from the north-west.

Northern elevation and the water garden.

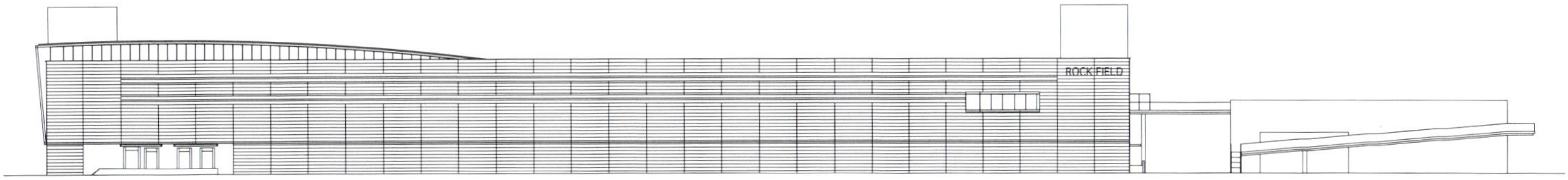

坂の上の雲ミュージアム

Location Malibu, California, USA
Design 2003
Building area 21 sq m
Total area 412 sq m

This site is located on the outskirts of Los Angeles on a hill in Malibu overlooking the Pacific Ocean. The main theme of the project was the attempt to build an architectural space that integrated light and sound.

First, part of the hill was excavated in order to gain living space that would meet two key requirements: protection of privacy and the creation of ocean views. The volume was rearticulated as a combination of pure geometric shapes – a box with a rectangular base, a triangular prism and a cube – that managed to provide a dynamic, interior spatial sequence of lighting effects.

The cube is the largest element. Here, light and sound are important components in defining the internal vacuum. From floor to ceiling, a continuum of laminated hyperbolic paraboloids give the space excellent acoustics.

The Electronic Poem (Philips Pavilion, Brussels World Fair, 1958) by Iannis Xenakis and Le Corbusier had the same hyperbolic paraboloids and cones that are used here, only here they are used to line the interior. In this house, every sound is enclosed within the volume and acquires different meanings in each block. Not only music, but also any natural sound in Malibu – the sounds of waves, wind and rain – is faithfully captured to create a fascinating flow of sound. It is a design inspired by invisible lights and sounds.

View from the sea and perspectives and plans.

Detailed perspective and a view of the southwest entrance.

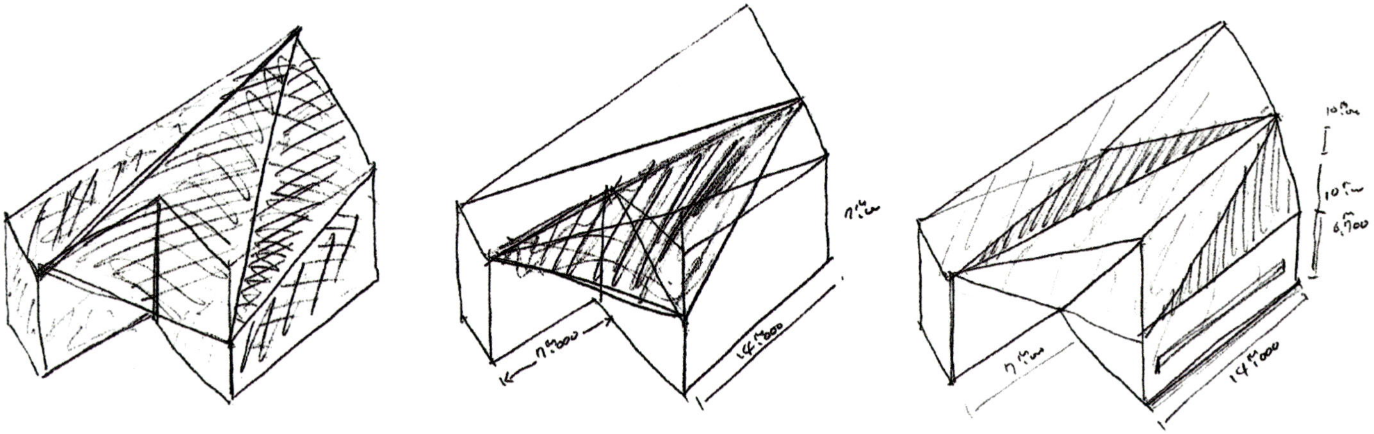

Opposite page: View from the south-west and studio sketches.

The front road and the loft level with skylights in the roof.

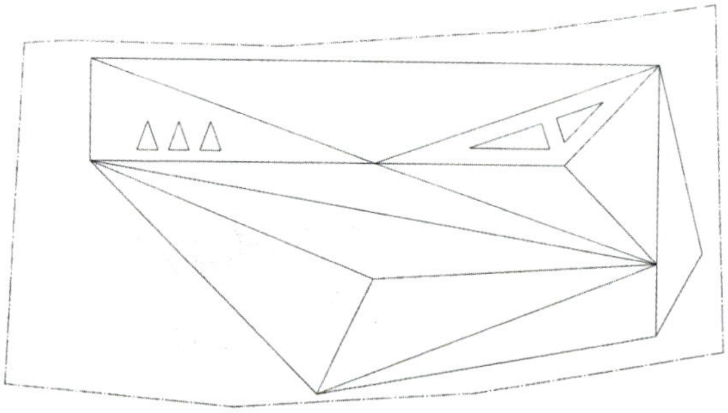

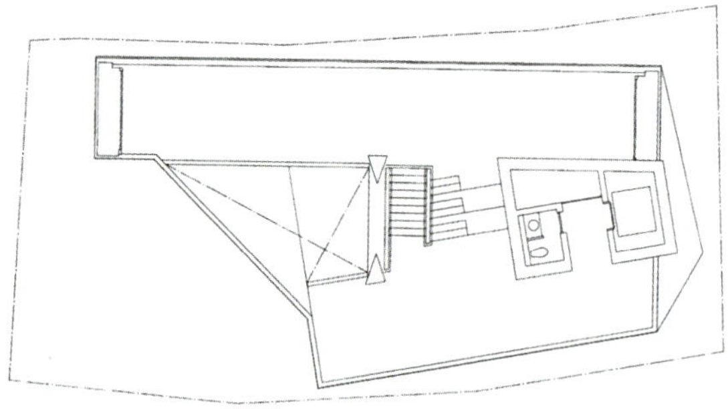

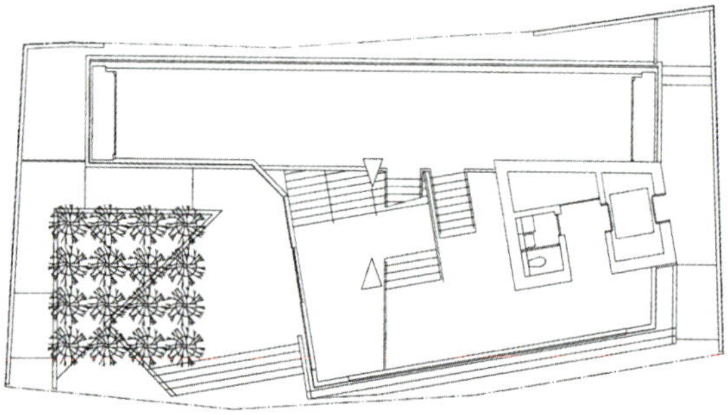

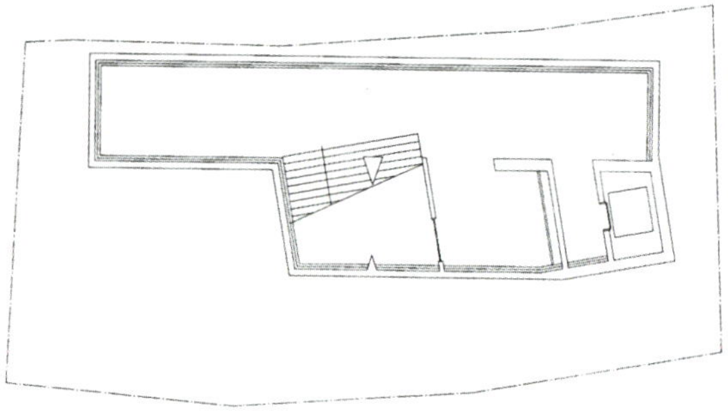

Opposite page: Plans of the covered floors, first floor and basement, and an inside view of the third floor as well as a staircase linking the second and third floors.

Prospects of the southwest, southeast and cross-sections.

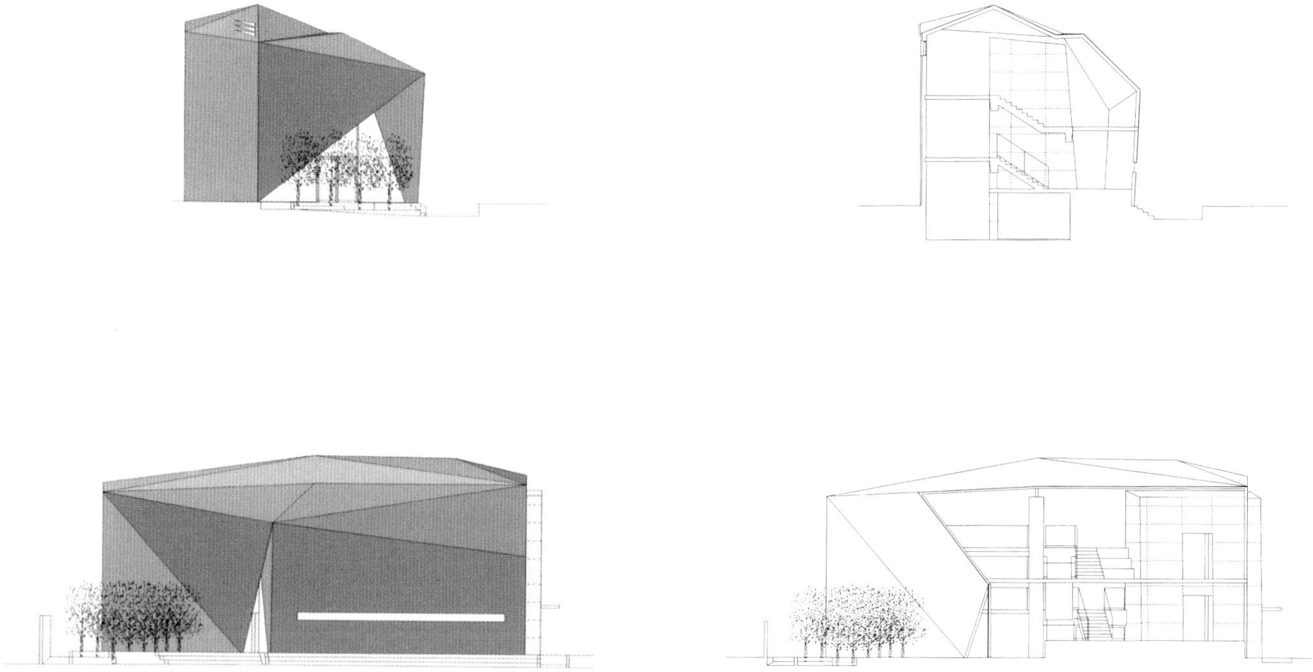

View and detail of the front of the house and from the road to the south.

trapezoid, with the last side overlooking Lake Biwa left completely open. The communal living space at the core of the house is located in this area.

Light and wind freely enter from the balcony, which extends horizontally along the front of the building and throws soft shadows on the area outside the ground floor below it. The space possesses a peaceful atmosphere that contrasts with the open and light foreground. A concrete block fence defines the property's boundaries and insulates the home from the surrounding area.

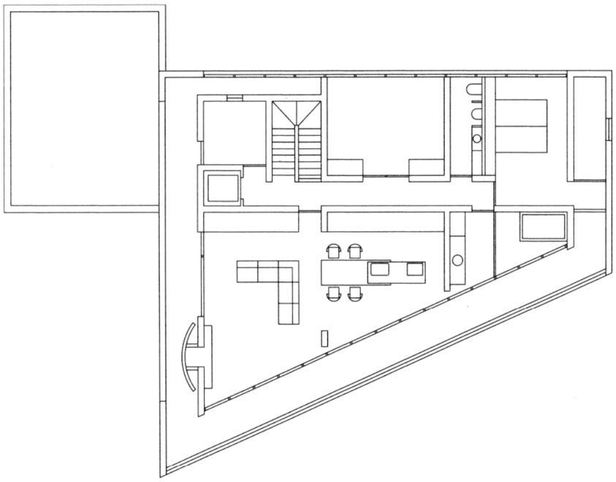

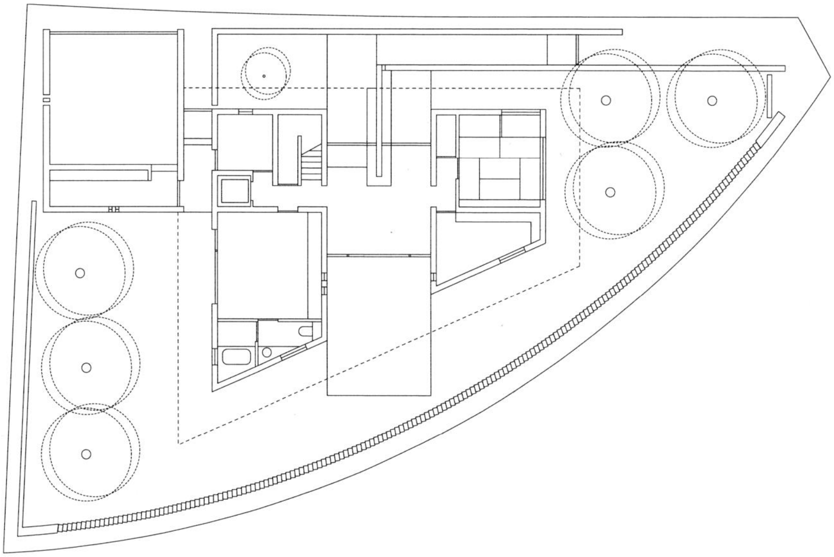

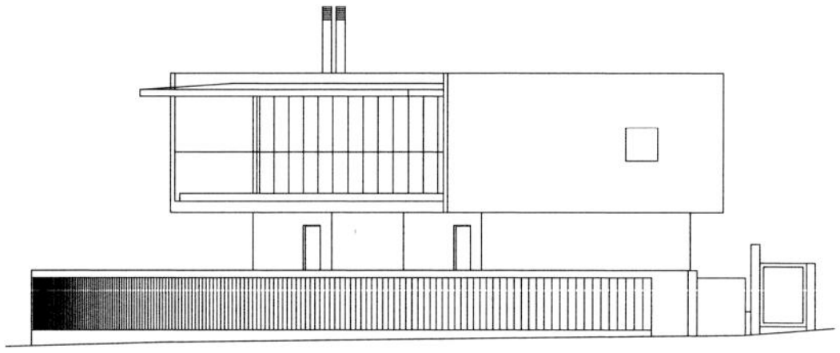

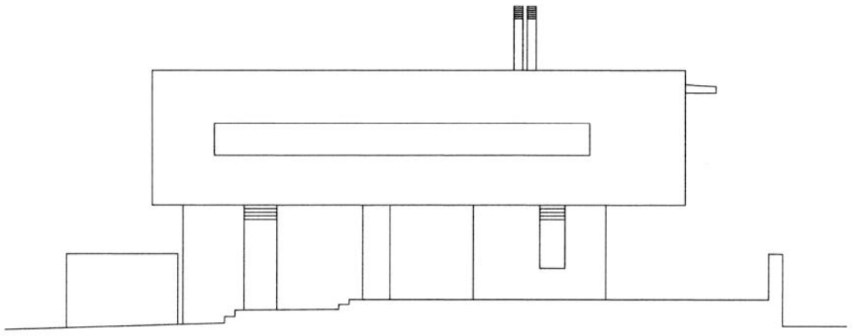

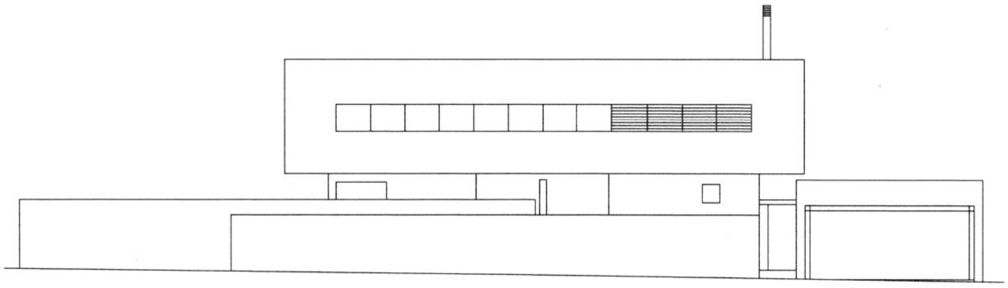

Left: Plans of the first and ground floors and elevations to the north, south and west.

The hallway and living space on the first floor.

Views of the lobby on the upstairs floor and the main gallery in the basement.

as well as the contours of the openings and the footprint that develops in the interior spaces. Steel plates 16 millimetres thick are used to provide continuous coverage of the 54-metre long roof, and they are mounted in such a flawless way that they recall the assembly techniques of the beloved wooden Japanese tea houses.

The concrete surfaces have been treated, like the steel surfaces, with a fluoride coating, whereas the glass frames were inserted in a simpler fashion, with a bare, austere look. They are not the only component with a modest appearance, however. The interior, built with concrete masonry, is also spartan.

The building consists of two volumes with a path from one side of the triangle that separates the wings and defines the courtyard entrance. At first, your glance is drawn in by the folds of the roof, and by the two inclined triangular surfaces. The building looks as if it has been placed under a finely cut piece of metal. A spiral staircase with a triangular footprint connects the upper level to the hypogean space.

The building is in central Tokyo, in the Akasaka district,

which has undergone heavy construction and revitalization in recent years. It is housed at the foot of a complex whose overall interest is inversely proportional to its vast size. A very tall tower dominates the campus, and an open space separates it from the new Design Museum, which recalls another project Ando completed two years previously in Tokyo, the hhstyle.com/casa. This building looks as if it were made from one material and its surface has been bent to make it systematically effective.

hhstyle.com/casa, however, does not have the rugged austerity that defines 21_21 Design Sight – an austerity similar to what Coco Chanel had in mind when describing her clothing designs as "pauvreté pour milliardaires", an austerity much like that which Ando has achieved with his building.

Jean-Marie Martin

Studio sketch and a view from the east.

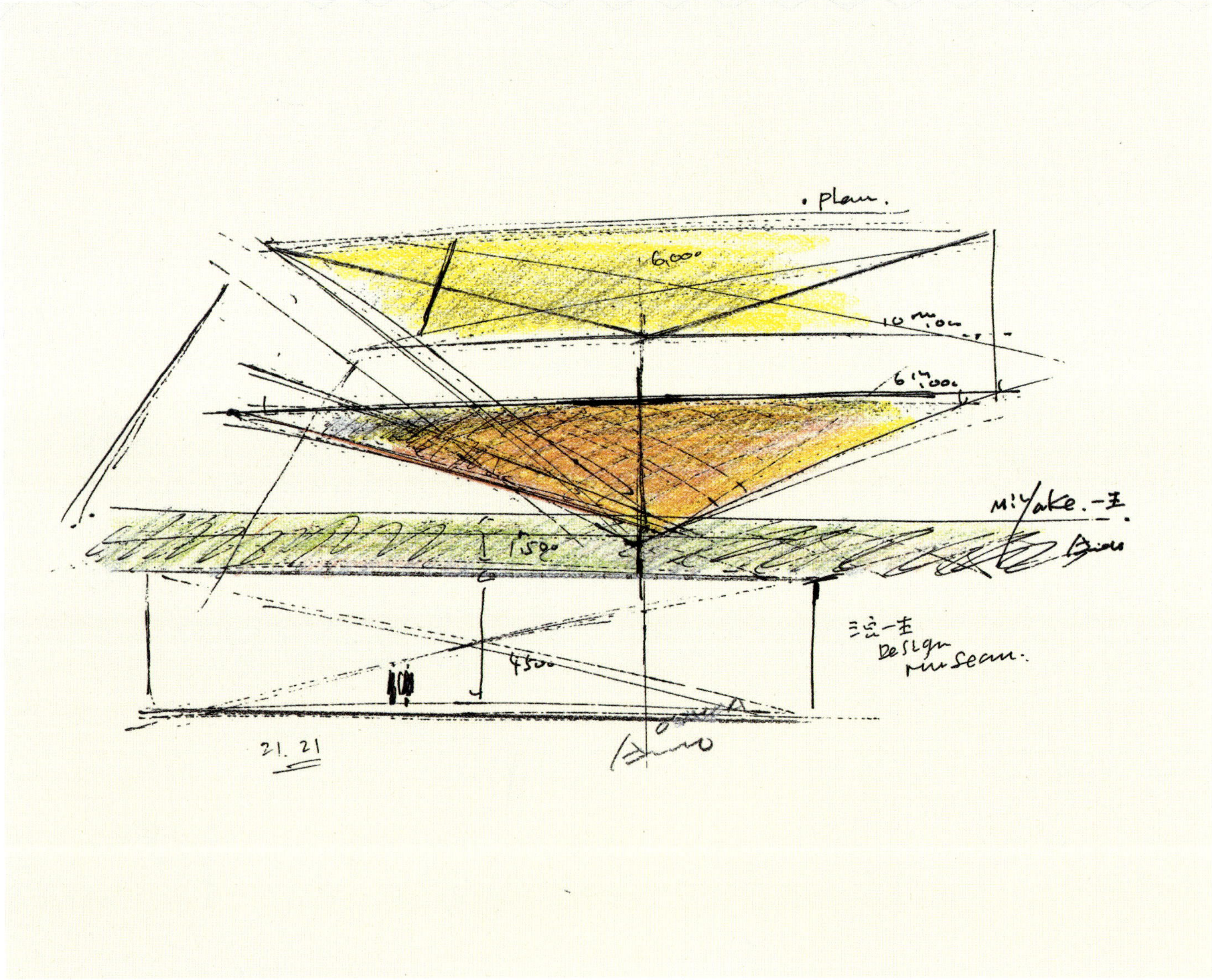

Location Minato, Tokyo, Japan
Design 2004–2007
Construction 2007–2008
Site area 58,641 sq m
Building area 642 sq m
Total area 987 sq m

This project involves the construction of a memorial hall to mark 100 years of the private, all-female Seishin University, located in a residential area of Shirogane Minato-ku in Tokyo.

Developed around a church designed by Antonin Raymond and immersed in a campus of greenery, the university buildings are organised like a horseshoe around a central courtyard. The room is placed at the extreme northeast point of the site, located between the indoor pool and gym.

Being a small site, the roof of the pool was used to create the "new wing". On the one hand, carrying out the expansion of a building from the 1960s posed a number of both technical and bureaucratic difficulties. However, it also presented an opportunity to develop a more organic learning environment.

Simultaneously to the construction of the new hall, the project included the renovation of the pool deck below, the nearby gymnasium and the neighbouring outdoor spaces. To avoid the overwhelming, traditional image of the *uragawa* (backyard), the path linking the gym and the pool was transformed into a plaza featuring a small-sized *engawa* (veranda).

From there a staircase leads up to the wooden roof terrace above the swimming pool, from which one can observe the verdant landscape and the campus. The memorial room rises above the terrace with a shape reminiscent of a piece of raw mineral.

Within this irregular polyhedron covered with metal panels, a foyer surrounds a circular room that makes up the core structure of the building. The casing of the circular room is composed in part by sliding elements that, without disappearing into the wall, make it possible to view the greenery from the inside too. The theme of the project was to introduce a new centrality integrated architecturally with the landscape of a school environment.

Left: Perspectives and cross-section.

View from the west with the new volume's roof hanging over the space between the pool and the gym to the left.

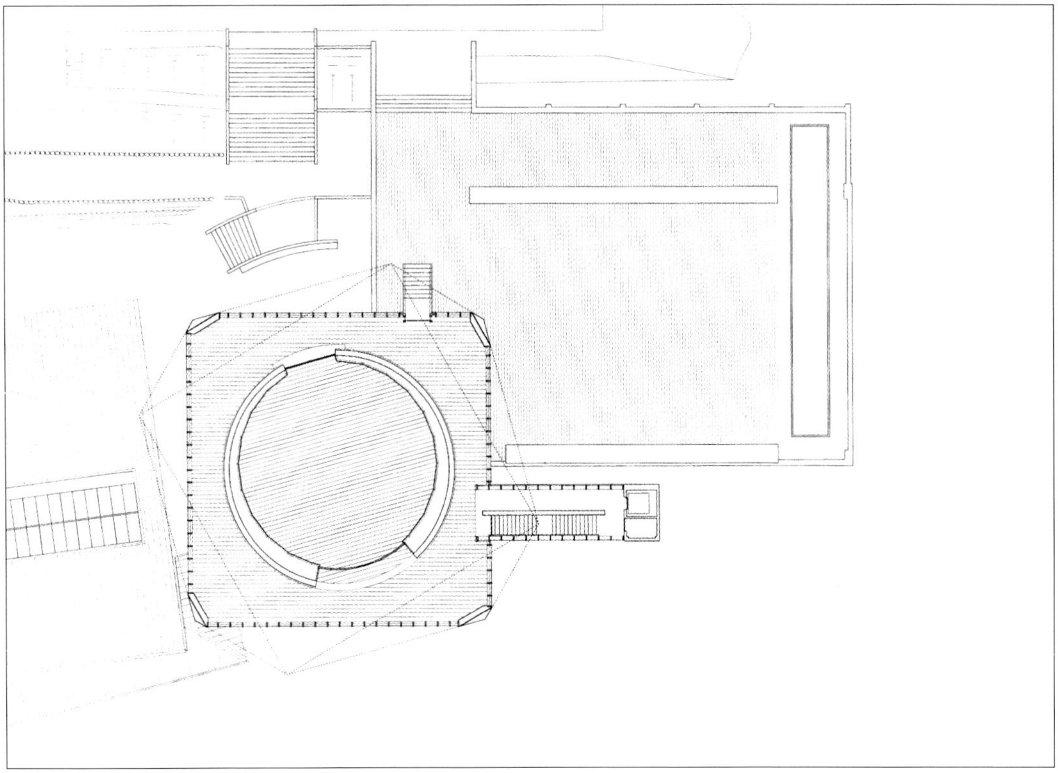

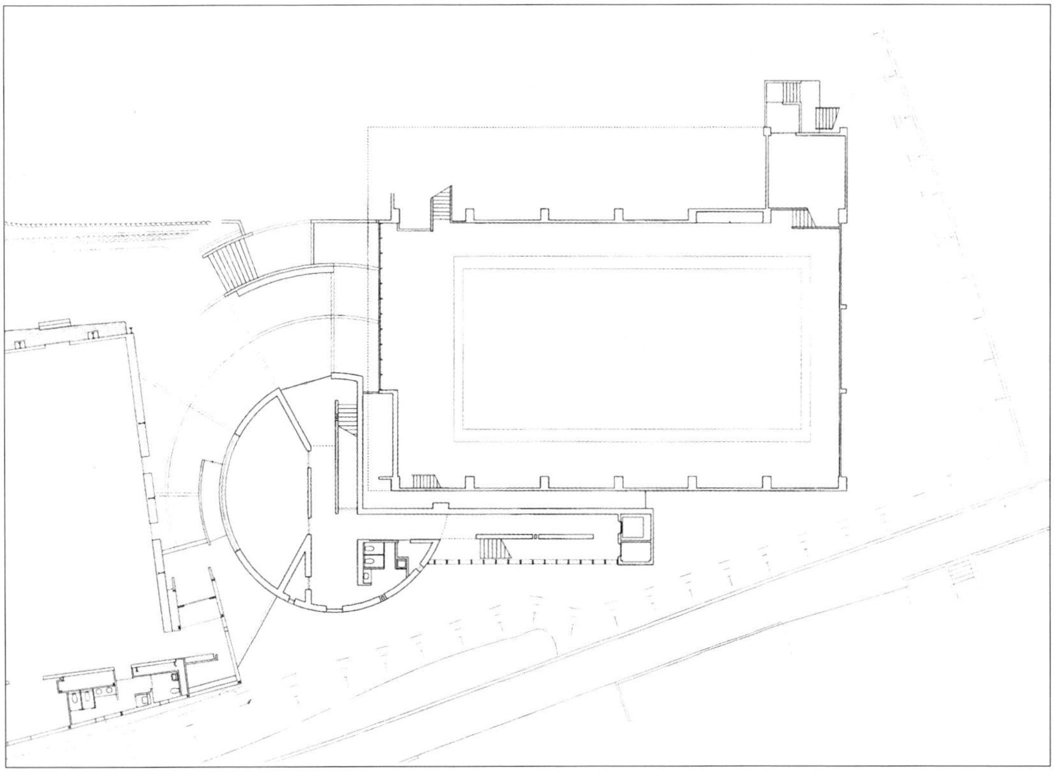

Plans of the second and ground floors.

Right: A northwest view and the panoramic roof terrace above the pool.

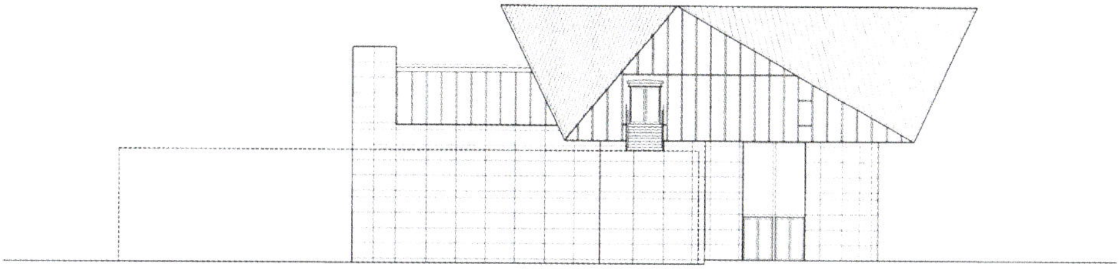

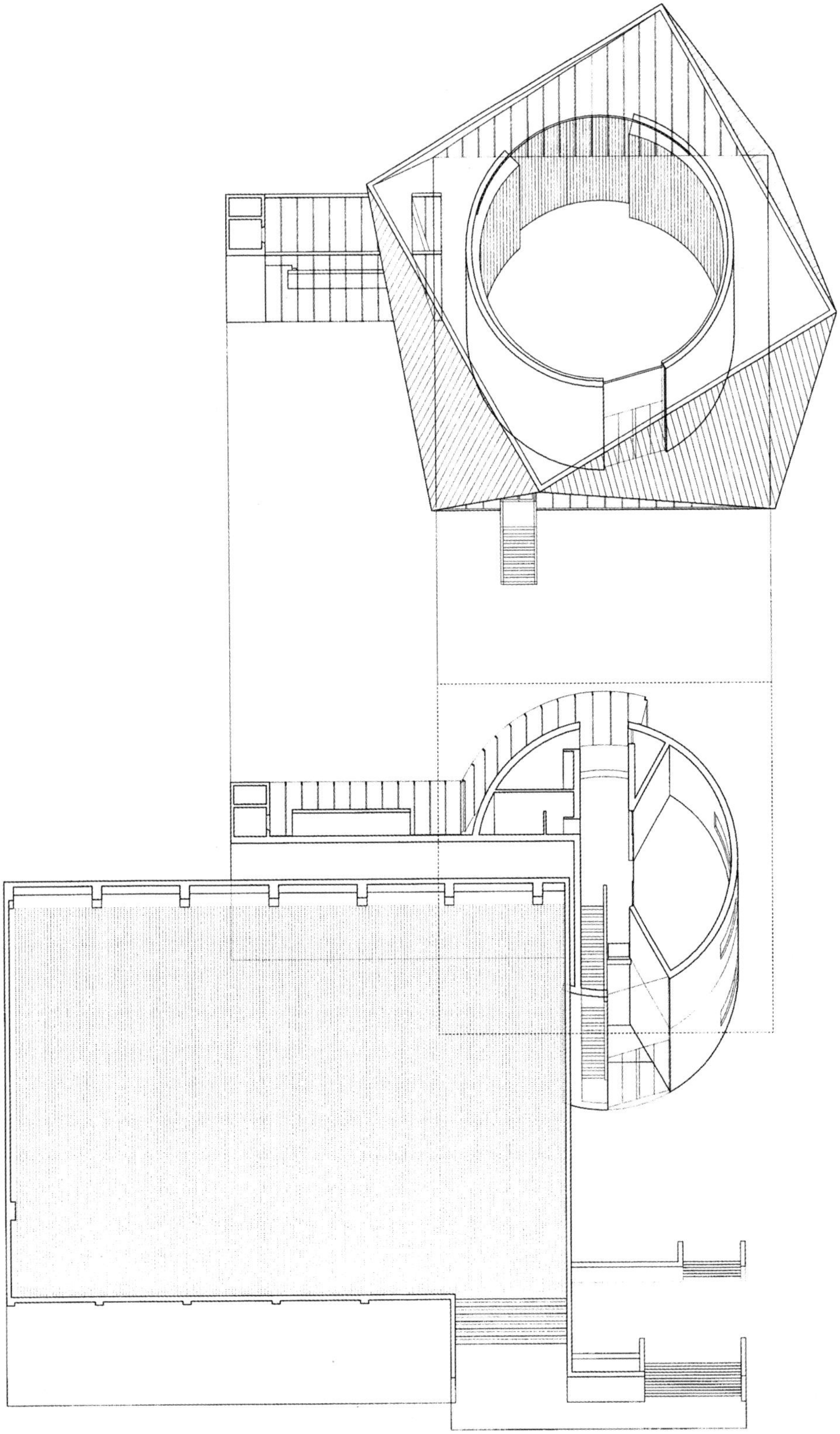

Axonometric diagram plus the view through the opening and the interior of the circular room.

Volumetric diagram and a perspective view.

Floor plans of the eleventh, tenth, third, and ground floors.

Opposite page: Views of the model.

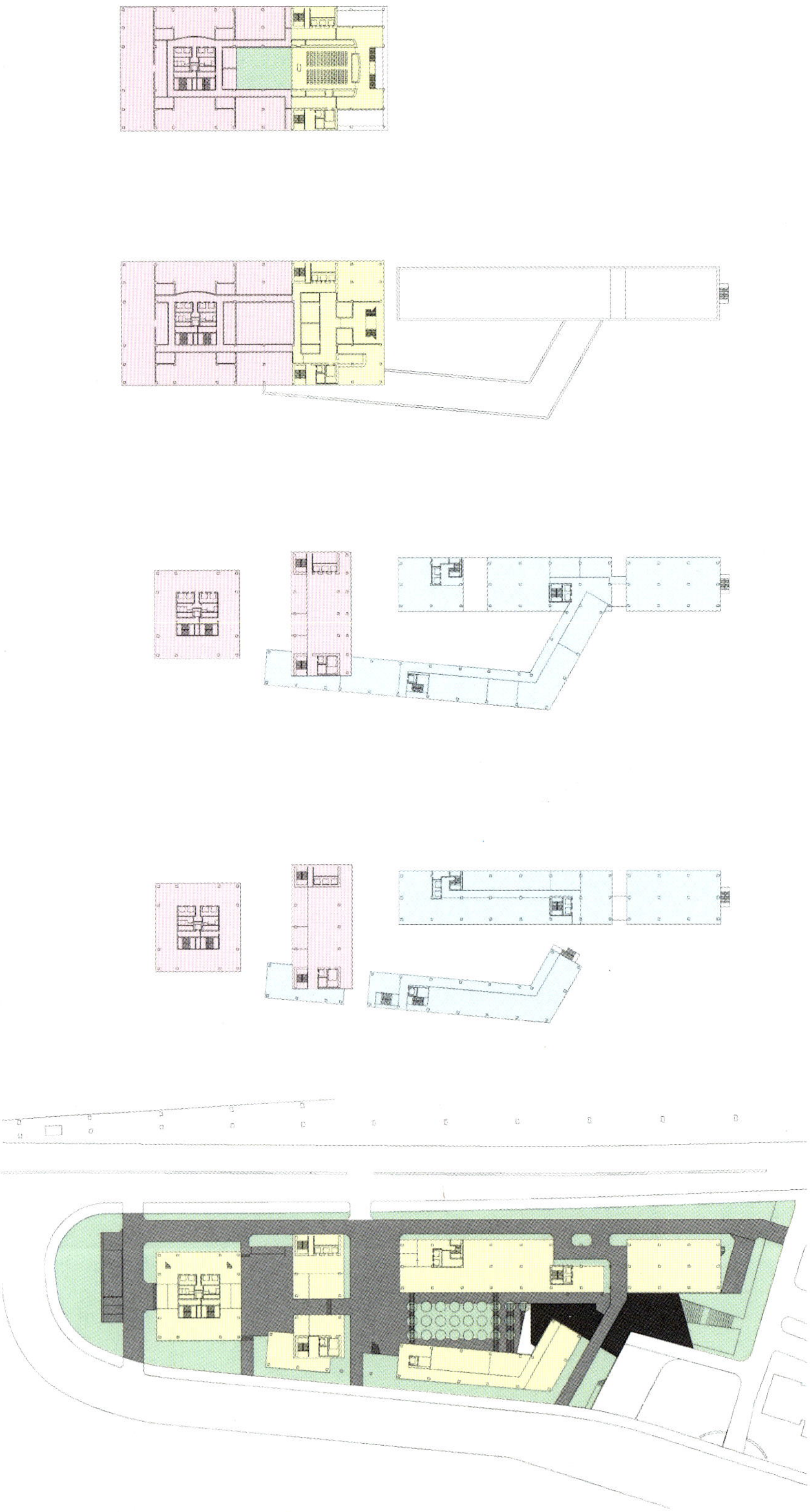

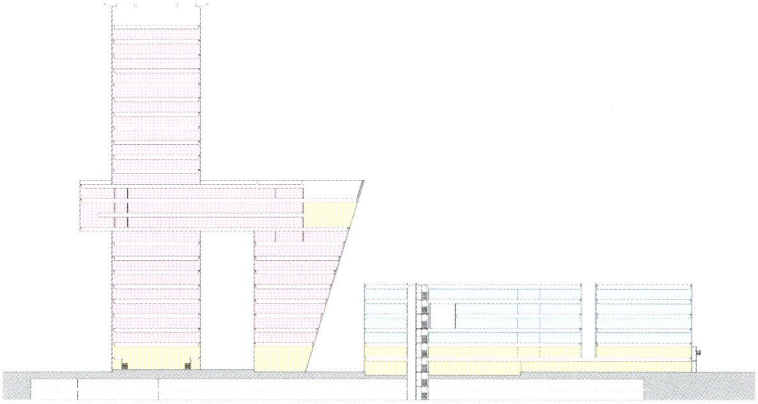

Location Bellevue, Washington, USA
Design 2004–
Site area 27,600 sq m
Building area 3,900 sq m
Total area 4,840 sq m

As its name would suggest, this place of worship sits on a gentle north-facing slope in a dense forest near the centre of Bellevue, a suburb near Seattle, Washington.

The chapel is shaped like an isosceles triangle with its tip pointing to the east. The altar is located near the apex of the building, which looks out over a body of water that helps establish distance from the trees of the forest.

The triangle is both a geometric figure that allows for an axis that can be clearly oriented towards the altar as well as a symbol of the Holy Trinity. This type of design was already explored in the International Design Competition for the 2000 Jubilee Church of the Year organised by the diocese of Rome in 1995–1996.

The nave, which can hold up to 144 faithful, descends gradually towards the altar and the water garden. At the foot of the triangular floor is a specially designed organ. The light that enters from the sides further emphasises the overall triangular shape. On the second level of the church are the organist's seat and the balcony that houses the choir.

In addition to daily religious services, the building can also accommodate conferences and concerts. Nestled in the tranquillity of the woods, there is a small semi-circular cemetery southeast of the chapel looking north across the body of water. Besides the fusion of architecture and landscape, the project has become a testament to how well the living, the deceased and nature can coexist.

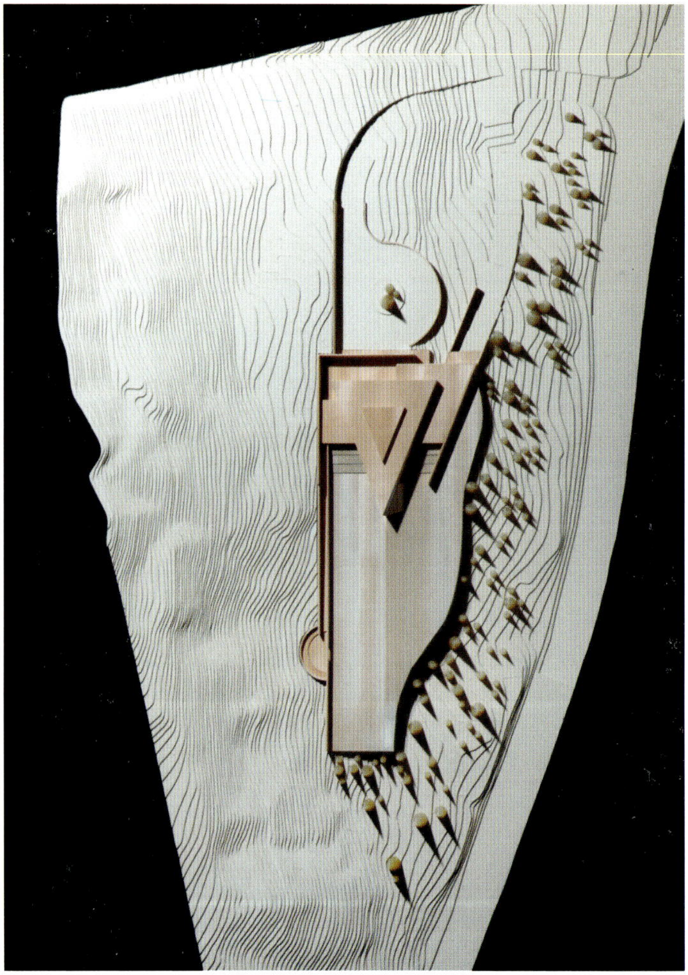

Left: Overhead view of the model.

Plans of the first and ground floors and a rendering of the interior.

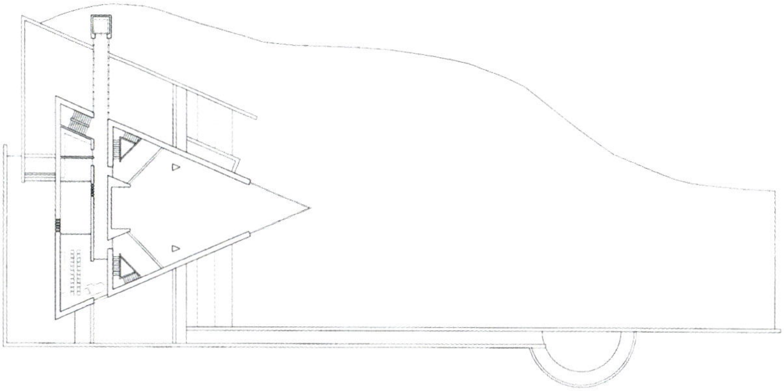

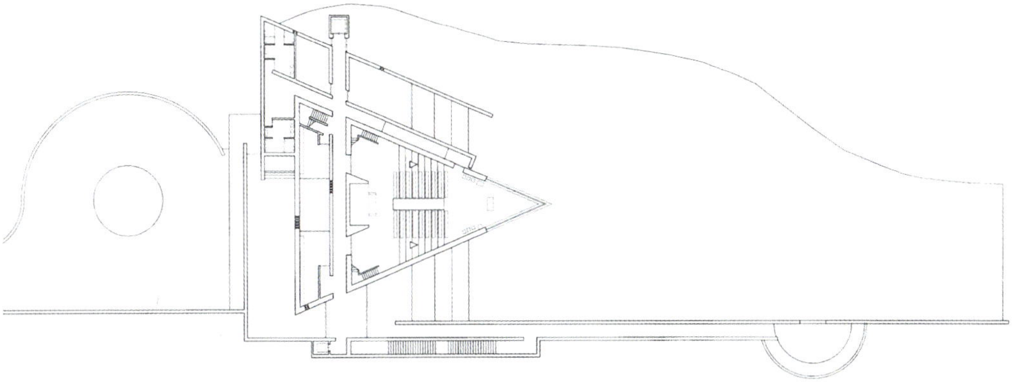

Location Venice, Italy
Design 2005–2006
Construction 2005–2006
Site area 1,450 sq m
Building area 1,400 sq m
Total area 6,320 sq m (reclassified area 2,900 sq m)

This project for the construction of a new Museum of Modern Art in the Palazzo Grassi in Venice was developed at the invitation of François Pinault. It followed an abruptly cancelled proposal (due to infrastructure issues) for the construction of the François Pinault Foundation's Contemporary Art Museum on the Île Seguin in Paris.

The proposal for the project had won an international competition to design the museum and although this was the same theme, the situation was quite different. It wasn't a question of building a centre for contemporary art from scratch, as was the case with the Île Seguin, but restoring and reusing an old neoclassical building, the Palazzo Grassi. Located on the Grand Canal near St. Mark's Square, and designed in the second half of the 18th century by Giorgio Massari, it had been used as an exhibition centre since 1983.

In Italy, the conservation of historic buildings is subject to strict regulations, so the project needed to comply with detailed government specifications with regard to both the restoration of façades – understandable due to their impact on the visible urban landscape – as well as the interior design. Based on these considerations, the initial idea to build a white box for modern art within an historic building might seem somewhat contradictory.

That contradiction would ultimately lead to a space that was full of vitality and capable of enhancing both the old and the new. As it happened, I had already explored this dilemma in a number of other projects, so the subject of a design based on a dialogue between the past and present was declined in the case of the Palazzo Grassi, in order to focus instead on a new study and attention to detail.

First, the masonry had to be restored to its original state. Second, the interior exhibition areas were redefined by white walls. Renouncing the idea of an independent white cube, the research instead focused on finalizing details that could enhance the existing structure.

The decorations on the walls and ceilings of the old building can thus be seen through openings in the white walls while the shimmering water of the Grand Canal filters into the halls and natural light from the atrium flows into the central gallery space. The works of art seem to suddenly materialize in a succession of surprises and discoveries. This spatial sequence is what captures the conversation between old and new.

Teatrino

Location Venice, Italy
Design 2005
Site area 800 sq m
Total area 1,800 sq m

Located in the garden of the Palazzo Grassi, this theatre was set up as an open-air stage in 1951, at which time the building was restored. Although this is not a structure of particular cultural value, the superintendent for architectural heritage in Venice did not consent to demolishing it and rebuilding the site from scratch.

The project was to restore the old outer walls of the building, thus preserving its appearance, and introduce a concrete cube to be used as an auditorium. The materials include white marble, widely available in this region, used for the steps that lead to the terrace. The objective of this design was to revive through contemporary architecture the old memories associated with the site.

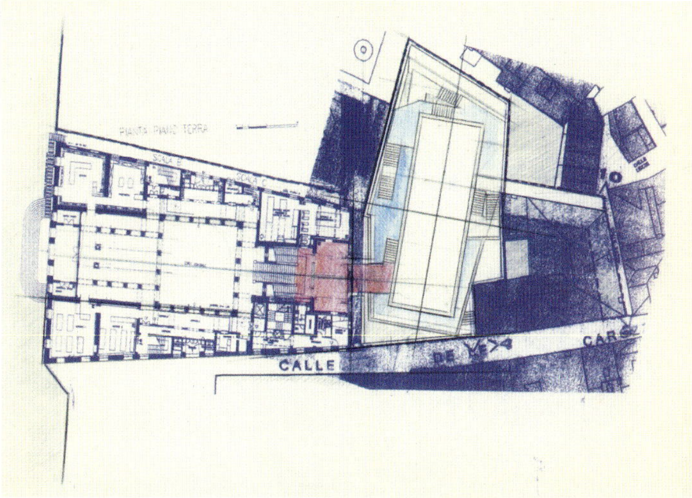

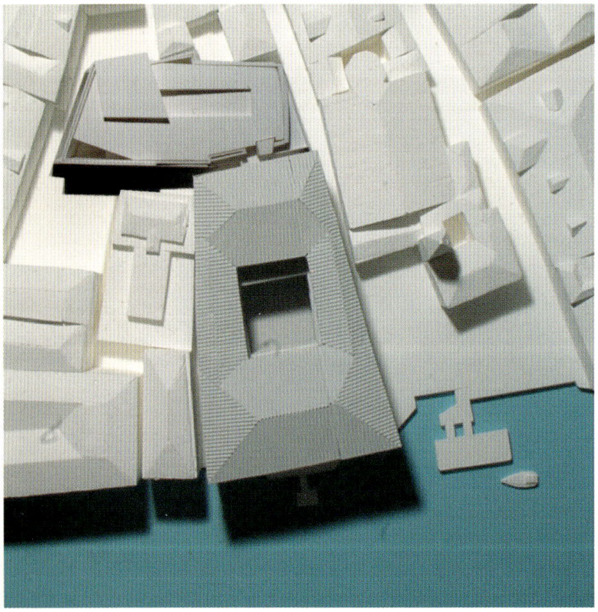

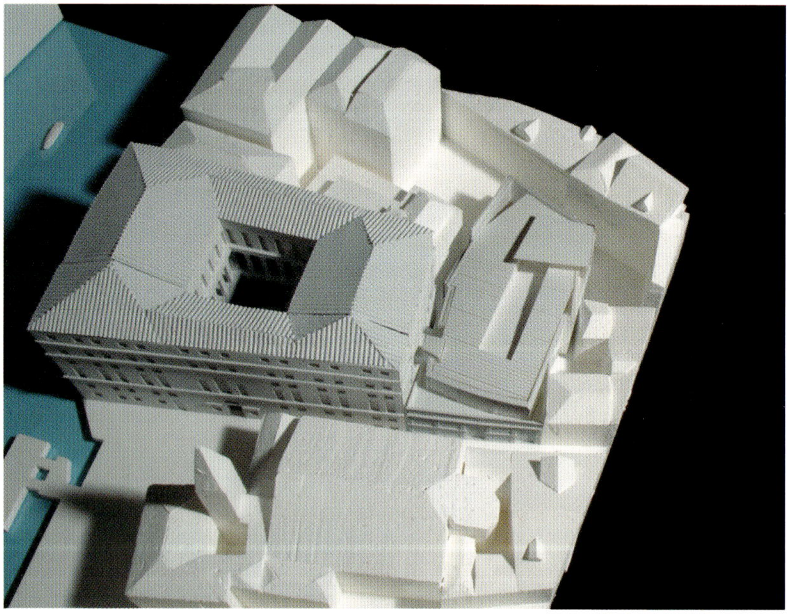

Left: Site plan and views of the model.

Plans of the top floor of access, the floor below and cross-sections of the model.

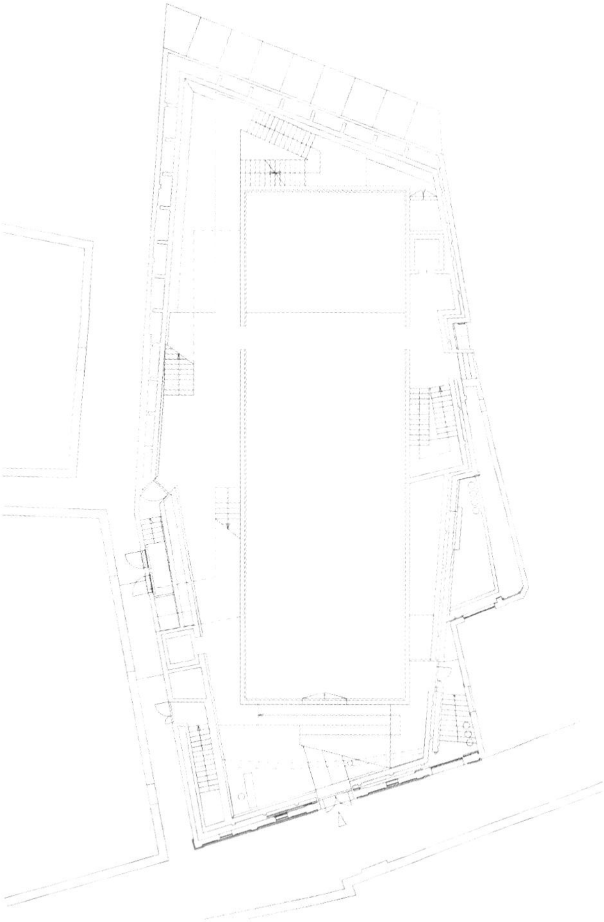

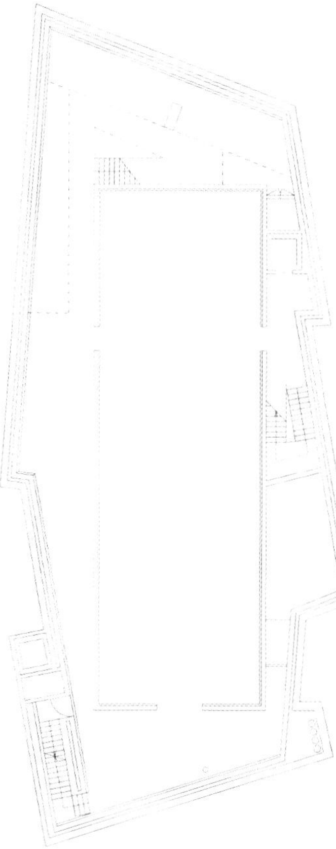

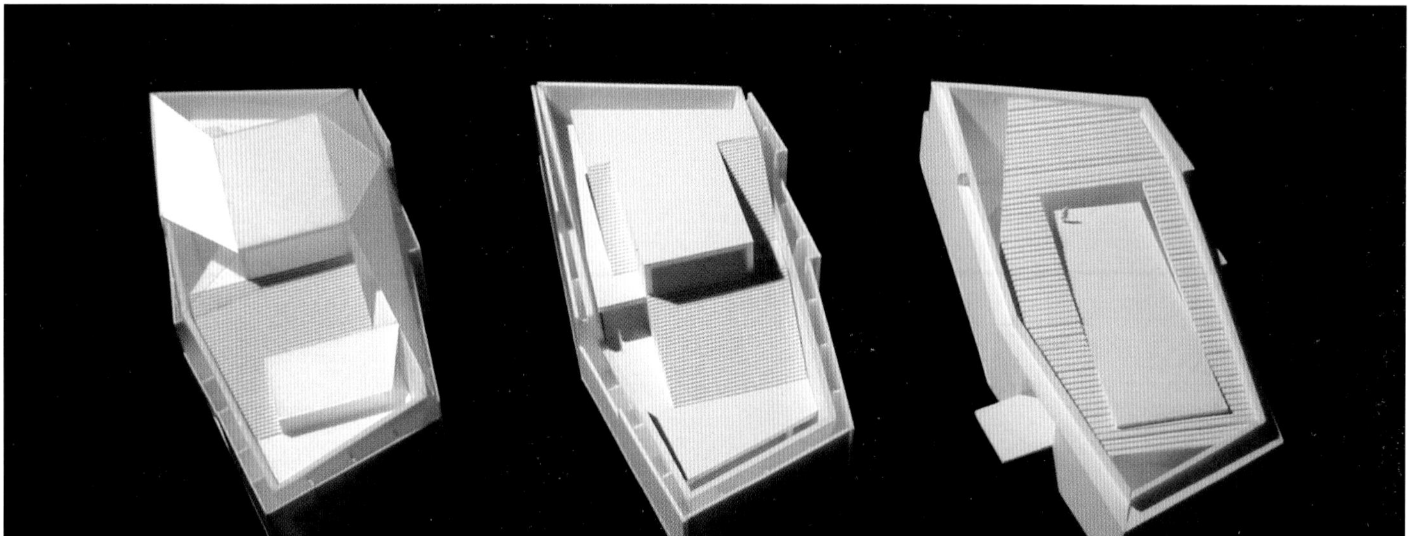

Location Makuhari, Chiba; Kadoma, Osaka; Chigasakai, Kanagawa; Toyonaka, Osaka, Japan
Design 2005
Construction 2005–2006

As part of a programme of environmental rehabilitation and reforestation in conjunction with the municipal administration of Osaka, a major Japanese electronics company decided to participate in the initiative to create a series of cherry tree parks.

Supported by regional subsidies, the company is taking its brownfield sites and turning them into public spaces. The first two sites were completed in 2006: one in the coastal suburb of Makuhari, Chiba Prefecture, and the other in the town of Kadoma, near Osaka. In 2007 they completed a park in the city of Chigasakai in Kanagawa Prefecture and in 2008 a fourth park was completed in Toyonaka near Osaka.

These public gardens adopt a very simple structure, organised as vast expanses of trees planted in a regular 6.5-metre grid. The scheme has allowed the creation of parks that in spring are bedecked with pink blossoms while in winter they remain bare to reveal an orderly grid. Since cherry trees do not reach full maturity for five years, local communities and citizens have begun helping the sponsors take care of the trees.

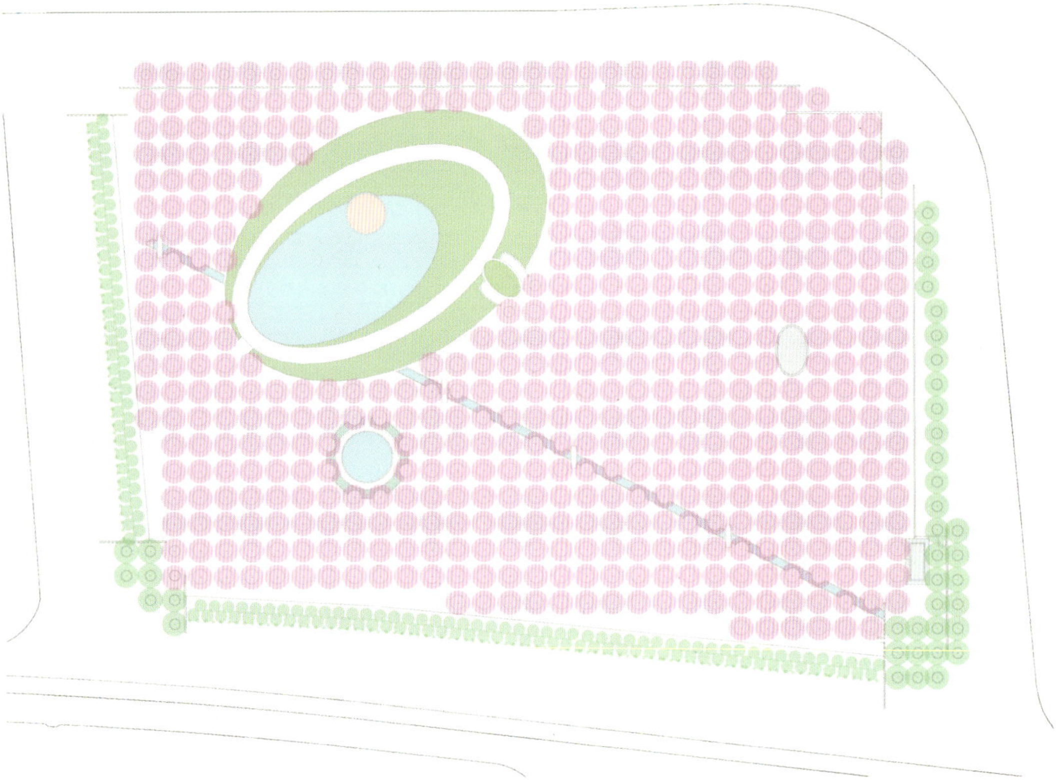

General plan, a regular grid of trees and a decorative canal.

Interfaculty Initiative in Information Studies · Fukutake Hall, the University of Tokyo

Location Bunkyo, Tokyo, Japan
Design 2005–2006
Construction 2006–2008
Site area 402,682 sq m
Building area 1,454 sq m
Total area 4,046 sq m

This building contains an auditorium with 200 seats and was built on the Hongo campus of the University of Tokyo to celebrate the 130th anniversary of the founding of the University.

Characterised by relatively homogenous neo-Gothic buildings, the Hongo campus consists of academic pavilions built in different eras and aligned along a verdant axis. Heavily planted, outdoor spaces are the connective tissue that joins all the structures in the area.

The site for the new building is near the Akamon (Red Gate), the oldest part of the campus, on a piece of greenbelt that separates it from the axis of Hongo-dori Street. In front of this long and narrow site (30 x 5 metres) is a row of 30-metre-high camphor trees that form a subtle border between the campus and the city.

The overall project comprises a rectangular four-storey building that preserves the tree line by extending two of its levels below ground. Initially it was proposed that a building would be completely hidden underground, but the concept was rejected when public pipelines were discovered below the site.

Later, during a second version of the project, a volume with one floor above ground and another below ground was attempted, but the final solution contained one floor above and two floors under ground.

We always wanted the buildings to stay below the height of the trees in order to achieve better integration with the surrounding environment. To complement the horizontal line of the building's overhanging roof, which extends along the entire edifice, a concrete ceiling highlights the character of the park behind the masonry and introduces a void on campus dedicated to meditation.

Tadao Ando

Left: View from the south with the Red Gate in the foreground.

Studio sketch and a view from the east looking towards the campus.

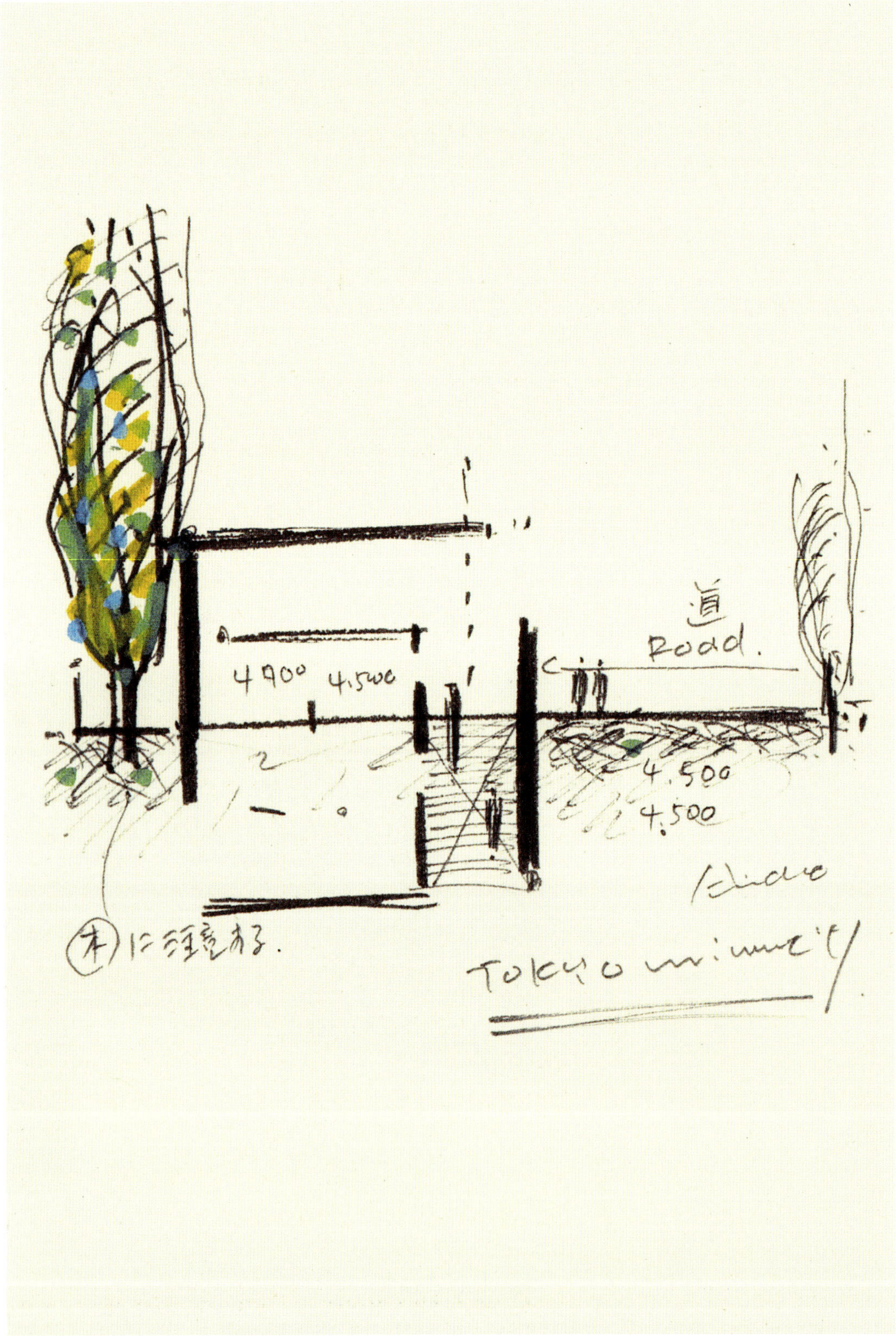

Cross-section sketch.

Right: Prospect of the entrenched system of ramps along the front entrance.

Location Bunkyo, Tokyo, Japan
Design 2007–present
Site area 829 sq m
Total area 1,367 sq m

Founded in 1878 (the first university in the country) and inspired by Western European models, the University of Tokyo has played a vital role in the modernization of Japan.

Under the direction of English architect Josiah Conder, the university's architecture and urbanism faculties boast alumni designers such as Kingo Tatsuno and Chuta Ito. Some leading figures of Japan's architecture scene also came through its ranks including Kenzo Tange, who won international recognition with his Peace Memorial in Hiroshima and the Yoyogi Olympic Gymnasium in Tokyo for the 1964 Olympics. The Library of Architecture was designed to preserve and showcase drawings and documents related to these architects.

The building is located in the middle of a green area adjacent to the Red Gate, opposite Fukutake Hall. Following compositional criteria similar to those applied to the Hall project, the structure consists of two underground levels that make the project as minimally invasive as possible in the surrounding landscape.

To ensure natural light gets into the subterranean levels and still preserve the camphor trees, an irregularly shaped skylight has been added to the Hongo-dori Street side of the site. In addition, stone has been chosen as the material for the masonry in order to establish continuity between the skylight and the environmental context.

The hope is that students will benefit from the vast wealth of drawings and documents stored in the library, using it as both a resource and as encouragement for the realisation of their dreams and aspirations for the future.

Left: Overview of the site and scale model.

Plans of the ground floor, first and second basements and cross-sections.

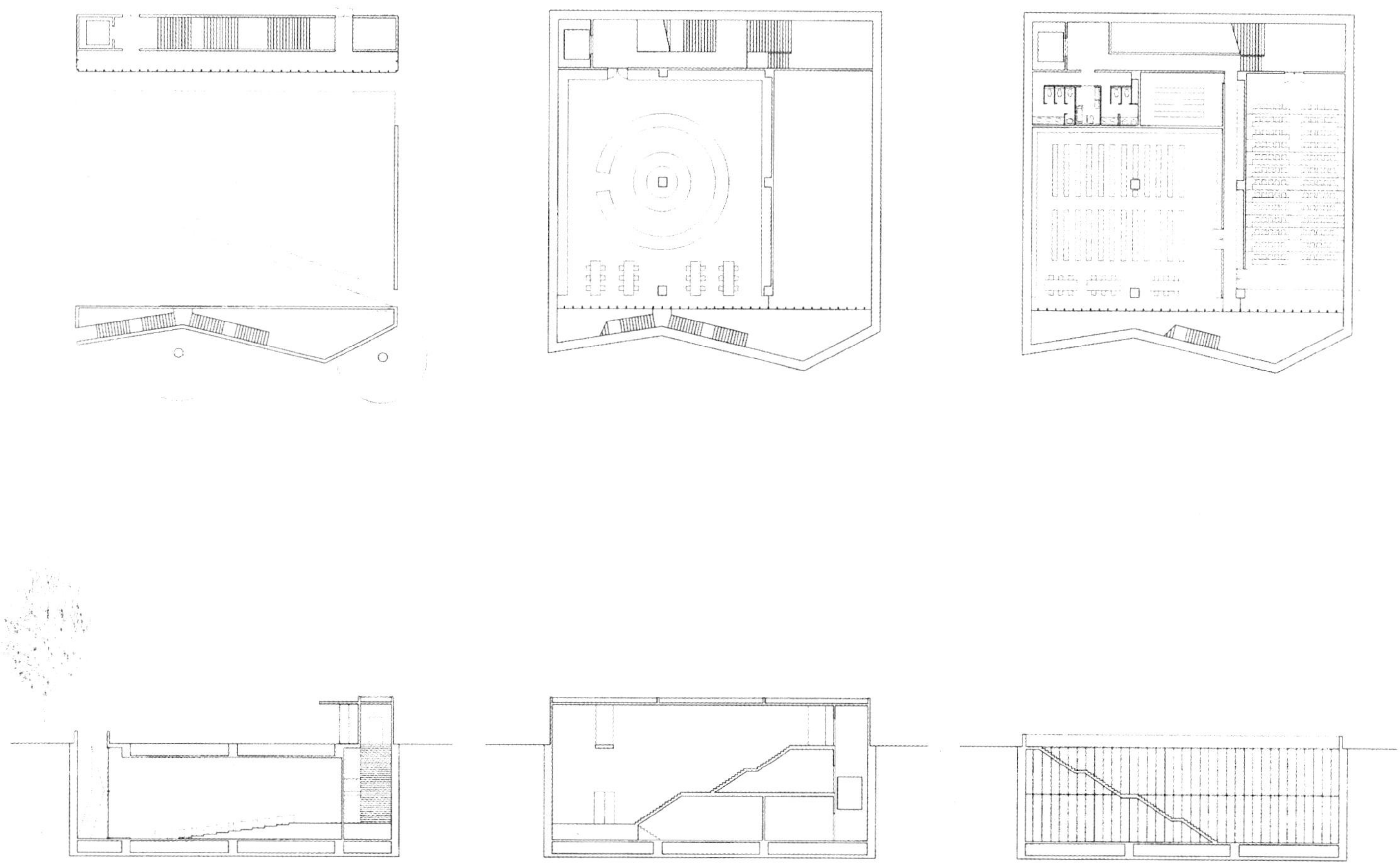

Rendering of the underground parking garage, a site plan and a plan of the ground floor.

Location South Korea
Design 2005–2008
Constuction 2008–present
present present
Site area 70,900 sq m
Building area 4,600 sq m
Total area 9,000 sq m

This museum was commissioned by a South Korean company that wanted to make its art collection available to the public. On a long and narrow lot, the museum was to be cut out of a mountain top at the edge of a vast tourist complex run by the same company.

I was immediately struck by the potential of the site and, having seen the landscape of valleys, I realised it offered me the opportunity to create a world completely isolated from the outside. Inspired by the client's enthusiasm, I decided to take the job.

To capitalise on the length of the lot (about 700 metres), the parking and reception centre were placed relatively close to the road so that the path to the entrance of the building, which is in the middle of the lot, would allow you to admire the view.

In essence, the building consists of a series of four staggered blocks, each in turn consisting of a layered structure of exterior stone walls and exposed concrete interior walls. The exhibition spaces are contained in the inner core. The stone and concrete volumes are separated by corridors pierced with large openings through which visitors can admire the surrounding environment.

The four blocks are interspersed with three void areas: a rectangular void, a triangular

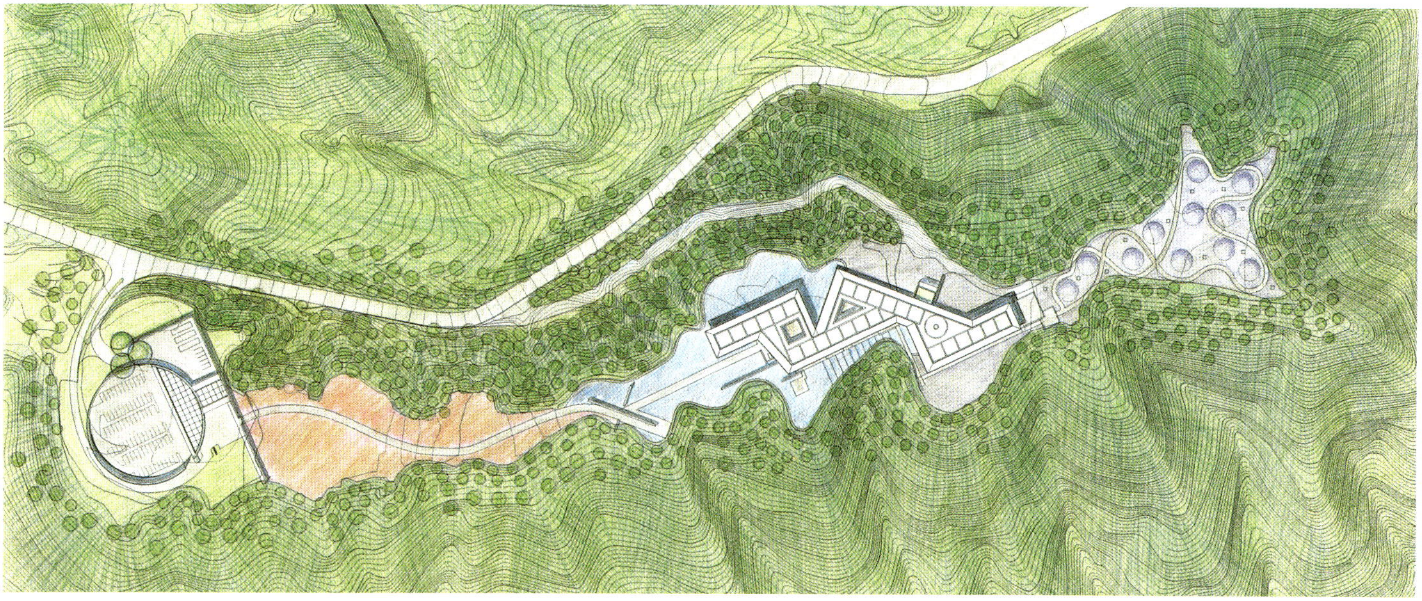

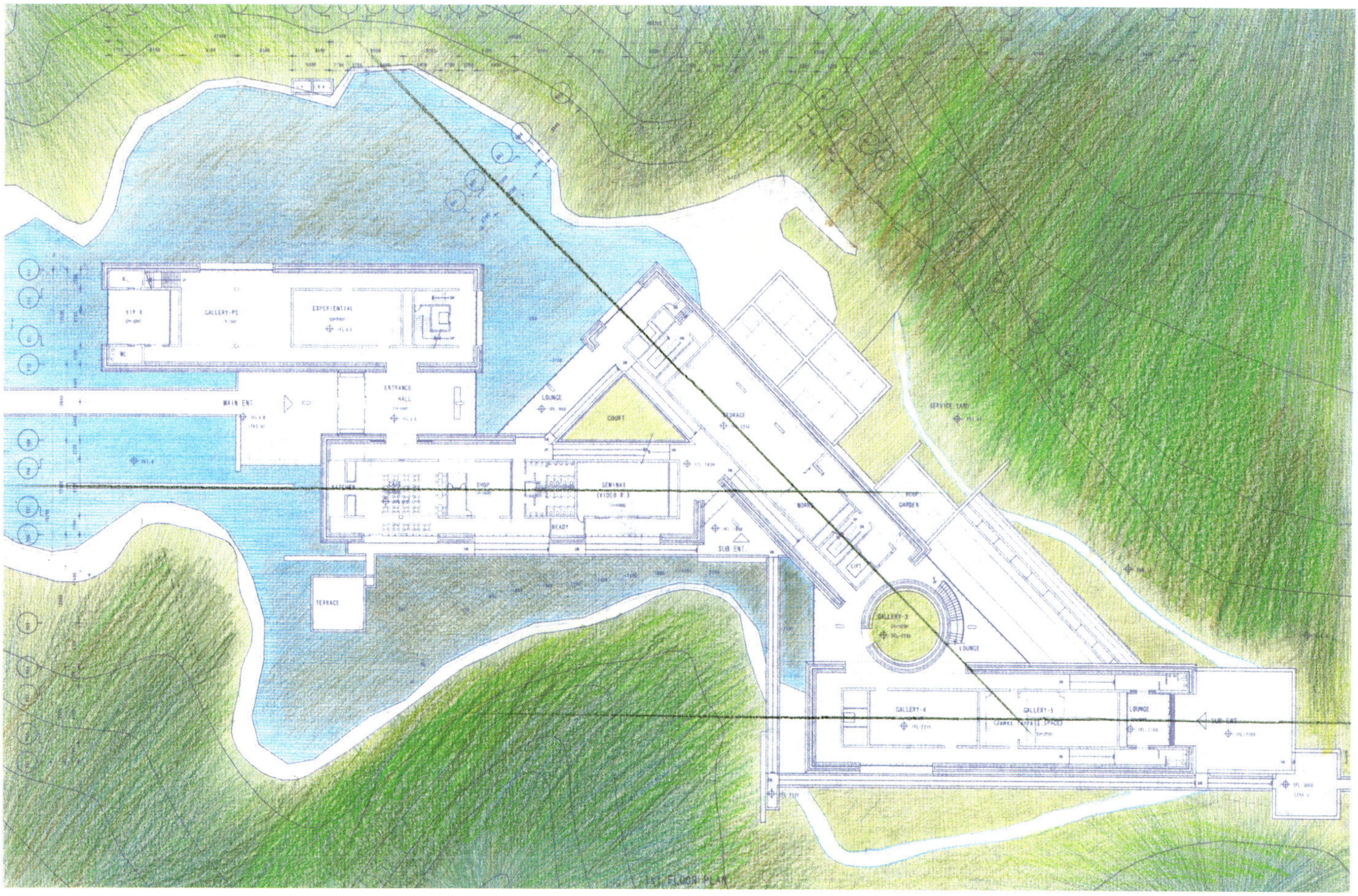

GALLERY-P5
EXPERIENTIAL
ENTRANCE HALL
MAIN ENT.
LOUNGE
COURT
SHOP
SEMINAR (VIDEO R.)
READY
SUB ENT.
TERRACE
SERVICE YARD
ROOF GARDEN
GALLERY-3
LOUNGE
GALLERY-4
GALLERY-5
LOUNGE
SUB ENT.

void and a circular void. Along with the corridors, these void spaces are designed to amplify the experience at the museum, where one can find time to stop and meditate.

In the inner sanctum of the design, a provision has been made for an outdoor museum. A floor made of local stone uses a motif inspired by the shape of an ancient tomb in Kyongju to define a nostalgic and yet new landscape. Exploiting the best position, the morphology of the terrain and indigenous materials and forms it was meant to give the public an opportunity to rediscover the environment, climate and culture of South Korea while also creating a suitable environment for admiring the art on display.

Tadao Ando

Left: View of the main entrance, the lounge and cross-sections.

First floor and elevations to the east and south.

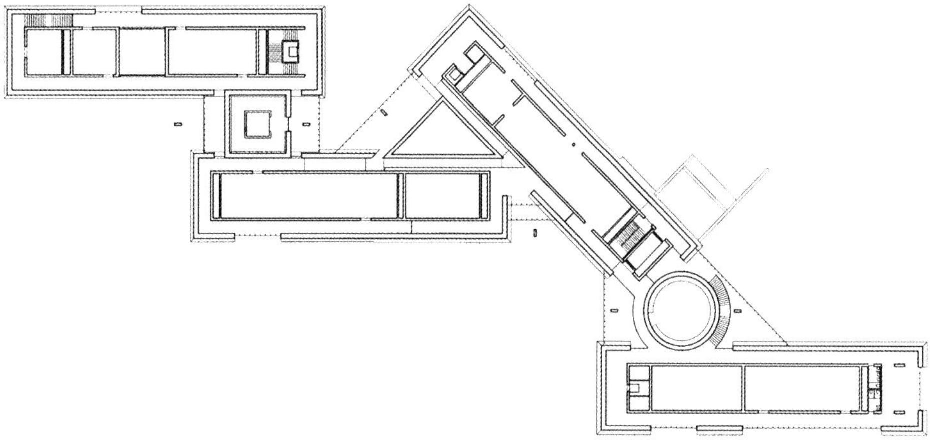

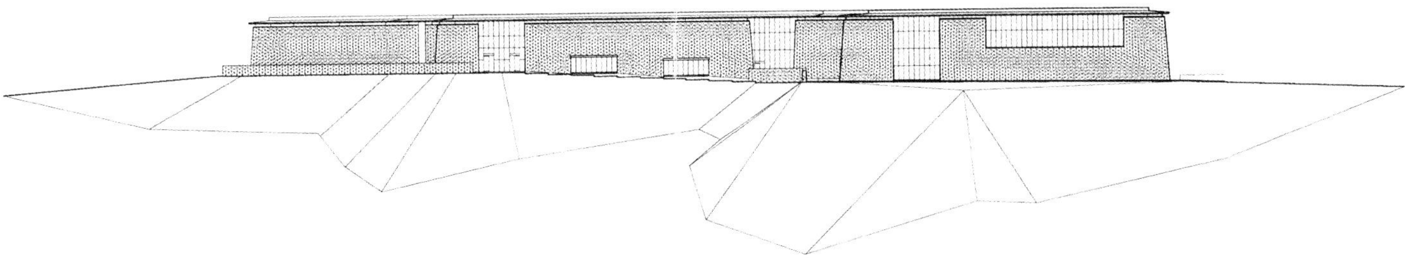

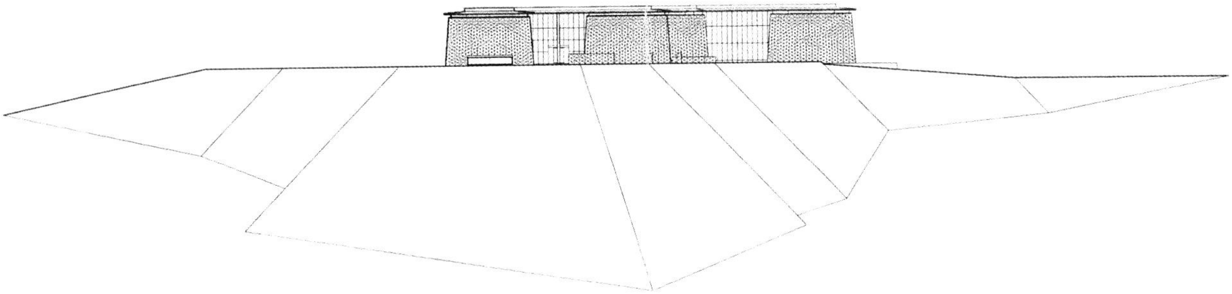

Tokyu Toyoko-Line Shibuya Station

Location Shibuya, Tokyo, Japan
Design 2005–2006
Construction 2006–2008
Site area 15,279 sq m
Building area 27,725 sq m

This project concerns the new metro station in Shibuya where the Tokyo Metro Fukutoshin and Tokyu Toyoko lines pass. Contrary to normal practice, in which the design of the underground station is adapted to the execution of the infrastructure, the two elements here have been developed simultaneously, thus enabling it to achieve a more integrated building design.

As a kind of landed mothership for underground travel , the new metro station has volumes that have been developed completely separately from its concrete shell. At the centre of the composition is an elliptical void enclosed within a large cement egg that penetrates the station. It is based on the second basement level and leads to the tracks located on the fifth basement level. This volume, which evokes the Urban Egg design originally proposed for Nakanoshima in Osaka, is appropriate for the railway hub at Shibuya because it creates a dynamic and highly functional space.

Firstly, it is set in an underground landmark where the central void of the egg allows orientation for commuters in the absence of other reference points related to the building. Secondly, the egg-shaped volume creates a cavity within the former site of the Tokyu Bunka Kaikan line to activate a system of natural ventilation inside the station.

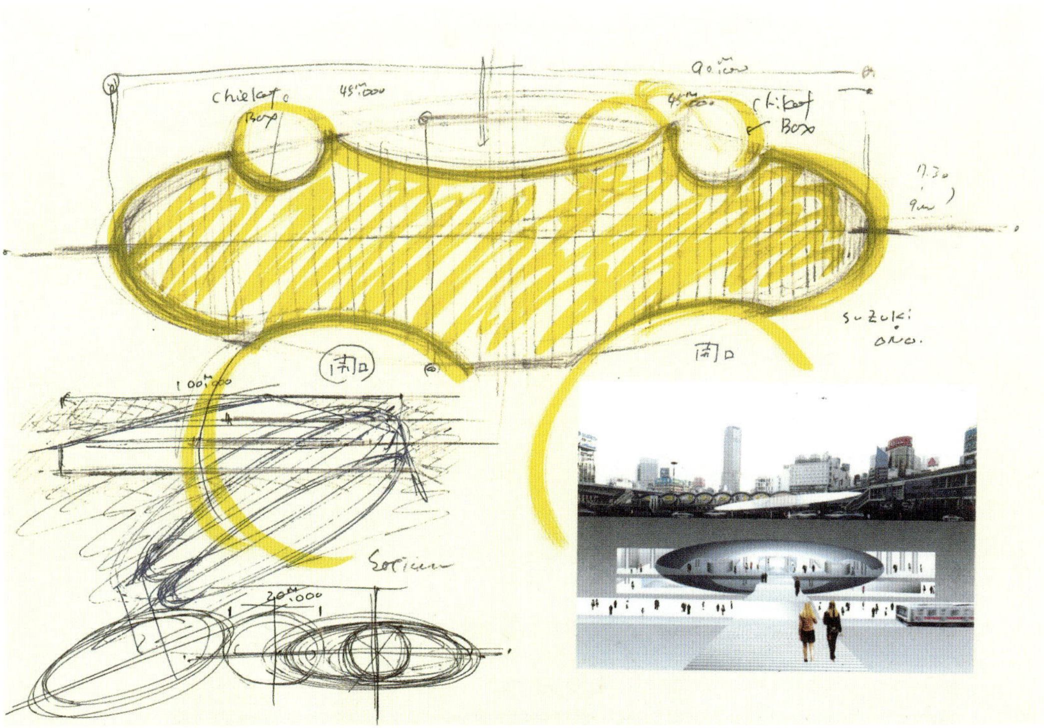

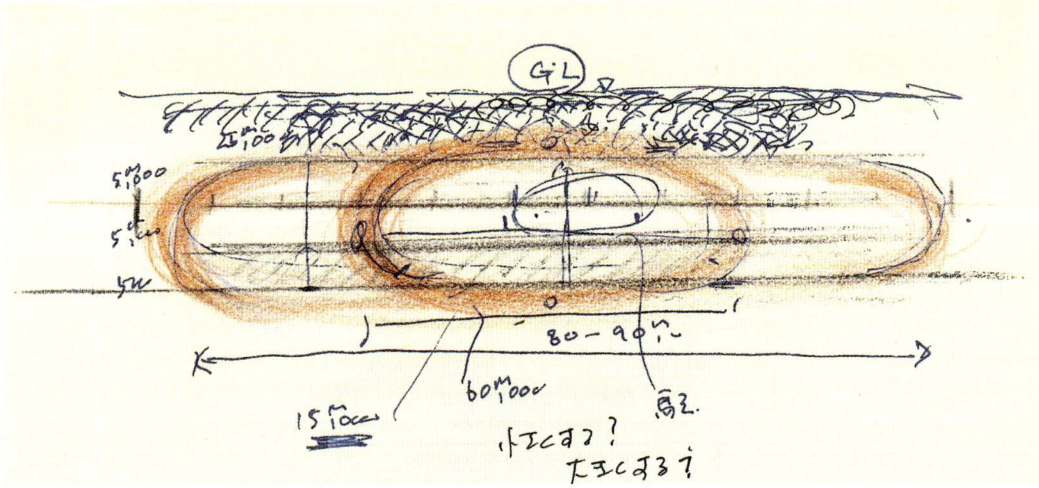

Left: Studio sketches and a digital concept.

The station and its position on the Tokyo subway network.

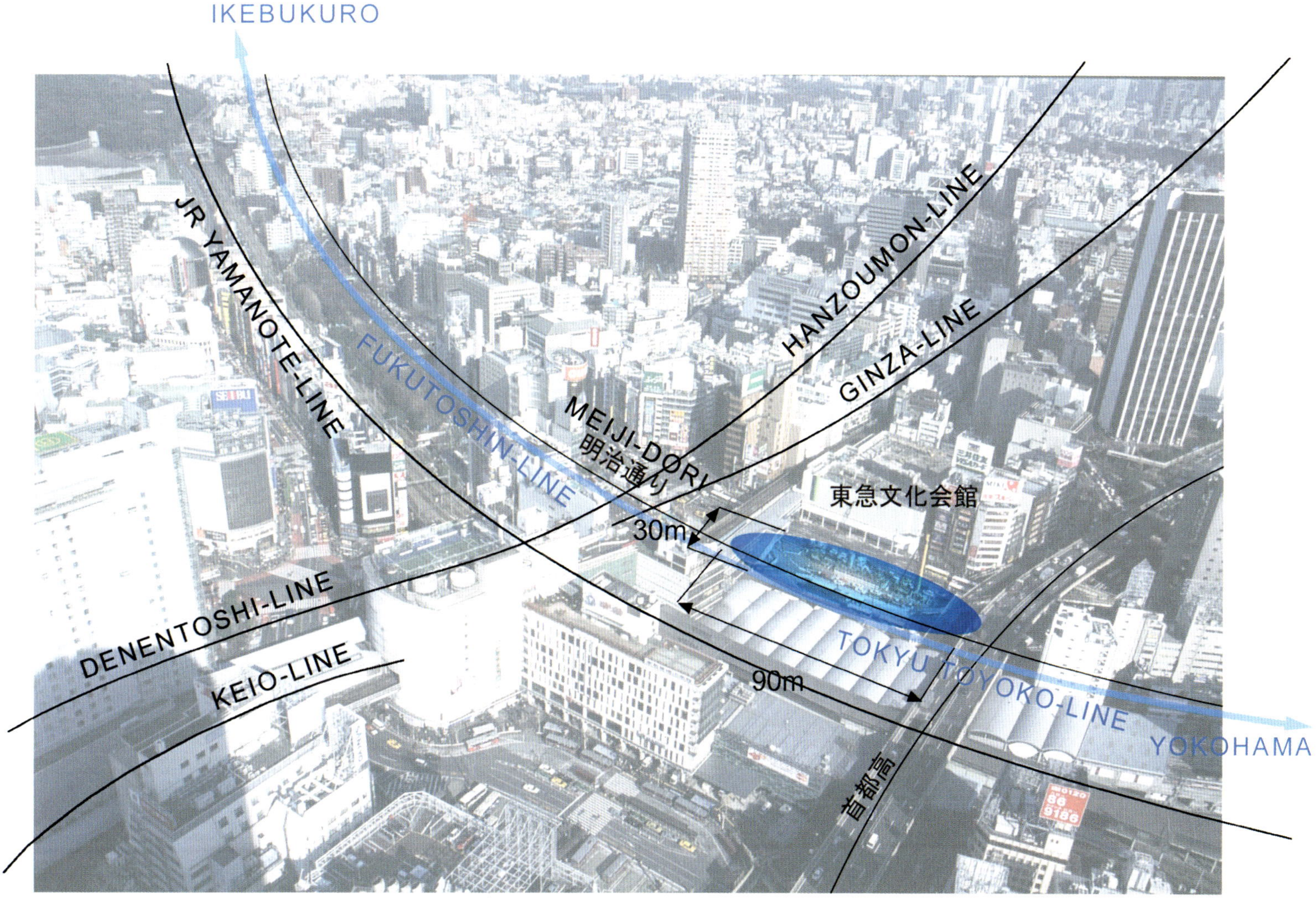

Plans of the first and third basement levels and a diagram of the natural ventilation system.

Opposite page: The full height of the central well.

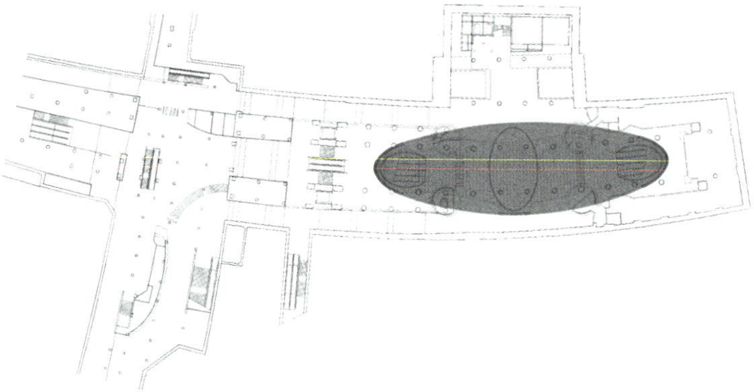

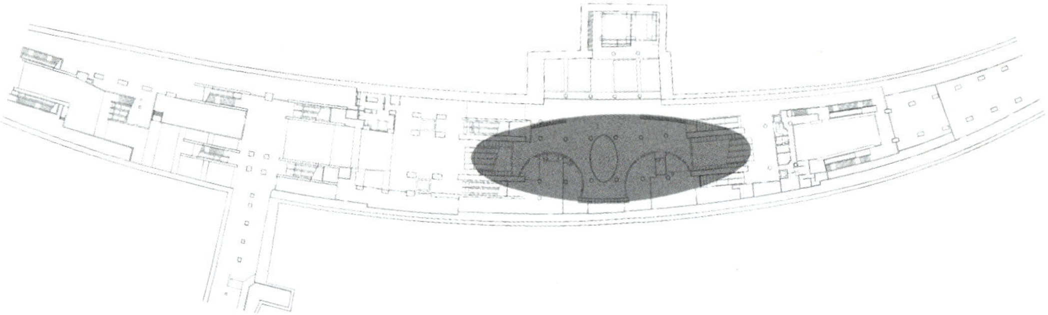

Another reason for the success of this work was the choice of fibre-reinforced concrete for the construction of the egg. The switch from the initial concrete option to fibre-reinforced cement was the result of a simple consideration of the technological situation. It ultimately alleviated the structural challenges associated with operating an air conditioning unit in the cavity of the egg, a feature that would be compatible with the natural ventilation mentioned above.

Being an urban service used daily by hundreds of thousands of people, a sufficiently durable space capable of withstanding the ravages of use was called for, but it also had to provide a sensible solution with regard to current environmental issues.

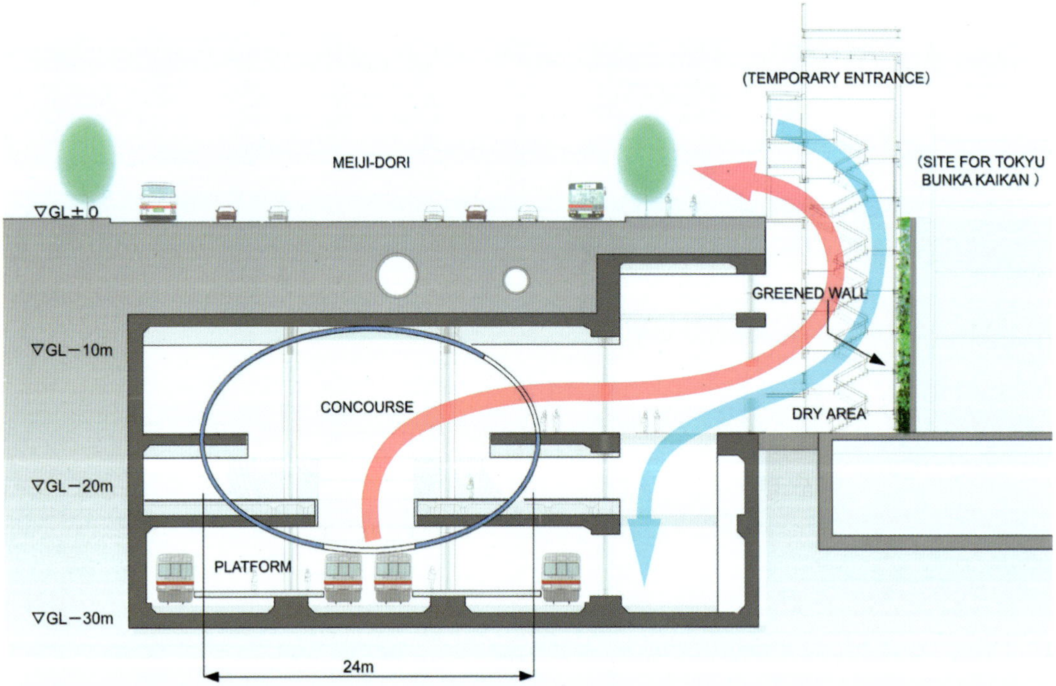

Left: Plans of the fourth, third, second and first floors and basement.

Cross-section perspective.

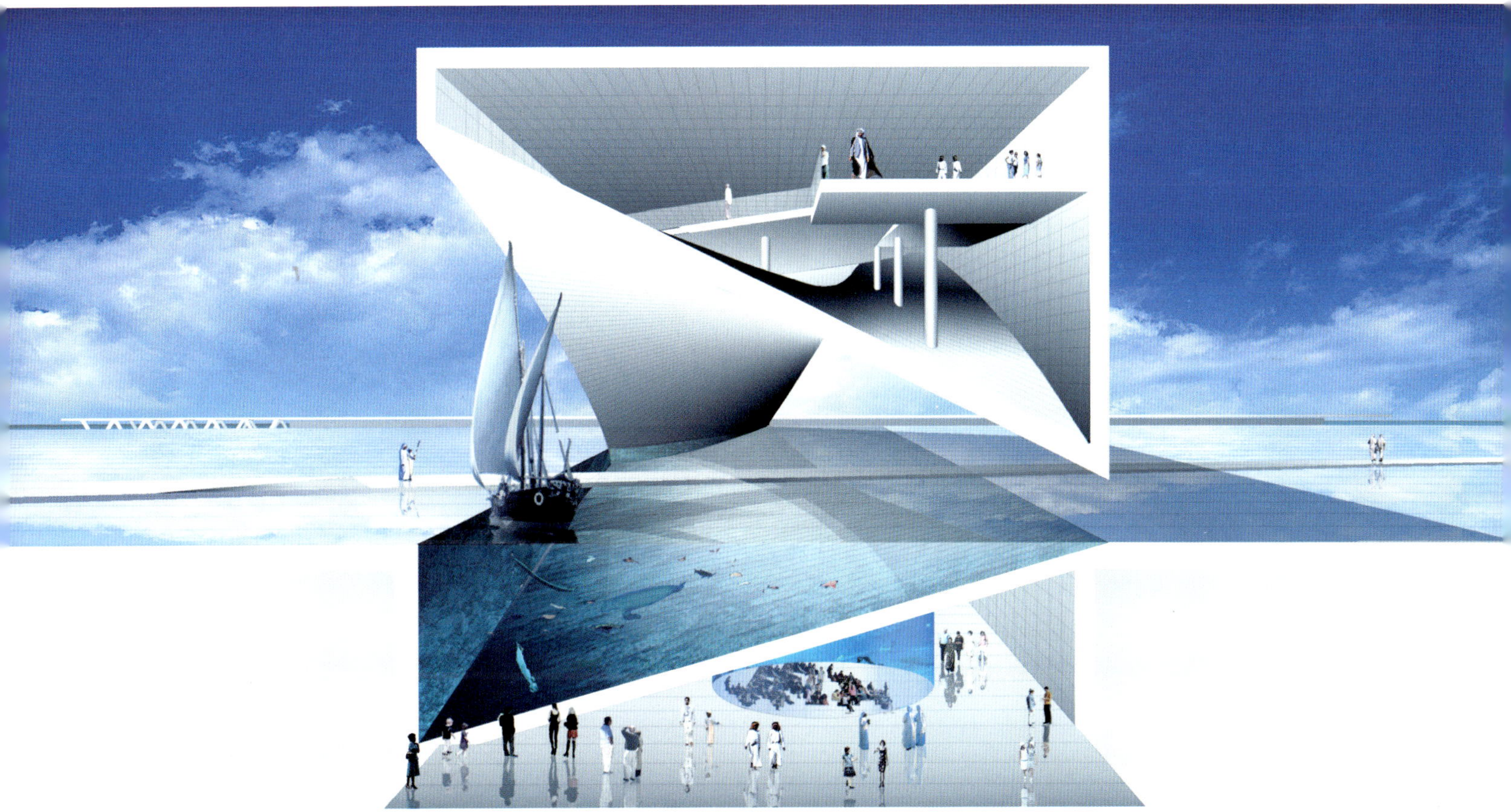

Detail of doorway with steel grille in the façade fronting the Grand Canal.

Right: Aerial view of the imposing complex of Dogana da Mar and Santa Maria della Salute.

Location Venice, Italy
Design 2006-2007
Construction 2007–2009
Site area 2,500 sq m
Building area 2,500 sq m
Total area 3,800 sq m

This project deals with the conversion of the Dogana da Mar into a museum of modern art. The historic state-owned complex was built in the 15th century on the banks overlooking Piazza San Marco.

The competition to design the project was held in Venice and attracted strong participants including Zaha Hadid from the Guggenheim Foundation. To our delight, our firm in conjunction with the François Pinault Foundation (the owner of the Palazzo Grassi) emerged as winners.

La Dogana da Mar, built on the tip of a spit of land in the Dorsoduro district, was originally constructed to cope with the increase in commercial traffic in the San Marco basin, and has been rebuilt several times over the years. Its present form is the result of a restoration carried out in the second half of the 17th century.

Although the La Dogana currently houses a Customs Office and warehouse, it remains a place of particular symbolic value and is loved by the Venetians. The building has a triangular layout that corresponds to the profile of the lot and features red-brick walls.

The project called for the structural consolidation of the unsafe building and the accommodation of a gallery for modern art inside once it had been provided with a system to protect it against rising water levels. Similar to the Palazzo Grassi project, the Punta della Dogana project had to take account of Italian architectural heritage laws. These require a detailed restoration of historic buildings that preserves the original state and prohibits changes to both the interior and exterior. Taking these constraints into account, the problem was once again how to achieve a modern space while developing the potential of the ancient monument – without altering it.

In addition to exposing the brickwork and wooden beams of the ceilings, which had been hidden by previous restorations, some of the few key changes include the introduction of some architectural elements designed to enhance the appeal of the environment and to give greater emphasis to the uniqueness of the building.

As with the cultural centre at the Palazzo Grassi, the Customs Office will be linked by ferries that cross the canal. The lively interactions between modern art and architectural heritage that abound in the city will offer the public a unique experience.

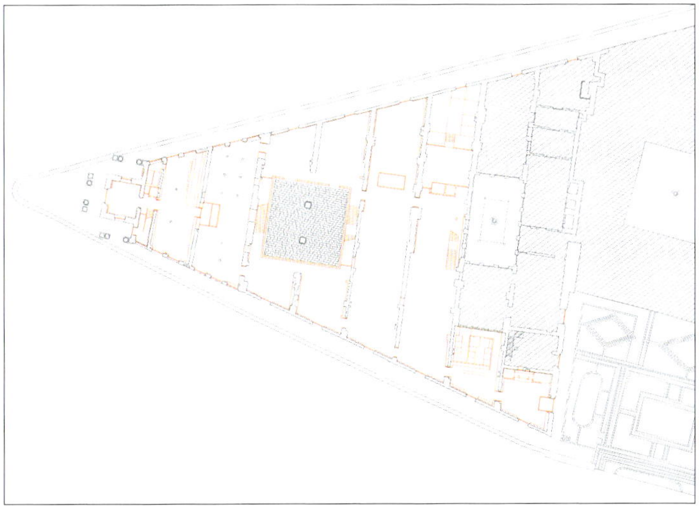

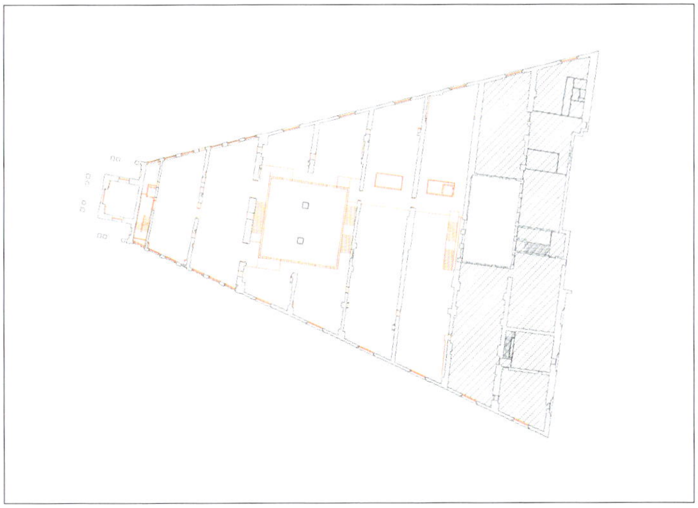

Interior views of the exhibition spaces formed from the floors surrounding the central court.

The concrete walls that enclose the central court provide a backdrop for Rudolf Stingel's oil on canvas, Untitled (Alpino 1976), *2006.*

Interior views of the central court.

Right: The full-height is open to the roof, which leads to a series of exhibition halls.

View of the exhibition space on the upper level of the last of the warehouses in the Punta della Dogana complex and a detail of a window casing overlooking the Giudecca Canal.

SITE

1995
Meditation Space, UNESCO, Paris, France

1997
House in Chicago, United States
TOTO Seminar House, Awaji, Hyogo
Daylight Museum (Hiroki Oda Museum), Hino, Shiga

1999
Rokko Housing III, Kobe, Hyogo

2000
Awaji-Yumebutai (Awaji Island Project) Awaji, Hyogo
Komyo-ji Temple, Saijo, Ehime
FABRICA (Benetton Communication Research Centre), Treviso, Italy

2001
Pulitzer Foundation for the Arts, St. Louis, United States
Armani / Teatro, Milan, Italy
Sayamaike Historical Museum, Osaka-Sayama, Osaka
Shiba Ryotaro Memorial Museum, Higashi-Osaka, Osaka

2002
Hyogo Prefectural Museum of Art, Kobe, Hyogo
The International Library of Children's Literature, Ueno, Tokyo
Piccadilly Gardens Regeneration, Manchester, UK
Modern Art Museum of Fort Worth, United States

2003
Noma Kindergarten, Ito, Shizuoka
4 x 4 House, Kobe, Hyogo

2004
Chichu Art Museum, Naoshima, Kagawa
Langen Foundation / Hombroich, Neuss, Germany

2005
hhstyle.com / casa, Shibuya, Tokyo
Iwaki Museum of Picture Books for Children, Iwaki, Fukushima

2006
Omotesando Hills (Omotesando Regeneration Project), Shibuya, Tokyo
Palazzo Grassi, Venice, Italy

2007
21_21 Design Sight, Minato, Tokyo

2008
Interfaculty Initiative in Information Studies · Fukutake Hall, the University of Tokyo, Bunkyo, Tokyo
Tokyu Toyoko-Line Shibuya Station, Shibuya, Tokyo

2009
Punta della Dogana Contemporary Art Centre, Venice, Italy

Representative projects

1988
Nakanoshima Project II (Urban Egg and Space Strata), Osaka

2001
Ground Zero Project, New York

Bibliography

1981
Tadao Ando, edited by Aiko Hasegawa, monographic issue of "SD", No. 201 (with essays from: Yukio Futagawa, Sei Kiyoshi Takeyama, Fumitaka Nishizawa, Fumihiko Maki, Tadao Ando); fully reprinted in *Gendai no Kenchikuka Tadao Ando*, Tokyo 1982.

1982
Tadao Ando, edited by Shozo Baba, monographic issue of "The Japan Architect", No. 301 (with essays from: Takamitsu Azuma, Hiroshi Watanabe, Tadao Ando).
AA.VV., *Gendai no Kenchikuka Tadao Ando*, edited by Kobun Ito, Kajima Institute Publishing, Tokyo (with essays from: Yukio Futagawa, Sei Kiyoshi Takeyama, Fumihiko Maki, Fumitaka Nishizawa, Tadao Ando).
AA.VV., *Tadao Ando. Obras y Proyectos 1972–1982*, edited by Alberto Campo Baeza, exhibition catalogue, Museo Espanol de Arte Contemporáneo, Madrid (with essays from: Alberto Campo Baeza, Kenneth Frampton, Yukio Futagawa, Fumihiko Maki).
AA.VV., *Tadao Ando Minimalism*, Electa Moniteur, Paris (with essays from: François Chaslin, Arata Isozaki, Vittorio Gregotti, Hiroshi Watanabe, Kiyoshi Takayama, Jean-Luc Dumesnil).

1983
Tadao Ando, Fumitaka Nishizawa, *Tadao Ando no detail genzushu*, Shokoku-sha, Tokyo.

1984
AA.VV., *Tadao Ando. Buildings, Projects, Writings*, edited by Kenneth Frampton, Rizzoli International Publications, New York (with essays from: Kenneth Frampton, Koji Taki, Toshio Okumura, Tadao Ando).

1985
AA.VV., *Tadao Ando. Edificios, Proyectos, Escritos*, edited by Kenneth Frampton, Editorial Gustavo Gili, Barcelona (with essays from: Kenneth Frampton, Koji Taki, Toshio Okumura, Tadao Ando).
Tadao Ando, edited by Frank Lowe, monographic issue of "The Architecture Show", December (with essays from: Masao Furuyama, Frank Lowe, Tadao Ando).
Emilio Ambasz, *Tadao Ando: Intercepting Light*, exhibition catalogue Urban Centre, New York.
Riichi Miyake, *Tadao Ando*, edited by Reinhard Gieselmann, monographic issue of "Prolegomena", No. 50.

1986
AA.VV., *Tadao Ando Chohatsusuru Hako*, edited by Kazuo Ogura, Maruzen, Tokyo (with essays from: Gozo Yoshimasu, Juro Kara, Tadao Ando).
AA.VV., *Tadao Ando Breathing Geometry*, edited by Richard Burdett, exhibition catalogue, 9H Gallery, London (with essays from: Kenneth Frampton, Richard Weston, Tadao Ando).
Tadao Ando Rokko Housing, edited by Mirko Zardini, Quaderni di Casabella, Electa, Milan (with essays from: Vittorio Gregotti, Riichi Miyake, Tadao Ando).

1987
Kenneth Frampton, *Tadao Ando*, edited by Yukio Futagawa, GA Architect 8, A.D.A. EDITA, Tokyo.

1988
Tadao Ando, edited by Shozo Baba, monographic issue of "The Japan Architect", No. 372 (with essays from: Riichi Miyake and Tadao Ando).
AA.VV., *Ando par Ando – Ando by Ando*, edited by François Labbé, Serge Salat, exhibition catalogue, Arc en Rêve, Bordeaux (with essays from: Tadao Ando, Mario Botta, Emilio Ambasz).
Giordano Tironi, *Tadao Ando, Ombres portées*, Halle SUD, Geneva.
Tadao Ando, edited by François Chaslin, monographic issue of "L'Architecture d'aujourd'hui", No. 255 (with essays from: Kenneth Frampton, Henri Ciriani, Yoichi Iijima, Tadao Ando).

1989
Tadao Ando, *Tabi – India, Turkey and Okinawa*, Sumai Library Publishing Company, Tokyo.
Tadao Ando, edited by Kobun Ito, monographic issue of "SD", No. 300 (with essays from: Peter Eisenman, Jackie Kestenbaum, Masao Furuyama, Katsuhiro Kobayashi, Sei Kiyoshi Takeyama, Norihiko Dan, Tadao Ando); fully reprinted in *Gendai no Kenchikuka Tadao Ando II 1981–1989*, Tokyo 1990.
Akira Asada, *Raika Headquarters Building Process By Tadao Ando*, Raika Co., Osaka.
AA.VV., *Tadao Ando. The Yale Studio & Current Works*, edited by David Morton, Rizzoli International Publications, New York (with essays from: Peter Eisenman, Kenneth Frampton, Tadao Ando, George T. Kunihiro).

1990
AA.VV., *Gendai no Kenchikuka Tadao Ando II 1981–1989*, edited by Kobun Ito, Kajima Institute Publishing, Tokyo (with essays from: Peter Eisenman, Jackie Kestenbaum, Masao Furuyama, Katsuhiro Kobayashi, Sei Kiyoshi Takeyama, Norihiko Dan, Tadao Ando).
AA.VV., *Tadao Ando et la maison Koshino*, edited by Pascal Bertrand, Mardaga Éditeur, Liège (with essays from: Pascal Bertrand, Augustin Berque, Daniel Treiber, Tadao Ando).
AA.VV., *Tadao Ando: Das Haus Koshino*, edited by Pascal Bertrand, Ernst Wasmuth Verlag, Tübingen (with essays from: Pascal Bertrand, Augustin Berque, Daniel Treiber, Tadao Ando).
AA.VV., *Tadao Ando Sketches – Zeichnungen*, edited by Werner Blaser, Birkhäuser Verlag AG, Basel (with essays from: Mario Botta, Werner Blaser, Tadao Ando).
Tadao Ando, edited by Fernando Marquez Cecilia, Richard C. Levene, monographic issue of "El Croquis", No. 44 (with essays from: José L. González Cobelo, Alain Bretagnolle, Frédéric Schoeller, Tadao Ando).
Tadao Ando, Masato Kawamukai, Mirko Zardini, *Tadao Ando*, Architectural Monographs 14, Academy Editions / St. Martin's Press, London / New York.

1991
Tadao Ando, edited by Takeshi Ishido, monographic issue of "The Japanese Architect", No. 1 (with essays from: Renzo Piano, Paul Andreu, Katsuhiro Kobayashi, Tadao Ando).
Tadao Ando, Peter Eisenman, *Tadao Ando Details*, edited by Yukio Futagawa, A.D.A. EDITA, Tokyo.
Tadao Ando, Kenneth Frampton, Stuart Wrede, *Tadao Ando*, exhibition catalogue, The Museum of Modern Art, New York.
AA.VV., *Tadao Ando Dormant Lines*, edited by Joseph Ryan, Rizzoli International Publications, New York (with essays from: Darell Wayne Fields, Jose Rafael Moneo, Kazuyuki Negishi, Katsuhiro Kobayashi).

1992
Frank O. Gehry, Issey Miyake, Makoto Ueda, Keiji Usami, *Tadao Ando. Beyond Horizons in Architecture*, exhibition catalogue, Tadao Ando Exhibition Committee, Tokyo / Osaka.
Tadao Ando, *Ando Tadao no Toshi Hoko*, edited by Hiroyuki Kushida, Magazine House, Tokyo.

Tadao Ando, edited by Kobun Ito, monographic issue of "SD", No. 333 (with essays from: Emilio Ambasz, Toyo Ito, Kazukiyo Matsuba, Yuzuru Tominaga, Atsushi Kitagawara, Tadao Ando), reprinted in *Unbuilt Project. Gendai no Kenchikuka Tadao Ando III*, Tokyo 1993.

1993
Tom Heneghan, *Tadao Ando 1988–1993*, edited by Yukio Futagawa, GA Architect 12, A.D.A. EDITA, Tokyo.
Tadao Ando, monographic issue of "Geijutsu Shincho", No. 525
Tadao Ando: Rokko Housing I, II, III, edited by Yasuhiro Teramatsu, monographic issue of "JA Library", No. 3 (with essays from: Daniel Libeskind, Hajime Yatsuka, Tadao Ando).
AA.VV., *Unbuilt Project. Gendai no Kenchikuka Tadao Ando III*, edited by Kobun Ito, Kajima Institute Publishing, Tokyo (with essays from: Emilio Ambasz, Kazukiyo Matsuba, Yuzuru Tominaga, Atsushi Kitagawara, Toyo Ito, Tadao Ando).
Günter Nitschke, *From Shinto to Ando*, Academy Editions, London.
Tadao Ando, edited by Richard C. Levene, Fernando Marquez Cecilia, monographic issue of "El Croquis", No. 58 (with essays from: Hajime Yatsuka, Jackie Kestenbaum, Tadao Ando).
AA.VV., *Tadao Ando*, edited by Alain Guiheux, exhibition catalogue, Centre Georges Pompidou, Paris (with essays from: Alain Guiheux, Yoichi Iijima, Tadao Ando.
Masao Furuyama, *Tadao Ando. Kabe no Tankyu – Studies on the Walls*, Artemis, Zürich.

1994
Masao Furuyama, *Tadao Ando. Kabe no Tankyu – Studies on the Walls*, Kajima Institute Publishing, Tokyo.
Masao Furuyama, *Tadao Ando. Kabe no Tankyu – Studies on the Walls*, Editorial Gustavo Gili, Barcelona.
Tadao Ando 1983–1992, edited by Richard C. Levene, Fernando Marquez Cecilia, monographic issue of "El Croquis", No. 44 +58 (with essays from: Hajime Yatsuka, Jackie Kestenbaum, Tadao Ando).
Tadao Ando, Yoichi Iijima, *Tadao Ando. Más álla de los horizontes en arquitectura*, exhibition catalogue, Ministerio de Obras Públicas, Transportes y Medio Ambiente, Madrid.
Tadao Ando, Yoichi Iijima, *Tadao Ando. Més enllà dels horitzons en l'arquitectura*, exhibition catalogue, Ministerio de Obras Publicas, Transportes y Medio Ambiente, Barcelona.
Francesco Dal Co, *Tadao Ando. Le opere, gli scritti, la critica*, Electa, Milan.
Concrete Poetics: Reconsidering Tadao Ando, edited by Cynthia C. Davidson, monographic issue of "Any", No. 6 (with essays from: Hiroshi Maruyama, Lynne Breslin, Fredric Jameson, Frederic Levrat, Frank O. Gehry).

1995
Tadao Ando, Yoshio Futagawa, *Tadao Ando*, edited by Yukio Futagawa, GA Document Extra 01, A.D.A. EDITA, Tokyo.
Tadao Ando, edited by Junichi Ishikawa, monographic issue of "The Sun", No. 413 (with essays from: Tomomi Muramatsu, Takeshi Umehara, Makoto Ueda, Kazukiyo Matsuba, Tadao Ando).
Riichi Miyake, *Suntory Museum "Tempozan"*, Kajima Institute Publishing, Tokyo.
AA.VV., *Tadao Ando no Yumekoso*, exhibition catalogue, Asahi Shimbun Sha, Tokyo (with essays from: Yoichi Iijima, David Stewart, Young Il Lee, Paul Goldberger, Tadao Ando).
Masao Furuyama, *Tadao Ando. Kabe no Tankyu – Studies on the Walls*, Birkhäuser Verlag AG, Basel.
Francesco Dal Co, *Tadao Ando. Complete Works*, Phaidon Press Limited, London.
Rudolf Klein, *Architect between East and West: Tadao Ando*, Pont Publishers, Budapest.

1996
Tadao Ando, *Jiyu ni ikiru*, Kyowa hakko kogyo, Tokyo.
Tadao Ando, Yasuyuki Takaguchi, *Houses*, Sumai Library Publishing Company, Tokyo.
Riichi Miyake, *Tadao Ando: Naoshima Contemporary Art Museum*, Kajima Institute Publishing, Tokyo.
Kazukiyo Matsuba, *Ando, Architect*, Kodansha International, Tokyo.
Philip Drew, *Church on the Water, Church of the Light*, Phaidon Press Limited, London.
Tom Heneghan, Richard Pare, *Tadao Ando. The Colours of Light*, Phaidon Press Limited, London.

1997
Tadao Ando, Francesco Dal Co, *Tadao Ando Details 2*, edited by Yukio Futagawa, A.D.A. EDITA, Tokyo.
Francesco Dal Co, *Tadao Ando. Complete Works*, Phaidon Press Limited, London, paperback.
Masao Furuyama, *Tadao Ando. Kabe no Tankyu – Studies on the Walls*, Zanichelli Editore, Bologna.
Masao Furuyama, *Tadao Ando. Kabe no Tankyu – Studies on the Walls*, Livraria Martins Fontes Editora, São Paulo.
Philip Jodidio, *Tadao Ando*, Taschen GmbH, Cologne.

1998
Yoichi Iijima, *Tadao Ando Prints 1998*, exhibition catalogue, Watanuki Inc., Tokyo.
Anatxu Zabalbeascoa, *Architecture monograph. Tadao Ando*, Editorial Gustavo Gili, Barcelona.
Tadao Ando, William J.R. Curtis, *Beyond Minimalism: The Architecture of Tadao Ando*, exhibition catalogue, Royal Academy of Arts, London.
Kazukiyo Matsuba, *Ando, Architect*, edited by David B. Stewart, Kodansha International, Tokyo / New York.
Tadao Ando, Lee Youngll, *Tadao Ando 1975–1998*, exhibition catalogue, C3 Group, Seoul.

1999
Tadao Ando, *Lectures on Architecture. Tadao Ando Lectures at the University of Tokyo*, University of Tokyo Press, Tokyo.
Tadao Ando, China Architecture & Building Press, Beijing.
Tadao Ando, *Orte der Kontemplation: Places for Contemplation*, exhibition catalogue, Galerie Aedes East, Berlin.
Tadao Ando, Steffen Barth, Werner Blaser, *Museum der Weltkulturen im Rhein*, Vice Versa Verlag, Berlin.
Yann Nussaume, *Tadao Andô et la question du milieu*, Editions Le Moniteur, Paris.

2000
Tadao Ando, edited by Toshiaki Shimizu, monographic issue of "The Sun", No. 472, (with essays from: Karl Lagerfeld, Yoichi Iijima, Jean Nouvel, Taichi Sakaiya, Norio Oga, Noboru Tsujihara, Kotaro Higuchi, Momoyo Kaijima, Oliviero Toscani).
Tadao Ando, William J.R. Curtis, *Tadao Ando 1994–2000*, edited by Yukio Futagawa, GA Architect 16, A.D.A. EDITA, Tokyo.
AA.VV., *Awaji Yumebutai. Tadao Ando*, edited by Takeshi Ishido, Shinkenchiku-sha, Tokyo (with essays from: Tadao Ando, Hiroyuki Suzuki, Hidenobu Jinnai, Tom Heneghan).

Tsuyoshi Hiramatsu, *Hikari no Kyokai. Tadao Ando no Genba*, edited by Takeshi Ishido, Kenchiku Shiryo Kenkyusho, Tokyo.
Tadao Ando 1983–2000, edited by Fernando Marquez Cecilia, Richard C. Levene, monographic issue of "El Croquis", No. 44 + 58 (with essays from: William J.R. Curtis and Tadao Ando).
Marina Fumo, Francesco Polverino, *Tadao Ando. Architettura e tecnica*, Clean Edizioni, Napoli.
Tom Heneghan, Richard Pare, *Tadao Ando. The Colours of Light*, mini edition, Phaidon Press Limited, London / Berlin / Paris.
Tadao Ando, *Lectures on Architecture. Tadao Ando Lectures at the University of Tokyo*, Kukje Publishing, Seoul.

2001
AA.VV., *Tadao Ando Museum Guide*, Bijutsu Shuppan-Sha, Tokyo (with essays from: Makoto Ueda, Akira Tatehata, Shigenobu Kimura, Riichi Miyake, Tadayasu Sakai, Shigeo Anzai, Tadashi Kawamata, Tadao Ando).
Tadao Ando, *Losing Battles, After Battles. Tadao Ando: Lectures at the University of Tokyo 2,* University of Tokyo Press, Tokyo.
Tadao Ando, *Losing Battles, After Battles. Tadao Ando: Lectures at The University of Tokyo 2*, Kachi Publishing, Seoul.
Tadao Ando, monographic issue of "Geijutsu Shincho", No. 621; entirely reprinted in *Le Corbusier no Yukiaru Jutaku*, Tokyo 2004.
Werner Blaser, *Tadao Ando. Architektur der Stille*, Birkhäuser Verlag AG, Basel.
Francesco Dal Co, *Tadao Ando. As obras, os textos, a crítica*, Dinalivro, Lisboa.
William J.R. Curtis, *Abstractions in Space: Tadao Ando, Ellsworth Kelly, Richard Serra*, The Pulitzer Foundation for the Arts, St. Louis.
Cara McCarty, *Tadao Ando Architect*, exhibition catalogue, St. Louis Art Museum, St. Louis.

2002
Inside Outside, edited by Yoshida, Nobuyuki, monographic issue of "A+U: Architecture and Urbanism", No. 378 (with essays from: Paul Goldberger and Tadao Ando).
Inside Outside, by Yoshida Nobuyuki, monographic issue of "AU: Architecture and Urbanism", ed. Chinese (with essays from: Paul Goldberger and Tadao Ando).
The Grand Tour with Ando, monographic issue of "Casa Brutus", No. 30.
Tadao Ando, *Kenchiku ni Yume wo Mita*, Japan Broadcast Publishing, Tokyo.
Tadao Ando, Michael Auping, *Seven Interviews with Tadao Ando*, Modern Art Museum of Fort Worth, Fort Worth.
Tadao Ando, *Ando Tadao no Toshi Hoko*, Garden City Publishing, Taipei.
Lorenzo Dall'Olio, *Tadao Ando. Antinomie senza contrasto*, Testo & Immagine, Torino.

2003
AA.VV., *Tadao Ando. Regeneration, Surroundings and Architecture*, exhibition catalogue, Delphi Inc., Tokyo (with essays from: Hiroyuki Suzuki, Yoichi Iijima, Yukio Ninagawa, Tadao Ando).
Tadao Ando, *Tadao Ando Details 3*, edited by Yukio Futagawa, A.D.A. EDITA, Tokyo.
The Grand Tour with Ando 2, monographic issue of "Casa Brutus", No. 42.
Paco Asensio, *Tadao Ando*, Archipocket, Loft Publications, Barcelona.
Tadao Ando, edited by Jianguo Wang, Xiaojian Ye, monographic issue, "World Architecture", No. 156.
Kenneth Frampton, *Light and Water*, The Monacelli Press, New York.
Tadao Ando, Marianne Langen, Marion Taube, *Langen Foundation: Tadao Ando*, exhibition catalogue, Galerie Aedes East, Berlin.
Tadao Ando, *Lectures on Architecture. Tadao Ando Lectures at the University of Tokyo*, China Architecture & Building Press, Beijing.

2004
Tadao Ando, *Le Corbusier no Yukiaru Jutaku*, Shinchosha Publishing, Tokyo.
Philip Jodidio, *Ando Complete Works*, Taschen GmbH, Cologne.

2005
Tadao Ando, Architecture Method – Kenchiku Shuho, edited by Yukio Futagawa, A.D.A. EDITA, Tokyo.
Tadao Ando, Werner Blaser, *Nähe des Fernen – The Nearness of the Distant*, Niggli Verlag AG, Sulgen, Zürich.
Tadao Ando, Sabine Langen-Crasemann, Andreas Rossmann, *Langen Foundation: ein Kunst- und Ausstellungshaus von Tadao Ando*, Langen Foundation, Neuss.
Tadao Ando, Weidong Ma, *The Grand Tour of Tadao Ando's Architecture*, edited by Weidong Ma, Ningbo Publishing House, Shanghai.
Tadao Ando, Hiroyuki Suzuki, *Tadao Ando*, edited by Weidong Ma, Ningbo Publishing House, Shanghai.

2006
Tadao Ando, Philip Jodidio, *Tadao Ando at Naoshima*, Rizzoli International Publications, New York.
Tadao Ando, *Ando Tadao no Toshi Hoko*, edited by Weidong Ma, Ningbo Publishing House, Shanghai.
The Complete Grand Tour with Ando, special issue of "Casa Brutus".
Tadao Ando, François Chaslin, Enrico Navarra, *Tadao Ando*, Galerie Enrico Navarra / Galerie Patrick Seguin, Paris.
Masao Furuyama, *Tadao Ando. The Geometry of Human Space*, Taschen GmbH, Cologne.

2007
Tadao Ando, *Hard-Fought Process – Akusen Kuto*, Tadao Ando Exhibition Committee, Osaka.
Tadao Ando, Kenichi Echigojima, Yoshinari Nakata, *Tadao Ando 1: Houses & Housing*, TOTO Shuppan, Tokyo.
Antonio Esposito, *Tadao Ando*, edited by Marco Casamonti, Motta Architettura, Milan.
Antonio Esposito, *Tadao Ando*, edited by Marco Casamonti, L'Architettura – I Protagonisti, vol. 6, La Biblioteca di Repubblica / L'Espresso, Rome.
Philip Jodidio, *Ando Complete Works*, Taschen GmbH, Cologne.
Tadao Ando, Werner Blaser, *Tadao Ando. Bauen in die Erde – Sunken Courts*, Niggli Verlag AG, Sulgen, Zürich.
Tadao Ando, *Tadao Ando Details 4*, edited by Yukio Futagawa, A.D.A. EDITA, Tokyo.

2008
AA.VV., *Tadao Ando 2: Outside Japan*, TOTO Shuppan, Tokyo (with essays from: Tadao Ando, Riichi Miyake, Emily Rauh Pulitzer, Renzo Piano, Giorgio Armani, Jean Nouvel).
AA.VV., *Tadao Ando. Modern Art Museum of Fort Worth*, Rizzoli International Publications, New York (with essays from: Philip Jodidio, Marla Price, Michael Auping, Tadao Ando).
AA.VV., *Row House, Sumiyoshi. Tadao Ando*, Tokyo Shoseki, Tokyo (with essays from: Manabu Chiba, Takamitsu Azuma, Osamu Ishiyama, Yukio Futagawa, Tadao Ando).
Tadao Ando, Hiroyuki Suzuki, *Tadao Ando 3: Inside Japan*, TOTO Shuppan, Tokyo.
Tadao Ando, *Tadao Ando, Architect*, Shinchosha Publishing, Tokyo.

97
Sergio Polano
Carlo Scarpa: Palazzo Abatellis
La Galleria della Sicilia, Palermo, 1953–1954

98
Sergio Polano
Santiago Calatrava
Complete Works

99
Enric Miralles
Works and projects, 1975–1995
Edited by Benedetta Tagliabue Miralles

100
Giuseppe Terragni
Opera completa
Edited by Giorgio Ciucci

101
David Whitney, Jeffrey Kipnis
Philip Johnson
The Glass House

102
Hans Sedlmayr
Die Architektur Borrominis

103
Claudia Conforti, Jacques Lucan
Alessandro Anselmi
Architetto

104
Lo specchio del cielo
Forme significati tecniche funzioni della cupola dal Pantheon al Novecento
Edited by Claudia Conforti

105
Anthony Blunt
Philibert de L'Orme

106
Wolfgang Lotz
Studies in Italian Renaissance architecture

107
William J Mitchell
City of bits
Space, place, and the infobahn

108
Francesco Cellini, Claudio D'Amato
Mario Ridolfi
Manuale delle tecniche tradizionali del costruire
Il ciclo delle Marmore

109
Marcello D'Olivo
Architetture e progetti 1947–1991
Edited by Guido Zucconi (With essays by Francesco Borella, Ferruccio Luppi, Paolo Nicoloso)

110
Françoise Fromonot
Jørn Utzon
Architect of the Sydney Opera House

111
Gonçalo Byrne
Opere e progetti
Edited by Antonio Angelillo

112
Walter Zschokke
Boris Podrecca
Arbeiten/works 1980–1995

113
Jean-Louis Cohen
André Lurçat
Autocritique d'un moderne

114
Francesco Venezia
L'architettura, gli scritti, la critica

115
Gabriella and Massimo Carmassi
Del restauro
Quattordici case

116
Christof Thoenes
Sostegno e adornamento
Saggi sull'architettura del Rinascimento: disegni, ordini, magnificenza

117
Manuela Morresi
Piazza San Marco
Istituzioni, poteri e architettura a Venezia nel primo Cinquecento

118
Matera
I Sassi. Manuale del recupero
Edited by Amerigo Restucci

119
Béla Lajta ornamento e modernità
Edited by Marco Biraghi

120
Roberto Masiero
Livio Vacchini
Works and projects

121
Antonio Pizza
Alberto Campo Baeza
Works and projects

122
Antonio d'Avossa, Francesca Picchi
Enzo Mari il lavoro al centro

123
Roberto Gabetti
Paolo Zermani
Costruzioni e progetti

124
Fulvio Irace, Vanni Pasca
Vico Magistretti
architetto e designer

125
Aldo Rossi Tutte le opere
Edited by Alberto Ferlenga

126
Modena 1598
L'invenzione di una capitale
Edited by Massimo Bulgarelli, Claudia Conforti, Giovanna Curcio

127*
Borromini
e l'universo barocco. I
Edited by Richard Bösel and Christoph L. Frommel

127**
Borromini
e l'universo barocco. II
Edited by Richard Bösel and Christoph L. Frommel

128
Alberto Ferlenga, Paolo Verde
Dom Hans van der Laan
Works and Words

129
Paul Wijdeveld
Ludwig Wittgenstein, Architect

130
Federico Bucci, Marco Mulazzani
Luigi Moretti
Works and Projects

131
Edoardo Gellner, Franco Mancuso
Carlo Scarpa e Edoardo Gellner
La chiesa di Corte di Cadore

132
Dominique Perrault
Projects and architecture
With an essay by Laurent Stalder

133
Franco Purini
Le opere, gli scritti, la critica

134
Antonio Monestiroli
Opere, progetti, studi di Architettura

135
Alessandro Mendini
Design and architecture
Edited by Peter Weiss

136
James S. Ackerman
Distance points
Essays in theory and Renaissance art and architecture

137
Toyo Ito
Works projects writings
Edited by Andrea Maffei

138
Enrico Bordogna
Guido Canella
Opere e progetti

139
Carlos Ferrater
Works and projects
Edited by Massimo Preziosi

140
I ponti delle capitali d'Europa
Dal Corno d'oro alla Senna
Edited by Donatella Calabi and Claudia Conforti

141
Giuseppe Vaccaro
Edited by Marco Mulazzani

142
La chiesa a pianta centrale
Tempio civico del Rinascimento
Edited by Bruno Adorni

143
Kenneth Frampton
Steven Holl, architect

144
Shuhei Endo
Paramodern architecture
Edited by Hiroyuki Suzuki

145
Nunzio Dego
Giorgio Grassi
teatro romano di Brescia
Progetto di restituzione e riabilitazione

146
Hans Kollhoff
Kollhoff & Timmermann Architects
Edited by Jasper Cepl

147
Roberta Albiero, Rita Simone
João Luís Carrilho da Graça
Opere e progetti

148
Christoph Luitpold Frommel
Der römische Palastbau der Hochrenaissance

149
Massimo Faiferri
Wiel Arets
Works and projects

150
Alessandro de Magistris and Michel Vernes
Odile Decq Benoît Cornette
Opere e progetti

151
Periferie e nuove urbanità
Edited by Federico Bucci

152
Marco Mulazzani
Massimo e Gabriella Carmassi
Opere e progetti

153
Francesco Repishti and Richard Schofield
Architettura e Controriforma
I dibattiti per la facciata del Duomo di Milano 1582–1682

154
Emmanuelle e Laurent Beaudouin
Opere e progetti
With an essay by Joseph Abram

155
Bolles+Wilson
Opere e progetti
Edited by Angela Germano

156
Sean Godsell
Works and Projects
With an essay by Leon van Schaik

157
Chiara Baglione, Francesco Benelli, Maria Teresa Sambin de Norcen
Nuovi antichi
Committenti, cantieri, architetti 1400–1600
Edited by Richard Schofield

158
Giorgio Grassi
Opere e progetti
Edited by Giovanna Crespi and Nunzio Dego
(With an essay by Juan José Lahuerta)

159
Federico Bellini
Le cupole di Borromini
La "scientia" costruttiva in età barocca

160
Waro Kishi
Works and projects
With an essay by Masao Furuyama

161
I musei e gli allestimenti di Franco Albini
Edited by Federico Bucci and Augusto Rossari

162
Francisco Mangado
Obras y proyectos
With essays by Luis Fernández-Galiano; Carlos Jiménez

163
Guillermo Vázquez Consuegra
Opere e progetti
With an essay by Víctor Pérez Escolano

164
Francesco Cellini and Claudio D'Amato
Le architetture di Ridolfi e Frankl

165
Luigi Alini
Kengo Kuma
Works and projects
(With an essay by Kengo Kuma)

166
Heinz Tesar: Architektur
Edited by Winfried Nerdinger

167
Mathias Klotz
Architecture and projects
With an essay by Miquel Adriá

168
Yuko Hasegawa
Kazuyo Sejima+Ryue Nishizawa SANAA

169
Carlos Ferrater
Works and Projects, Volume 2

170
Roberto Gargiani
Archizoom Associati 1966–1974
Dall'onda pop alla superficie Neutra

171
Alejandro Aravena
Progettare e costruire

172
Gonçalo Byrne
Opere e progetti, Volume 2

173
Allestimenti tra le quinte di Palladio
With essays by Donata Battilotti and Sergio Polano

174
Marco Mulazzani
Ipostudio
La concretezza della modernità

175
Giampiero Bosoni and Federico Bucci
Il design di Franco Albini

Prestel Verlag
A Member of Verlagsgruppe Random House GmbH

Prestel Verlag
Königinstrasse 9
80539 Munich
Tel. +49 (0)89 24 29 08-300
Fax +49 (0)89 24 29 08-335

Prestel Publishing Ltd.
4 Bloomsbury Place
London WC1A 2QA
Tel. +44 (0)20 7323-5004
Fax +44 (0)20 7636-8004

Prestel Publishing
900 Broadway, Suite 603
New York, NY 10003
Tel. +1 (212) 995-2720
Fax +1 (212) 995-2733

www.prestel.com

Library of Congress Control Number: 2009942603

British Library Cataloguing-in-Publication Data: a catalogue record for this book is available from the British Library; Deutsche Nationalbibliothek holds a record of this publication in the Deutsche Nationalbibliografie; detailed bibliographical data can be found under: http://dnb.d-nb.de

Prestel books are available worldwide. Please contact your nearest bookseller or one of the above addresses for information concerning your local distributor.

Translated by: Miranda Denenberg, Jim Potter
Editorial direction: Curt Holtz with Anita Dahlinger
Copyediting & typesetting: Kevin White for bookwise GmbH, Munich

Printing and binding: Mondadori, Verona

FSC
Mixed Sources
Product group from well-managed forests, controlled sources and recycled wood or fibre
www.fsc.org Cert no. SGS-COC-004313
©1996 Forest Stewardship Council

Verlagsgruppe Random House FSC-DEU-0100
The FSC-certified paper Ecotecno Satin *is produced by mill Burgo s.p.a, Italy.*

Printed in Italy
ISBN 978-3-7913-4454-6

About the Author

Francesco Dal Co teaches architectural history at the University Institute of Architecture in Venice and has taught at the Yale School of Architecture and at the University of Lugano.
He directed the architecture section of the Venice Biennale, is editor of the magazine *Casabella* and has numerous publications to his name.